SECURITY AND PEACE

The Imperatives for National Development in Nigeria

Published by
Adonis & Abbey Publishers Ltd
P.O. Box 43418
London
SE11 4XZ
http://www.adonis-abbey.com

Nigeria:
No. 3, Akanu Ibiam Str.
Asokoro,
P.O. Box 1056, Abuja.

Year of Publication 2014.

British Library Cataloguing-in-Publication Data
A catalogue record for this book is available from the British Library

ISBN: 978-1-909112-28-5

SECURITY AND PEACE

The Imperatives for National Development in Nigeria

BY

J. ISAWA ELAIGWU

Security and Peace

TABLE OF CONTENTS

ACKNOWLEDGEMENT

It is my pleasure to acknowledge the support and contributions of many people which made this publication possible. Not all those whose help I sought and got can be mentioned here. But I am grateful for their assistance in various ways.

I acknowledge, with gratitude, the assistance of my colleagues, Celestine Ukatu, Ali Garba, Amedu Oteikwu, Thadeus Faruk, Simi Cole, Jonah Apeh, and Stephen Isawa-Elaigwu, whose regular research provided the raw data for this book. My gratitude and thanks also go to Hadiza Umar Bala, Patience Joseph, Rose Ogbuzuo, Ramatu Ocheja, Rihanat Agboola, Bunmi Alademoni and Nicodemus Beska – for all their various contributions in the production of this volume.

I would like to appreciate all those who found the time to read and make invaluable suggestions, especially Prof. Habu Galadima, and Ms. Victoria Onyechi Isawa-Elaigwu

Finally, inspite of all the above, I take full responsibility for all errors contained in this book.

PREFACE

This book on *Security and Peace: The Imperatives of National Development in Nigeria* was inspired by two invitations to public discourses. The first was an invitation by the Federal Radio Corporation of Nigeria (FRCN) to give the Fifth edition of the *FRCN Annual October Lecture*, scheduled for October 27, 2011. The Second was the invitation by the Arewa Consultative Forum (ACF) to make a presentation on – *Socio-Economic and Political Imperatives for Peace and Security in Northern Nigeria,* at the Arewa Peace and Unity Conference in Kaduna, December 5, 2011. While the FRCN Lecture was postponed and then cancelled, the Arewa House Conference held.

It is important to make the point that the issue of security had taken the front burner in the concerns of Nigerians so much that the two invitations asked one to address virtually the same issue. Armed robbery and kidnapping had posed challenges for conventional institutions for the maintenance of law and order and for criminal cases, such as the Nigeria Police Force (NPF). However, the year 2011 witnessed the advent of aggressive insurgency/terrorism illustrated by the progressive expansion of serial bombing incidents and even suicide bombing of public and private institutions and places. Nigerians, who had believed that their compatriots loved life too much to engage in suicide bombing, got the shocker of their lives when a suicide bomber attacked the Nigeria Police Force Headquartersin Abuja. Since then suicide bombers have terrorized Nigerians in Maiduguri, Kano, Kaduna, Gombe, Yobe, Jos, Suleja and other cities.

Hardly any week passes by without fierce engagements between the extremist Islamic sect, *Juma'atul Ahlis Sunnah Lidda'awati Wal Jihad* (otherwise known as *Boko Haram)* and security forces. There is a pervasive sense of insecurity in the geopolitical North, while the South is gripped by anxiety. In the first two months of the year 2012, there were violent battles between security agencies and members of the Boko Haram. Thus far, while the *Boko Haram* has continued to terrorize the northern states; armed robbers dominate the crime space in the Western States, and the South-eastern and South-southern states suffocate under the grip of kidnappers.

The police seem to be overwhelmed by the escalation of insurgency and/or terrorism which requires more than law and order techniques and skills. In about 28 of the 36 states of the federation, the military has deployed soldiers to assist the police in dealing with domestic violence and terrorism. For over one year, governments at different tiers have had difficulty implementing development projects, even among the few of them who are determined to do so. In essence, insecurity of lives and property has virtually put all other activities on hold, especially in states such as Kano, Gombe, Kaduna, Borno and Yobe.

If *Security* is the first *order of the state,* what is happening in Nigeria? Why has Nigeria become so prone to insurgency and terrorism? What can be done to arrest the situation; reverse the trend, and establish a peaceful environment for national development?

In this short book, the writer speaks directly to Nigerians and proffers solutions. Our challenges as Nigerians are not unique in the current global setting, but we need unique solutions because of the peculiarity of our socio-political environment.

There is no suggestion in this book that the proffered solutions to the challenges facing the country are the best. Nor are we suggesting that immediate solutions can be found to some of these problems, the identification of which are only approximate. This book is intended to generate discussions on how to get our dear country out of its current web or quagmire. If this book has tickled your mind sufficiently, to proffer some solutions to Nigeria's current security challenges, then it has been partially successful.

As I travel all over the country and the world, I am very much aware of the level of apparent despondence, disappointment and anger of many Nigerians with their country. Many Nigerians have lost confidence in their leaders and government. They no longer trust those who claim to be the vanguards of societal transformation. This became very clear during the eight-day demonstration in January 2012 by Nigerians against the removal of subsidy on the pump price of petrol. In addition, many Nigerians believe that we have been crawling in fifty-one years instead of walking or even running. They may be right. Others believe that our little progress over the years had been through a strategy of piecemeal somersault. Maybe. Yet others believe we should disintegrate, or dissolve by mutual agreement, because 1914 has been an irremediable mistake. This I do not agree with.

I believe that my bias must be stated at the beginning so that the reader is not in doubt about where I am coming from. Yes, we have reasons to be disappointed with our leaders and ourselves in our 51 years of sojourn as a nation-state. We have reasons to be angry or to even be mad with ourselves. We could have done better and we can still do much better. My belief is that, staying together as a country for 51 years is an achievement. While we –leaders and followers – have not lived up to expectations, let us not allow ourselves to be drowned in the vortex of cynicism. Let us not sit down as *grumbletonians* - grumbling about everything but doing nothing. We must stop playing the whining children wallowing in self-pity. We must get up and put our acts together and take our destiny in our hands. The fault is not in our stars but with us. It is our fault that we have not adequately corrected whatever was the *'mistake'* of 1914. Other countries have tried to correct their own 'mistakes'. Let us learn from the experiences of the United Kingdom, India and Malaysia. I believe that **while the ship of the Nigerian nation-state may be battered severally on the high seas, with discipline, hard work, selflessness, patriotism and dedication, the Nigerian ship will safely anchor and be renewed to the surprise of everyone in the world**. I am passionate about my commitment to a single and indivisible Nigeria and I have no apologies for it or for my views on the necessity for a **rebirth** of my country. However, I shall try not to allow my passion to overwhelm my intellectual objectivity.

This book is also designed to be a primary source book for researchers. This is why a substantial part of the book (the appendices) has data on selected violent crises in which there is loss of life and/or destruction of properties. One hopes that these data are also useful to the reader.

CHAPTER ONE

INTRODUCTION

1. Current State of National Security

Since the return to 'democratic' civil rule in May 1999, there have been dramatic increases in the numerous violent conflicts among Nigerians. The research carried out by the Institute of Governance and Social Research (IGSR, Jos, indicates that the numbers of selected violent conflicts in which one or more lives were lost and/or properties destroyed are over 1000 cases. There are more cases of violent clashes which do not fit into this selected category. This number is about four times the number of similar violent conflicts, between1980-1999.

Nigeria has experienced numerous electoral, ethnic, political, ethno-religious, communal (land), economic and other violent conflicts since May 1999. Nigeria, within the period witnessed the emergence of ethnic militias – such as, *the Odu'a Peoples' Congress (OPC),* the *Arewa People's Congress (APC), the Igbo People's Congress (IPC*), the *BakassiBoys,* the *Egbesu Boys* and others. These ethnic *militias* had taken on the causes of their ethnic groups. In some cases, some of these have played the role of *vigilantés* – showing that the capacity of the police force was inadequate to demonstrate government's monopoly of the legitimate use of force to maintain law and order.

In addition to these, has been inter-ethnic violence, such as, *Itsekiri-Urhobo*; *Tiv/Jukun, Tiv-Fulani, Berom-Fulani*, and others. While the period 1980-1999 were marked by few serious religious violence, such as, the Maitasine, these increased tremendously in number after May 1999.

Militant ethnic and religious protests transformed themselves from the level of criminality to insurgency/terrorism. The activities of Niger-Delta militants, especially the Movement for the Emancipation of Niger-Delta, (MEND), the kidnappers of South Eastern and South-South Nigeria, and the activities of the *Jama'atu Ahlis Sunnah Lidda'awati Wal Jihad*, better known as the *Boko Haram,* are examples of these. Not only did Nigeria witness an escalation in the technology of violence – from guns to bombs – Nigeria has begun to experience *suicide* bombers.

Ironically, these insurgents are very sophisticated in style, and have at times, beaten security agencies checks to get at their targets. The October 1, 2011 celebration was allegedly postponed because of the challenge of security in Abuja. The National Youth Service Corps (NYSC) did not hold a passing-out parade in October 2011, reportedly because of security challenges. Candidly this is State submission to forces of terrorism and an acceptance that it lacks the capacity to protect the lives and property of Nigerians. Government, having the monopoly of the instruments of violence must always show that while seeking peace, it can bite. As Yasser Arafat once said:

> I come bearing an olive branch in one hand, and the freedom fighter's gun in the other. Do not let the olive branch fall from my hand[1].

It must be clear that governments' olive branch must not be allowed to fall by insurgent and terrorists.

Our very young ones have also had their hands awash in human blood – the blood of their compatriots. What kind of younger generations are we producing? Our current state of insecurity and lack of patriotism are reflected in the perception and behavior of the young ones. The impressions of a 23 year old Nigerian in her – **A Letter to Nigeria, My Country** – expresses the concern of the youth.

A LETTER TO NIGERIA, MY COUNTRY

Dearest Nigeria,

Sweet and beautiful Nigeria.Home of the strong and happy. How have you been?

I hear that the soil of your land harvest no more because, it is soaked with the blood of the innocent.

I hear that your beautiful and serene plateau where the weather is so cool is now covered with smoke from the burning of houses and cries of pain.

I hear that your greatest resources have become a great burden in the lands of the Delta.

I hear that the unity achieved through your civil war, has gone down in flames.

---

[1]Yasser Arafat in *55,000 Amazing Quotes, No. 11506.*

I hear that, the knights of your round table do not fight for the justice and welfare of your people but only for their bank accounts because your democracy has become <u>*government*</u> *of the* <u>*government*</u> *by the* <u>*government*</u> *for the* <u>*government*</u>

I hear that, like the farmer chases his cattle in the field, so do your people chase themselves in the name of religious differences.

I hear that, you're once happy nation, in spite of all your trouble in the 3rd world, are no longer happy; for they live in fear and wonder when it will ever get better.

I hear that, the hope that used to linger on the lips of your people "e go better" is no longer a reality to hope for, because it has become a shattered dream.

I hear that, you are now branded the "good people, great nation" but the Irony of this is that your people are now their own worst enemies. So the question is, can you really be the good people, a great nation?

In spite of all these, the most painful thing I have heard is that with the crises taking place within your borders, your future is becoming your past as the children, the leaders of tomorrow, are dying today in your meaningless squabbles and violence.

Oh Nigeria, Dearest and sweet Nigeria………………! I ask you, where is the love? Where is the hope? When would you fight for the future that you deserve? Would you lean back and watch yourself fall? Or would stand and stop the violence?

Lots of love, prayers and hope
From your very own [2]

We must therefore develop the courage to get to the root causes our current state of insecurity, underpinned by criminality and terrorism. This leads us to our major questions in this volume.

2. **Suggestions**

What is **Security**? What do we mean by **Peace**? What is the relationship between security and peace? What impact do these have on national development in Nigeria? What are the major threats to peace and security in Nigeria? What are the main threats to democratic governance? What are the desirable socio-economic and political measures which can be put in place to enable us to achieve relative peace and stability for development?

---

[2] Rose Elaipu Isawa-Elaigwu, '*Letter to Nigeria, My Country*', a copy of which was sent to her father.

In order to answer these questions, we suggest that:

a. **Security** is the *first priority of the State* – for without security, peace and/or law and order, all other functions of the state cannot be effectively carried out.
b. There can be no national development without relative peace and stability.
c. Since May 1999, there have been greater challenges of security than at any point in time in our history, thus rendering our political stability fragile, democratic institutions and processes weak and fluid, and our economy debilitated.
d. Government, political leaders and followers, and all of us, must have the courage and honesty to get to the root causes of our current state of insecurity, underpinned by criminality and terrorism.
e. Our leaders and followers have taken the issues of security for granted; yet urgent and immediate steps (short and long–term) must be taken to consciously respond to current threats, by architectonically designing and building a security system which would create a stable and relatively peaceful environment, conducive for national development.
f. unless we all (leaders and followers) rise up and decide **now** to:

    - Create an ecumenical society in which all religions can peacefully cohabit.
    - Establish a civil and democratic society which accommodates our ethnic and lingo-cultural differences, in the context of **justice**, **equality** and **fairness**.
    - Put pressure on our governments to take emergency measures to drastically reduce **Poverty** among the populace.
    - Establish mechanisms for enforcing the rules guaranteeing the promotion of a democratic polity in which no man is oppressed by hunger or by the violent pangs of sectarianism, and the dictates of authoritarianism.

We will be handing over to our children an unenviable and unstable society with an incurable propensity for undermining its own development; andsecurity is the duty of all Nigerians, and we must take our destiny into our hands, determined to face the sssfuture with confidence, discipline, patriotism and demonstrable honesty.

3. Security, Peace and National Development: Toward Operational Definitions.

Since this is not strictly an academic volume, we shall skip theoretical arguments on the key terms – *security*, *peace* and *national development*. However, we shall give operational definitions which will guide our discussions.

Every Nation-State Has At Least Three Functions

a. Security (law and order)
b. Welfare of its citizens
c. The pursuit of national interest in the global setting.

Of all of these, **security**[3]is the most important in the establishment of the State. That is why; one of the important characteristics of a State is the monopoly over instruments of violence. For our purposes, *security* refers to a set of measures taken to guard against espionage, sabotage, crime, attack, terrorism, insurgency and other forms of danger to the State. These measures are aimed at preventing the State and its citizens from experiencing dangers, fears and /or anxiety. It means the ability of a State to ward off all forms of threats external to its survival, and these may include ensuring the internal stability and predictability of the system. The **soft** side of security refers to those socio-political and economic factors/values that are central to the harmonious working relations of members of the state. These include,

[3] Securityis the first order of the State. All other attributes of the State hang on it. It is pertinent, therefore, to note that the monopoly over the instruments of, and the legitimate use of, violence is a cardinal attribute of the State. Also, see J. Isawa Elaigwu, 'African Security in a Changing International Environment' in M. A. Vogt and L. S. Aminu (eds.) *Peace-Keeping as a Security Strategy in Africa: Chad and Liberia as Cases Studies*, (Enugu: Fourth Dimension Publishing Co. Ltd., 1996) PP. 2-22; Institute of Peace and Conflict Resolution (IPCR, *Strategic Conflict Assessment of Nigeria: Consolidated and Zonal Reports* (Abuja, IPCR, 2003, 2008); J. Isawa Elaigwu, 'Crisis and Conflict Management in Nigeria since 1980' in A. M Yakubu, R.T Adegboye, C.N. Ubah and B. Dogo (eds) *Crises and Conflict Management In Nigeria Since 1980,* Volume I (Kaduna: Nigeria Defence Academy 2005) pp 28 – 79; National Institute of Policy and Strategic Studies, *Research Reports on Conflict and Integration In Nigeria* (Kuru: National Institute, 2003).

food, environmental, political, economic, health security. The **hard** elements of security refer to the most obvious material elements of the State designed to maintain law and order, the defence of the country, and the security of lives and property, such as the police, and military outfits. It is therefore important to see security in holistic terms.

In essence the concept of security has become wider than military security. Security has come to be defined in wider terms including political, economic, health, environmental and others. This is often referred to as *Comprehensive Security*.

Let us illustrate the point. If there is no 'good' governance, food and health insecurity could be potent sources of political instability. Similarly, in the context of a weak economy and an ever-enlarging army of the unemployed, violence becomes democratized as young men get enlisted as political thugs by politicians. It is however, important that **only the State has the monopoly of the legitimate use of force** in order to guarantee freedom, security of lives and property, and relative peace.

We may also discuss, at this point, a few relevant concepts. For us, **Insurgency** is a condition of violent revolt against constituted authority or established leadership through sabotage and harassment in order to undermine its authority. It is not an organized war with recognized belligerents in the field. In addition, **Terrorism** is used to refer to systematic use of violence or destructive acts to intimidate or cause fear in a population or government, with the objective of securing demands or concessions.

What do we mean by **Peace? Peace** is not the absence of conflicts. There will always be conflicts where more than one person lives. Interests often clash, thus resulting in conflicts. It is not the conflicts but how they are managed that is important. Peace is about how conflicts are managed to ensure relative stability, law and order in order to enable human beings carry out their daily activities. Peace is a societal condition which ensures relative social stability and order through the dispensation of justice, fairness and opportunities for accommodation by formal and informal institutions, practices and norms[4]. It does not refer to the peace of the graveyard which often seems still and peaceful to human beings at night, but active for the

---

[4] Christopher A Miller, *A Glossary of Terms and Concepts in Peace and Conflict Studies* (Geneva: University of Peace, Education for Peace in Africa Programme) p.29.

spirits. It refers to our ability to successfully manage conflicts below a threshold which does not threaten the freedom and the security of lives and property. In such contexts regular institutions and processes deal with emerging conflicts which permit the system to carry out national development.

For us, **national development** refers to the delivery of services which achieve the ends of the state – security, welfare and the pursuit of national interests in the global setting. While the United Nations has indicated some Millennium Development Goals (MDGs as welfare goals of the state[5], national development is a multi-dimensional process of change which affects political, social and economic growth and sustainability. It directly and positively changes the quality of life or welfare of the people. Meaningful national development has to be people-centric.

Most politicians and analysts agree that there is a positive link between security and 'good' governance. This is because, unless there is relative peace and stability, development would be elusive.

Governments need to ensure the maintenance of law and order, and the security of lives and property in order to enable people to move freely about to carry out normal activities of development. Insecurity created by instability does not provide a conduscive environment for development. **Thus security and a relatively peaceful environment are imperatives for national development**. Yet, there are socio-economic and political imperatives for security and peace in Nigeria.Let us now turn to sources of insecurity in Nigeria.

---

[5]The Millennium Development Goals to be achieved by 2015 – to which Nigeria is a signatory are:

- Eradication of poverty and hunger
- Achievement of Universal Primary Education
- Promotion of gender equality and empowerment of women
- Reduction of child mortality
- Improvement of maternal health
- Combating HIV/AIDS, Malaria and other diseases;
- Ensuring environmental sustainability; and
- Developing global partnership for development

CHAPTER TWO

SOURCES OF INSECURITY: TOWARDS CAUSALITY

Conflict is the spice of every State. It tests the fragility or otherwise of the State and creates the basis of future amelioration or adjustments. However, conflicts beyond certain thresholds are detrimental to the very survival of the State, precisely because they threaten the consensual basis of the association. Conflicts which **emanate from the non-recognition of the claims of others** to issues of conflict (for example, excluding others from sharing in crucial items of allocation) could be very dangerous for the system. Such conflicts mobilize total loyalties of the people and tend to defy all attempts at effecting desirable compromises. The events which led to the Nigerian civil war provide useful illustrations of the perceived non-recognition of mutual claims among Nigerian groups.

On the other hand, conflicts which result from the **nature of distribution** are less dangerous to the survival of the State. Since the claims of others are recognized in this case, the only issue of conflict is the nature of distribution of the items of conflict (such as how allocatable items) are shared or how conducive compromises are struck between competing claims. This form of conflict is less dangerous to the process of nation-building, than those which totally exclude the claims of others.Finding **causes** of human and societal problems can be very difficult. As any good social scientist would explain, tracing causality is a very difficult exercise. As an illustration, to what extent is the ostensible reason of "bad food" the cause of students' riot in a given university? Were the Ekiti riots of 1965 or the Agbekoya riots of 1969, necessarily over tax or politics? Or were these events the result of multi-variable causation and the reasons given, mere verisimilitudes?

In addition, **human and societal conflicts are often multivariable and multidimensional in causation.** Often it is a daunting task to accomplish in a few pages. This means brevity in many aspects of our analysis which may not do justice to the above topic. Our objective here, therefore, is to raise issues for further debate.

Conflicts may be caused by actions which trigger mutual mistrust, polarization of relations, and/or hostility among groups in apparently competitive interactions within a country. Conflicts may even be the result of frustrations arising from unsatisfied human needs – physical, psychological, social, and economic and others.

Conflicts may also arise from explosion of identity as groups begin to ask for greater participation and rights. Threatened identities of groups have also led to conflicts in a State. Seeming cultural incompatibility among groups with different communication styles could generate conflicts in a polity. In addition, demonstrable and/or perceived inequality and injustice expressed through competitive socio-political, economic and cultural frameworks, have been known as potent causes of conflict, as groups react to their perceptions of the situation.

The principle of power-sharing and perceived political and economic domination by one group or the other in the state can lead to the frustration and disenchantment/alienation of one group or the other from the polity. It is therefore difficult to adequately identify causes of conflicts in contemporary Nigeria.

We cannot claim to know all the causes of conflicts which have created challenges of security and peace in Nigeria. However, we shall briefly mention a few of these for purposes of analysis and discussions.

1. The Foundations of Nigerian Federation:

It is our contention that the period 1914 to 1946 had witnessed the mere *co-existence* of Nigerian groups which hardly knew of one another nor interacted in any substantial way horizontally. Like most colonial authorities, the British administration encouraged vertical relations between the individual communities and their administrators. Close horizontal relations among Nigerian groups would have nailed the colonial coffin earlier than the British would have wished, assuming they had any intentions of leaving. It was the *Richards Constitution* of 1946 which formalized the division of Nigeria into three regions within a unitary colonial state. If the year 1914 marked the birth of colonial Nigeria, 1946 marked the establishment of the structure of effective horizontal relations among Nigerian groups.Thus within this period; there was no concept of colonial Nigeria as a State. Nigeria evolved in the context of British colonial policies in West Africa, in piecemeal fashion.

Once it became evident that the colonial administration would soon go in response to a combination of international and national events, Nigerians began to organize to inherit colonial power. This realization came as Nigerians had begun to establish contacts with one another. No sooner had they started to interact than they realized that they were strange bedfellows in the same polity. They had not interacted long enough with one another to work out an acceptable mechanism of conflict resolution. Given the competitive setting in which they found themselves; Nigerian politicians withdrew into their ethnic/ethnoregional or geo-ethnic[1]cocoons in order to mobilize their followers effectively for competition. The new parochialism was not the old one (based on ignorance of one another) but *parochialism based on the awareness of others* in a competitive setting. As Mallam Aminu Kano told this writer in an interview:

> I think regional grouping was a result of sudden awakening. I think there was a period of sudden awakening in Nigeria, but the awakening was misdirected.... The sudden realization of 'we can take power' resulted in ethnic grouping and therefore regionalism.[2]

If the very process of decolonization had spurred regionalism, regionalism also determined the form of government Nigeria was to have - **one based on the mutual fears and suspicions among Nigerian groups.**

The mutual distrust among Nigerians and the prevalence of centrifugal forces in the colonial state were amply demonstrated at the Constitutional Conferences between 1957-1958. The result was the federalization of Nigeria with three component units (the North, West and Eastern regions), the structural imbalance among these units and the suppression of the fears of the minorities, inspite of the *Willink Commission* Report.

---

[1] See a more detailed account in J. Isawa Elaigwu, *The Politics of Federalism in Nigeria* (Jos: Aha Publishing House, 2005), and (London: Adonis and Abbey, 2007).

[2] Interview with Aminu Kano, 1974

Our argument is that the **pattern of colonial administration had partly led to the emergence of federal government in Nigeria. We argue that, in part, federalism emerged as a compromise formular to assuage the mutual fears and suspicions of domination among Nigeria's heterogeneous population.** One legacy of this process was the *structural imbalance in Nigeria's federation* which the military tried to resolve through the creation of additional subnational states. Like any medicinal prescriptions, the creation of states produced its "political rashes".[3]

Under this 'democratic' polity, the suppressed *angst* of various groups within the Nigerian federation has found expressions in many ways. The emergence of a fiscally and politically titanic centre has questioned the basic sense of security of groups. Some groups have begun to wonder aloud if the federal association was meeting their objectives, and if desirable adjustments should not be made in the federation to give everyone a sense of belonging.

2. Structural Adjustments of the Nigerian Federation and the Majority/Minority Divide

The creation of states (from 12 in 1967 to 36 in 1996) from the original 3 (later 4) regions in the country created new sets of problems, even as it attempted to resolve the problems of the structural imbalance in the federation. The first is the emergence of new boundary problems among the new states. Secondly, while inter-communal boundary conflicts had been intra-regional, with the creation of states, some of these became inter-state problems, thus giving these conflicts higher saliency and visibility. As an illustration, the *Tiv-Jukun* land/border conflict, was transformed, after the creation of 'Taraba and Benue States, to inter-state conflict; so also is the conflict between the Tivs and Fulanis in Southern Nassarawa State.

Similarly, after every creation of additional states, emerged *new majorities* and *new minorities*. Often, many of the '*new majorities'*

[3] The creation of States was a structural medicinal prescription to correct the imbalance in Nigeria's Federation. However, like many medicinal prescriptions, it produced side-effects or political rashes. This became evident with the emergence of *New Majorities* and *New Minorities*, with each act of the creation of additional States. In addition, the creation of additional States came to be seen by many political leaders as an *elixir* for all political problems emanating from inter-group relations. Ironically, the *new majorities* are often more *vicious* than the *old majorities.*

(who were old minorities) are even more vicious than the old majorities, thus creating new basis of conflicts in the new setting. In addition, public servants in the old public services faced new problems. As an illustration, after the creation of Enugu State, husbands and wives who now belonged to different states and served in the public services of the old state were under pressure to transfer their services. In most cases, the wives were under pressure to transfer their services to the home state of their husbands.

In 2011, in reaction to the ₦18, 000 minimum wage demand, Abia state transferred the services of all those Igbos who were not from Abia, but were in her public service, to their respective states of origin. Thus, while solving some problems, the creation of additional states, has had its *political rashes* which require new medication.

It has also been observed that while the old regions had grazing paths mapped out, these became obsolete in the context of the new states. It has been seen as one of the main reasons between cattle herders and farmers. Kaduna, Katsina, Benue, Plateau States are examples of states with many incidents of these types of violent conflict.

3. **Competition for Control of Resources**

Many of the ethno-religious and other conflicts we have today are related to nature of interactions among groups as they compete for scarce but allocatable resources. As the state or government at all levels, serves as the main allocator of resources and also sets the terms for such distribution, the control of government becomes an object of group competition. Controlling government also means the control of resources and the power for their distribution. As groups contest for political power, ethnic and religious sentiments and loyalty get easily regimented for the achievement of goals. Yet ethnic and religious sentiments are issues of primordial identity with large emotive content. Often the contest for the control of state and policy generates religious and ethnic interests which serve as mechanisms for mobilizing loyalties. These resources could be land for farmers, or boundaries for claimed lands or grazing lands. The creation of additional states heightened these problems in certain areas.

A variant of this is when those in control of government discriminate against others who then perceive gross injustice in the polity. As an illustration, the Niger-Delta sense of deprivation did not start today. Isaac Adaka Boro, Nothingham Dick and Owomero, had embarked on secessionist bids to protest this perceived injustice as far back as 1966.[4]

Yet another variant which generates conflicts, is that in some newly created states, their composition is such that one ethnic group dominates the political arena perpetually – to the exclusion of others who are considered permanent minorities. The creation of permanent and excluded minorities often generates frustration, disenchantment with the state, and anger which can degenerate into violent reactions.

Currently, Nigerian political leaders are busy quarrelling over the revenue allocation formula – that is, how to share resources in the Federation Account.

While the Northern States want a revision of the formula to distinguish between on-shore and off-shore oil (as in the past), South-South states are opposed to this. The arguments over the distribution of resources in the federation will continue, but no one seems to be concerned about resource generation.

4. **Decisions of Government**

Decisions of government must be properly thought through before execution, or they could generate violent conflicts. Given the competitive setting among ethnic and religious groups, you need **fairness, justice and equity.** In the struggle for the control of government policy, many people believe that if one group has an ascendancy, government decisions may not favour the other group. The aggrieved group in the absence of fair avenues for seeking redress goes violent. As an illustration; the creation of local government, (re)location of local government headquarters, the citing of government projects or even appointments into political offices, can generate violent conflicts, which utilize ethnic and religious bases for mobilization. The violent conflicts between Ife and Modakeke in Osun state, Urhobo and, Itsekiri in Delta State and in Gwantu of Sanga Local Government Area of Kaduna State, are good examples of cases in which government decisions sparked off violent conflicts that are traceable to deep-rooted rivalry between different groups. The

[4] J. Isawa Elaigwu, *Gowon: A Scholarly Biography of a Soldier-Statesman* (Jos: Aha Publishing House, 2009 ed.) p. 76 and p. 144.

negative perception of government policies by the various groups in a polity (especially poor delivery of services) could, generate violent ethnic, religious and other forms of conflicts.

5. **Migration and the Indigene/Settler Problems**

In some parts of the country, especially in the Middle-Belt area, there have been substantial migrations in the last 20 years. The rapidly encroaching desertification of the north does not help matters. In the context of competition for scarce resources and the importance of the control of the state and instruments of political power for the distribution of these resources, new lines of cleavages develop among groups. As *indigenes* organize for the control of their polity and economy, so do the *settlers* press for their rights of participation in these processes. Beyond a threshold, *settler* communities threaten the indigene's position of hegemony and control. While the 'settler' gets *defensively aggressive* in its relations with the indigenes, the indigenes get *aggressively defensive*, often resulting in violence with the full mobilization of ethno-religious loyalty and commitment. This is a general problem all over the country which requires urgent constitutional amendment, to give the country a lease of peace and life.

6. **Deliberate Manipulation of Ethnic and Religious Identities**

There are instances when politicians, traditional and religious leaders deliberately manipulate ethnic and religious identities of groups. There are enough evidences to show that quite a number of ethno-religious conflicts are caused by politicians and other members of the elite. The level of hypocrisy among our political leaders is nauseating. Some of these politicians have no constituencies from which to demonstrate their relevance except through their narrow ethnic and religious groups. Without being religiously judgmental, they are not genuinely religious in their actions and faith—whether they claim to be *'born again'* (or is it *'born against'* God?). Their personal lives do not show that God has a place in them. They exude religious bigotry and ethnocentrism with demonstrable arrogance. They symbolically use churches and mosques as their theatres of operation in the day time, while consulting *babalawos,* cultists and/or *juju men* or even ritualists at night. It is important that they maintain this semblance of *churchianity* and *mosquianity*, bereft as these may be of the core values of Christianity and Islam. This is because it is their lifeline for survival. They pollute the minds of young children with their bigotry and encourage them to exhibit ethnocentric arrogance. Many of the ethno-religious conflicts in Nigeria (especially in Northern Nigeria) are generated or exacerbated by this group. Since no commission of inquiry ever recommends them for punishment and government does not punish them, they hide behind their ethno-religious curtains as *untouchables*—constantly brewing and dispensing new forms of violence. Genuinely religious people respect the ways of life of others and treat human lives with care and dignity. They know that since they did not *create,* they could not *take* the lives of others.

7. Traditional Social Stratification and Ethnocentrism

Very often some citizens of ethnic and religious groups consider themselves as hailing from aristocratic traditional backgrounds, and arrogantly exhibit ethnocentrism in relations with other groups. At times, these people relate to other groups (that is when they care to) with disdain, extending their ethno-religious status recklessly to domains of others' socio-cultural preferences. Politicians do this with nauseating efficiency. It is no wonder that traditional leaders 'sell' or 'award' traditional titles more under democratic polities than under military regimes in Nigeria. As a matter of fact, the character of the recipients hardly seems to matter. How they acquired their wealth is often considered unimportant. No wonder some young men struggle for these titles, in some parts of Nigeria, as if it is a matter of life and death. This often offends the sensibilities of other people who find other platforms for checkmating the nuisance of these '*leaders*' or persons.

8. Partisanship of Security Agencies

In potential conflict situations security agencies may be useful in creating a sense of safety and security among groups. The partisanship of security agencies usually tips the balance, resulting in the lack of confidence in the security agencies. Thus, instead of preventing violent conflicts or effectively controlling conflicts, they exacerbate conflicts. The perception of the security agencies as neutral arbiters is useful in conflict management. There have been allegations of partisanship of security agencies which helped to escalate rather than dampen conflicts. As an illustration, in Plateau State, there were allegations of partisanship of soldiers and the police, by various groups.

9. **Economic Woes and Poverty**

There can be no durable democracy nor can governance be qualified as 'good', without a viable economic base. **No one cares for democracy on an empty stomach.** We must not forget that democratic culture and political stability cannot thrive in a society where there is **abject poverty**. Our poverty alleviation/eradication programmes have so far failed to tackle the problem. Our economy is still in bad shape: the exchange rate is about ₦160.00 to one USA dollar; inflation still haunts our hopes for a good take home pay; some banks are still tilting towards collapse; the manufacturing sector has experienced closures in spite of our privatization process; there seems to be greater *invasion* of our market by external forces than investment; our infrastructure are dilapidated; our educational system is collapsing and the health sector is severely in pains. Perhaps, the financial sector has been transformed. But there is still the need for more regulation of the banking industry. In addition the private sector is still small and heavily tied to the apron-strings of the public sector, which is anchored on a monocultural economy.

It is not enough to mention that there are poverty alleviation programmes. The truth is that our experience since 1999 shows that these programmes are not well thought-out nor coordinated. While some state governments in the North have shown relative concern about the plight of their people, others are more concerned about structurally grandiose projects than projects which would liberate their people from the pangs of hunger, poverty and diseases. In addition, the disease of corruption has accentuated existing problems of poverty. At state and local government levels, we all know how the poverty alleviation money is thrown down the drain-pipe. When programmes tend to contribute to poverty escalation than alleviation, government should stop and review its activities. In less than a decade to 2020, how can we launch the economy to the desired position with poverty still ravaging our people; with power supply still very epileptic, and our factories closing down one after the other? How can we become one of the 20 largest economies at the rate we are going, by 2020? We can, but only if we put our act together and act with urgency and purposeful determination.

a. Unemployment

Given the economic hardship and high level of unemployment, 'armed youths for hire' are available at cheap price. While the Federal Government 'deregulates' the economy, politicians 'deregulate' violence and the control of the instrument of violence, which is supposed to be the cardinal duty of government. Members of the army of the unemployed are always willing to find new jobs as body guards, assassins, and canon-fodders in communal and electoral violence. The conspicuous consumption of political office holders (whose backgrounds were well known before they assumed offices) amidst the abject poverty of the people, not only alienates, but generates hatred and aparthy. Candidly our level of unemployment is directly related to our security.

b. The Corruption Conundrum.

Some Nigerians have no doubt earned their only country a bad reputation in terms of corruption. No nation is free from the corruption cancer. But the fact that we are always, rightly or unfairly, rated among the most corrupt nations is devastatingly irritating. Corruption is real in our society. It is a menace to our individual, societal and national life. It happens in the open and in the dark. How can we fight it?

Many Nigerians have observed that there are some people with unclean hands in and around the government, thus casting shadows of corruption over Jonathan's administration. Is the President a victim of the political context in which he rose to office? Have our Governors, Ministers, Legislators, Permanent Secretaries, Local Government Chairmen and Councilors also gotten the message? Are the policemen on the streets, the messengers in the offices, the classroom teachers, businessmen and contractors alike conscious of the desirability for change? Herein comes the need for aggressive advocacy.

The wind of change against corruption has been sweeping from Peru, Chile and Argentina through Italy, Japan, France, and Thailand to Taiwan, Philipines and Costa Rica.[5] — witnessing how former Presidents and leaders have been brought to trials with some convicted and jailed for corruption. What is happening in this country? Can we amend the laws of our anti-corruption agencies to give them enough teeth to bite? What about the establishment of an anti-corruption court? The lesson is that the anti-corruption crusade must start from the top.

It is even more perturbing when one hears and reads rumors of members of the executive branch (at Federal and State government levels) bribing legislators and members of the judiciary. How cangovernment reduce the level of corruption when our leaders bribe one another to pass through certain legislations and /or policies adjudged to be unpopular with the masses? Scandals over billions of dollars wasted on power projects and on subsidy of refined petrol and petroleum products are mind-boggling. In Delta State, former governor James Ibori pleaded guilty of money laundering charges at a London court.

This money was carted out of State treasury. The same story is true of many state governors, ministers and others. Corruption corrodes the wheels of the machine of development; weakens the process of service delivery; robs the people badly needed funds for improving their welfare; enriches a few and impoverishes many; and often even knocks the engine of national development and renders the prospects of development and nation-building bleak.

[5] Taiwan's ex-president and his wife were sentenced to life imprisonment, while two of his children were sentenced to 2-year jail term. Members of the former first family were sentenced for embezzling public funds, accepting bribes, committing forgery and/or money laundering. (*ThisDay*, Sept. 13, 2009, p. 21). Former Costa Rican President, Rafael Angel Calderon, was convicted and sentenced to 5 years in prison for embezzling funds from Finish loan intended for Medical equipment for public hospitals in 2004. The amount he embezzled was $520,000.00. (*Daily Trust*, October 7, 2009, p. 22). The Italian Prime Minister, Berlusconi, has had his immunity removed by Italian Constitutional Court, in order to face trials.

10. Lack of Political

It is clear that many political leaders know who are fuelling violence in the country. In known cases, such as Plateau State, probe panel reports have repeatedly indicted people, but nothing has been done about these reports. In some cases, political leaders are afraid that taking necessary action to bring these sponsors of violence to book might trigger off additional incidences of violence, given the connections of these people to people at high government levels – state or federal.

It is sad that the Northern states are among the poorest states, yet perennial violent conflicts prevent the establishment of a stable and peaceful environment for development. In addition, the membership of ruling political parties by these conflict generators, tend to give them protection to break the law with passion. Political leaders must summon the will to implement **White Papers** on Probe Panel Reports. A crime is a crime, and there are laws for dealing with these crimes. The recurrence of violence is often related to the lack of political will of leaders to enforce the law dispassionately. Leaders must strive to keep their oaths of office.

11. Security, Law and Order, and Conflict Management

The greatest problem in the country today is the security of lives and property. This is not unrelated to the lack of 'good governance' which has alienated people from government. For a long time, citizens have had to live with armed robbery and kidnapping. In the northern parts of the country, in particular, ethno-religious or communal violence has led to the death of thousands of people, the destruction of property, and the displacement of millions of people from their homes. Young people (in their teens) have had their hands stained in human blood, and it is not clear how these young people will turn out at the age of thirty.

From violations of law and order, Nigeria now has upgraded its technology to bombs. From the Niger-Delta bombs, we are now plagued by the *Boko Haram* bombs and street gun-fights with security agencies. No town or place is sacrosanct. Church and Mosques, police stations, and even military barracks, have become targets. Primary

Schools in Borno State have been bombed by the *Boko Haram* rendering thousands of children without schools.

Unfortunately, the Nigeria Police Force (NPF is overwhelmed, while the presence of the military in the streets is not good for a democratic polity. Insecuritylooms large in the horizon, and the average citizen is sceptical of assurances given by government. In essence, the average Nigerian feels insecure and wonders if his/her government has the capacity or capability of providing a stable and peaceful environment for carrying out of other socio-economic activities.

Given these security challenges how do we proceed from here? Do we give up? This is not an option, because we owe our children a relatively stable polity within which development can take place. The only option available to Nigerians seems to be – taking up the challenges, facing these challenges collectively, with courage, discipline, determination, and patriotism. We cannot afford to be overwhelmed by these challenges; rather our resolve and actions should help us to overcome these challenges.

CHAPTER THREE

SOURCES OF INSECURITY: THE CHALLENGE OF DEMOCRATIC GOVERNANCE.

1. Democracy and Democratic Deficit.

The sources of insecurity in Nigeria go beyond socio-economic or ethno religious or communal conflicts. For purposes of emphasis and better understanding of the dynamics of violence in Nigeria's polity, we have deliberately separated the challenges of democratic governance from other sources of conflict, it does seem, from available data (see appendix AxB) that there are greater incidences of violent conflicts under civilian 'democratic' regimes than under military regimes. The reasons are perhaps obvious to any good observer of the Nigerian polity.

Some of the causes of conflict stated here may overlap with the ones discussed above. However, for purposes of a deeper understanding of the setting, this apparent repetition may be tolerable.

For us, democracy is a **system of government based on the acquisition of authority from the people; the institutiona-lization of the rule of law; the emphasis on the legitimacy of rulers; the availability of choices and cherished values (including freedoms), and accountability in governance.**

This definition brings out the principles of democracy. For us, these principles include the locus of authority in a democratic polity. Authority emanates from the **people**. Any authority which does not emerge from the consent of the people is not democratic. How consent is operationlised may vary from one system to the other. Secondly, a democratic polity must be based on *the rule of law*. Law cannot be arbitrary in a democracy. There are specified limits to power and how it can be used. In addition, there should be an acceptance of the "rules of the game" of politics by all the players, if arbitrariness is not to creep in at a later stage. There are no sacred cows before the law, and no individual takes law into his/her hands because the system provides opportunity for redress for the aggrieved.

The third characteristic of a democratic polity is that it must be *legitimate*. Legitimacy involves two processes. One of these is that the leader has the right to rule - that is to say - that given the law or the rules for accession to power he is the right person to be there. The institutional mechanism for his accession to power would depend on the particular country and people. The other is that he is *ruling rightly*. This is to say that he is performing well, given the mandate he was given by the electorate.

In addition to these, is the fourth, the element of *choice*. The people should have the right to effect changes in the leadership or the government of their country, given available alternative leadership. In some countries the plebiscetarian system is used. In some others, other mechanisms for providing choice are used. Choice also includes all basic human *freedoms* of thought, movement, association, worship and others, in relative terms. It must be emphasized that all freedoms have their limits and are often accompanied by obligations. Fifthly, there must be *accountability*. Leaders must be held responsible for their actions as representatives of the people who are trusted with power to achieve particular ends, and must also account for such actions periodically.

These five principles may be seen as the minimum characteristics of democracy. However, the institutional framework for their operation may differ from one country to the other. Does democracy mean Western democracy? No! It is also important to note that *democracy is not necessarily the most efficient and inexpensive system*. In fact, it is very expensive and at times, slows. It will really be wishful thinking to assume that democracy is the *elixir* to all problems of development. It is not. It *provides for relative peace and a conducive medium for development to take place*. In fact, it generates its own problems, to which solutions must constantly be found.

Most of the conflicts and crises which have characterized Nigeria's democratic path are associated with undemocratic values which underpin our national life – that is, **building supposedly democratic structures on undemocratic foundations and values.** Let us illustrate some of these:

a. The Electoral Process (Electoral Malpractices)

Democracy is not all about elections. Elections are vehicles for the establishment of representative government. The 2003 and 2007 elections were blatantly rigged. The judiciary has exposed the shame we called elections by the various judgments of its tribunals, and in essence enforcing political rectitude. The 2011 elections were an improvement on earlier ones, but were also seriously flawed. Again the various reversals by tribunals of election results, the Court of Appeal and Supreme, all illustrate the problems of the 2011 elections.

Given the perception that the control of state power is important, groups often decide which political platform is the best for the pursuit and the promotion of their interests. Thus, politics in Nigeria *is not game but a battle*. Nothing succeeds as much as success and nothing fails as much as failure. The exclusion of political failures has been a major source of conflict.

In addition, the blatant rigging of elections creates a reservoir of ill-will for the so-called winners. Seeing no prospects of peaceful change, the aggrieved often take the violent route. Even the judiciary could not, in such circumstances be trusted. Similarly, the intolerance among members of political parties generates intra-party and inter-party conflicts. At times, ethno-religious support gets mobilized to achieve targets. The Jos crises of 2001 and 2008 are good examples of violent conflicts which started apparently because of elections but which later took on ethno-religious colouration.

Furthermore, the *Tazarcemania* (self-succession) of political incumbents generates conflicts as there are often zones or groups which are opposed to the self-succession agenda of the incumbents. Thus, electoral malpractices offend the sensibility of those already dissatisfied with the incumbent. Often politicians hire thugs and young people to visit violence on their opponents – even within the same political parties. It has been alleged that the militancy in the Niger-Delta took on criminal dimensions after the 2003 elections. Politicians reportedly recruited young cult members into their army of political thugs over whom they lost control, after the elections. These groups became monsters and were even threats to their erstwhile masters. In addition, some governors courted and pampered religious and youth groups for political purposes, only to abandon them after elections. These eventually boomeranged on them, as well as on the system. Groups such as "*ECOMOG*, *Kaleri*, *and Sara Suka* are examples of these extra-constitutional armed groups which specialize in democratizing violence on behalf of their masters. As Aliyu Tishau, a leading member of the *Jama'atu Ahlis Sunnah Lidda'awati Wal Jihad* (otherwise known as *Boko Haram*) claimed:

> The truth is that politicians are the root cause of this Boko Haram problem .... I was contacted by a governorship candidate to kill an opponent for a fee ... some politicians are now taking the advantage of the conflict between Boko Haram leadership and the authorities to execute their own agenda.[1]

Boko Haram has consistently denied that it did not kill the ANPP Governorship candidate in Borno State. Similarly, as Senator Matori once observed:

> ...If we can all be honest to one another, especially our leaders, by demonstrating transparency and accountability, Nigeria will begin to enjoy peace. But as far as we still have elite, people with selfish motives, Nigeria may not witness any meaningful development; so the earlier we bury our selfish and political motives the better. We should come together and start seeing ourselves as One Nigeria, because whether Christians or Muslims, we belong to one God. No religion preaches that you should kill or destroy properties...so politicians should desist from using innocent youths to ferment trouble because these youths are powerless, but it is politicians that supply them arms and money for Indian hemp and after taking such drugs they begin to kill because they have lost control of their memory.[2]

It is illegal and unconstitutional for politicians to keep armed groups and body guards, not so deployed by security agencies. But these are daily scenes at political party rallies and with politicians. Politicians, in and out of government, are therefore the greatest generators of conflict, because they do not perceive politics as a *game*, but a *battle*. If president Obasanjo had referred to the 2007 elections as 'a do or die affair', he saw the 2011 elections as a 'Total War'.

Similarly, *political parties*, which are expected to aggregate and articulate the interests of their members, as well provide alternative governments, are largely undemocratic, fragile and ridden with 'deadly' fractionalization. Party elections and primaries generate violence and even lead to assassinations.

---

[1] Aliyu Tishau's interview on the television channel – *Africa Independent Television (AIT)* quoted in *Sunday Nation* (Lagos) September 25, 2011, p. 13. It was also reproduced in the *Sahara Reporters*.

[2] Interview with Senator Isa Matori, *Vanguard* (Lagos), March 22, 2009, P. 22.

The intolerance of the opinion of others is another challenge of democracy. Leaders of political parties are intolerant of different views and often see these as 'anti-party activities', which deserve to be punished. It is not surprising that the political *pilgrimage* (or cross-carpeting) of politicians from one party to the other by membershas been on the ascendancy since 1999.

b. Leadership and Statesmanship

Since we started our journey in democratization in May 1999, three major political groups have emerged in the political arena. These are the *politicians,* the *political contractors* and the *political thugs.* The *genuine politicians* know how to acquire and use political power for the ends or goals of the state. These are few and have become endangered specie.

The *political contractor* is a businessman for whom democracy is a tolerable nuisance in his calculus of profitable investments. The electoral process is a commercial process in which deals can be made in the form of investments in politics. Thus, from the Ngige-Ubah saga in Anambra State to the Ladoja-Adedibu showdown in Oyo State, the political contractors insisted on their pounds of flesh[3]. There are more political contractors than politicians. It is hoped that the political contractors in 20 years, may transform themselves into genuine politicians.

The *political thugs* often brazen and rough, are usually the hirelings of the political contractor. The only value of this group is the maximum dispensation of violence and/or threats of violence as may be requested by the political contractor. The political thug democratizes violence—thanks to the big unemployment market which swells up its rank.

Good governance and accountability entail the tolerance of divergent views, the accommodation of political opponents and the widening of the frontiers of politics through inclusiveness but not alienation and exclusion. Our leaders, once in the State House must

---

[3] In the Anambra case, Chris Ubah made it very clear that he funded the election of Dr. Chris Ngige as an investment on which he expected returns when the latter became Governor. He felt betrayed that Dr. Ngige refused to give any returns on his investment from the Anambra State public treasury. Similarly, Chief Adedibu of Oyo State could not understand why Chief Ladoja, whom he "installed" as governor of the state, could not give monthly returns of mere N10 – 12 million from the state security vote. He expressed dismay over the governor's reluctance or refusal to make returns on his investment, from Oyo State public treasury.

accept that they have become *statesmen* and no longer soap box politicians. They must accept that they are no longer ethnic and religious champions or parochial opinion leaders. They have become the *fathers* of all irrespective of the ethnic group, language, geopolitical unit, or religion to which they belong. They now transcend all these and must respect the country's *unity in diversity* and *diversity in unity*.

In essence, our leaders have not learned that once elected, they must transform themselves into **statesmen**. Often many of them remain *politicians* in State Houses. There is no principle they cannot mortgage, no value they cannot adulterate, and there is no law they cannot bastardize. Genuine critics of their actions are dubbed 'saboteurs' and reactionaries, as if this country does not belong to all Nigerians. Many politicians and political leaders have learnt nothing from the past. They behave as if Nigeria belongs to them to milk and exploit, while the rest of us are mere tolerable nuisance. It is no wondered that there is a big disconnect between leadership and followership, and between government and the people. This is one major problem that must be sorted out.

Leadership thus remains a vital factor in effecting desirable compromises in our democratic federation. The way our political leaders respect the rules of the games of politics; their ability to imbibe the democratic value of accommodation, tolerance of opposition and participation; and their ability to demonstrate gallantry in defeat and grace in victory, will determine the extent of harmony in our democratic polity in the future.

Letus now turn more specifically, to electoral violence with sources manifestations and consequences.

2. Electoral Violence

Electoral violence is really a form of *anomic participation* in the political process. Electoral violence often takes place where there are political or electoral grievances which have been ignored or have not been adequately addressed by the relevant institutions or agencies. Let us illustrate this. The problems of electoral violence do not always start during elections but well before. They may even start during the voter registration process or within political parties. These unaddressed grievances may climax in violence during elections in the polity.

In addition, how does one distinguish between electoral violence and other forms of violence? Is it an electoral violence because it took place during the elections? Could elections be catalyst to existing political cleavages? To what extent were the Jos crises of 2001 and 2008 electoral crises or were they indigene/settler problem? Or were they religious? The Tiv riots of 1964 might have taken place during elections, but were there underlying deep-seated resentments to which the elections of 1964 merely gave vent? There are many cases like these in Nigeria. The difficulty in analysis is clear.

Social conflicts are usually multivariable in causation. Causation is usually multivariable. To what extent is an apparent cause, really a manifestation of electoral violence? To what extent do causes, manifestations and consequences exchange places, given the context and time? Could an apparent manifestation at a point in time be a consequence or a cause as another point time? These questions are only meant to illustrate the difficulty in analysis.

Often, people see the beginnings of elections as the setting for identifying electoral violence or conflicts. In Nigeria, intra-party nominations for electoral posts, voter registration, and even old political cleavages such indigene/settler problems, exist long before elections or even electoral campaigns. Often, inter-party violent clashes also take place over one issue or the other, well before elections.

For our purposes, while not ignoring our experiences in the past, we shall concentrate on illustrations from 1999 elections to date, while looking at the past for comparative purposes.What are the causes of electoral violence? In what ways are these forms of violence manifested? What are the consequences of these forms of violence for the democratic polity?

In our attempts to answer these questions, we suggest that:

a. Electoral violence is often multivariable in causation.
b. Such forms of violence are also multidimensional in their manifestations.
c. The consequences of electoral violence for Nigeria's democratic polity have often been enormous, distractive, disruptive, and even destabilizing in certain circumstances.
d. Unless conscious efforts are made by all political actors/institutions or agencies of democracy to abide by the "rules of the game", the electoral process will continue to be

laced with thick veneers of threat of violence or actual violence.

e. The duty of curbing or containing electoral violence belongs to all of us – governors and governed; leaders and followers.

Electoral Violence: Towards Causal Analysis

Tracing the causes of electoral violence in Nigeria is a daunting task. For our purpose, however, there are three broad categories of causes of electoral violence – 1) **Structural** (or situational), 2) **Institutional**; and 3) **Attitudinal** (or political culture). Electoral violence is usually multicausal and is related to underlying societal issues such as – poverty, unemployment, illiteracy, and ethno-religious/regional cleavages.

1. *Structural Sources of Electoral Violence*

The structural sources of electoral conflicts refer to those societal cleavages which make electoral violence, at times, inevitable. While these cleavages may pre-date and transcend electoral matters, they may have important impact on the electoral process. In other words, the structural contexts often provide conduciveenvironment for electoral violence. Let us briefly survey a few of these sources.

a. The Federal Grid

The federal structure which was unbalanced provided the basic historical and political source for mutual fears and suspicions among Nigerian groups. The Nigerian State at independence was already bedevilled by problems arising from mutual suspicion and fears of domination among various groups which had established contact with one another during the terminal colonial period. These suspicions were really not unusual; they were also understandable.

A federal structure in which the Northern Region accounted for 79% of the total geographic area and 54% of the population, made groups from the Southern regions to feel seriously disadvantaged. In the context of Nigeria's ethnoregionalism and democratic framework of one man, one vote, the South saw the Northern *tyranny of population* as detrimental to their political interests. Thus the fear that the North would continue to provide political leadership in the country created an intense sense of political deprivation in the South. The North-South dichotomy became sharper and clearer.

On the other hand, the North was disadvantaged educationally. The Southern states had a headstart in Western education which had become a passport into the modernizing sectors of the society - parastatals, the federal civil service, and even in private economic sectors. The North was very keenly aware of this handicap. It was therefore not surprising that the North adopted a *Northernization policy* of recruitment as a defensive mechanism against the perceived Southern *tyranny of skills.* The North feared the economic domination by the South. Thus while the North had political power, economic power resided in the South.

By 1965, the graph of Nigeria's political temperature had risen very high. The rules of the game of politics had been ruthlessly violated; corruption and conspicuous consumption of politicians amidst the abject poverty of the masses became very glaring; census exercises were inflated and politicized because of mutual suspicions among groups; and the rigging of elections disenfranchised the Nigerian masses.

Thus, the 1961 elections in the Northern Region and the Tiv riots of 1961 and 1964 were directly related to the perception of the ruling party by the opposition. Similarly, inter-regional crises over the 1962 and 1963 census exercises, the federal elections of 1964 and the Western Region elections of 1965 – were all related to the fears generated by Nigeria's federal structure at independence. Ironically, efforts to correct the structural imbalance in the federation through the creation of additional states in 1967, 1976, 1987, 1991 and 1996 – only created new *political rashes.* The political rashes include the creation of *new majorities* and *new minorities;* the additional demands for the creation of states as a political *elixir* to cure all political ills; and the emergence of smaller and weaker states and a titanic federal centre. Nigerians are now busy debating how to reduce the power of the centre.

Given the imbalance in Nigeria's federal structure, numerical superiority became an important factor in Nigerian politics. The NCNC[4], the Eastern government, and many southern peoples had hoped that the 1962 census figures would give the south numerical

---

[4] The *National Council of Nigerian Citizens (*NCNC*)* – was a partner with the *Northern People's Congress* (NPC) at the federal level, and the ruling party in the Eastern Region.

superiority over the north. In such a situation, a coalition of the southern parties with a few seats from the disaffected areas in the north would give the south the majority with which to control the federal government.[5] On the other hand, the Northern Region continued to fear the concentration of numerical and technical superiority in the south. Such concentration of power, to them would be "utterly disastrous".[6]

In addition, census figures were tied to revenue sharing among the regions. The 1962 census exercise was therefore politicized. Discrepancies in the actual figures led to its cancellation and the initiation of another census exercise in 1963.

In the 1962 census exercise, the population of the Eastern and Western Regions had shown an average increase of about 70%. In five Eastern divisions (Awka, Brass, Degema, Eket, and Opobo), increases of about 120-200% were recorded. The total for the south was then about 23 million. The southerners had hoped that, for the first time, the North would be in a minority with its 22.5million (on the basis of 30% increase). Mr. Warren the officer in charge of the census felt the figures for the north were "reasonable."[7] He dismissed the southern

---

[5] It may be important to remember that all the three parties, the NCNC, the NPC, and the AG, had become identified with particular regions: the East, the North, and the West, respectively. The NCNC, still had many non-Ibos as members, but had become identified mainly as the party of the Eastern Region. When Azikiwe returned to the Eastern Region and displaced Prof. Eyo Ita as the Chief Minister, Eastern minorities were furious. The selection of Michael Okpara as the successor to Nnamdi Azikiwe as leader of the party had led to accusations of Ibo dominance of the party, and by 1965, Yoruba-Ibo conflict in the party became open.

[6]Awolowo had observed in 1963:

> I believe that the problem of Nigeria cannot be solved until that of Northern Nigeria has been solved... If the Action Group and the NCNC, both of which have a monopoly of political following in the South, and at least one-third of the political followership in the North, could come together, then they would serve as a catalyst to the political situation in the North, entrench liberal democracyin the country, and infinitely increase the tempo of progress in the federation as a whole. I hold it as a fact that such a combination is sure to win alandslide victory at a subsequent election.

Quoted in Walter Schwarz, Nigeria (London: Praeger, 1968), p. 152.

[7] Similarly, Ahmadu Bello had expressed the same fear of a Southern coalition in My life, when he contemplated that:

> Eighty years have passed since the last crisis and we see clearly now that Nigeria must stand as one and that, as things are, the existing external boundaries cannot readily be changed--nor can those of the regions... As things are in the present situation, the North has half the seats in the House of Representatives. My party might manage to capture these, but it is not very likely for the present to get any others; on the other hand, a sudden grouping of the Eastern and Western parties (with a few members from the North opposed to our party) might take power and so endanger the North. This would of course

figures as "false and inflated," particularly in the five divisions of the Eastern Region.[8]

However, in its revised 1962 figures, the north claimed to have "missed out all of 8.5 million people, presenting a total of 31 million,"[9] giving it an increase of about 80%. In the light of these discrepancies, Prime Minister Balewa decided to abandon it and conduct a new census exercise.

In 1963, another census exercise was undertaken. It was probably as unreliable as the previous one, but was even more controversial. The 1963 official census figures showed the north with a population of 29.8 million, the East with 12.4 million, and the West and the new Midwestern Region with a population of 12.8 million. The figures for the north and the east increased by 67% and 65% respectively, while the West and Midwest together recorded an increase of about 100%.[10]

Clearly, the NPC[11]-NCNC's coalition which had started "souring" or weakening from the Midwestern Regional elections showed an open rift between the two parties over the census issue. While Ahmadu Bello, the Premier of the North, accepted the census as "fair and reasonably conducted," Michael Okpara of the Eastern Region rejected the census figures, which he regretted disclosed inflations "of such astronomical proportions that the figures… taken as a whole, are worse than useless."[12]Together, the Midwestern and Eastern Regions

be utterly disastrous. It might set back our programme of development ruinously; it would therefore force us to take measures to meet the need. What such measures would have to be is outside my reckoning at the moment, but God would provide a way. You can therefore see that the political future must rest on an agreeable give and take between the parties. So long as all respect the common purpose, all will be well."Sir Ahmadu Bello, *My Life*, (London: Cambridge University Press, 1962) *pp. 228-229)*.

[8]Mackintosh, J.P. (ed.) *Nigerian Government and Politics* (Evanston: Northwestern University, 1966), pp. 547-549.

[9] W. Schwarz, *op. cit.*, p. 159.

[10]*ibid.*, p. 160

[11] Northern People's Congress (NPC)

[12]Quoted in Mackintosh, *op cit*, p. 552.

(Revised Population Figures, 1952 – 3, 1963, in Millions)

	1952-53		1962		Revised 1962		Revised 1963	
North	16.8	55.3	22.5	49.3	31.0	57.4	29.8	53.5
East	7.2	23.7	12.4	27.0	12.3	22.8	12.4	22.3
West	4.6	15.1	7.4	17.1	7.8	14.4	10.3	18.5
Midwest	1.5	4.9	2.2	4.8	2.2	4.1	2.5	4.5
Lagos	0.3	1.0	0.7	1.5	0.7	1.2	0.7	1.3
Total	**30.4**	**100.4**	**45.6**	**99.7**	**54.0**	**99.9**	**55.7**	**100.1**

(Adapted from Schwarz, Nigeria, *op, cit.*, p. 163).

rejected the figures, while the Northern and Western Regions accepted them. Actually, the Midwestern Region was as much under NCNC leadership as was the East, while Akintola's Western Region had not gotten over her gratitude to the NPC for the latter's support during the political crisis in the Western Region.

To the NCNC leadership, the census controversy was indicative of the Northern Region's determination to use its size to maintain its hegemony at the centre. Subsequently, the Premier of the East, Dr. Okpara's suit in the Supreme Court alleging irregularities in the census exercise was dismissed. This court judgment was more painful for him because of the impending federal elections of 1964.

The politics of demography as a source of violence before and during elections is aggravated by the importance of population in revenue or resource distribution. Thus, General Gowon's attempt in 1973 to hold another census exercise was also drowned in political crises. As General Gowon observed in 1974: "I was really surprised that the people were politicizing the whole exercise".[13] While the figure of 79.76 million was hotly contested under the military government of General Gowon, the succeeding administration of Murtala/Obasanjo admitted that Nigeria was over 80 million.[14]

Similarly, in 1991, General Ibrahim Babangida's administration conducted a census of Nigerians. The population was declared to be 88.9 million for the whole country. While there were hues and cries over this exercise, it was generally regarded as probably the most acceptable exercise since independence, even though protests by different groups continued for years after. In March 2006, there was another exercise under President Olusegun Obasanjo. Without any results declared, there were protests against the handling of the exercise and complaints from groups which claimed not to have been counted. The finally approved census figure for 2006 was 140.4 million for the whole country,[15] even though many observers believe that Nigeria has about 200 million people. Does this have serious implications for planning?

**Totals do not add up in some cases because of rounding.*

[13] Elaigwu, J. I, *Gowon (2009 ed.) op. cit. p. 254.*

[14]The Nigerian High Commission, *Nigeria Today* (Budget Edition) London, No. 89, April 1978, p.34.

[15] Federal Republic of Nigeria, *Official Gazette*, Abuja, No. 2, 2nd February, 2009, Vol. 96, provided the legal notice on publication of 2006 Census Final Results. For details, also see Federal Republic of Nigeria; *Nigeria: Demographic and Health Survey, 2008* (Abuja: National Population Commission and ICF Macro, 2008).

Why is the census exercise so easily politicized? It is so politicized because census figures are important for development planning and the distribution of resources, and representation in political institutions of democracy. These figures have political saliency in the content of one man, one vote, especially in the competitive relations between the North and South geopolitical divide.

b. Revenue Distribution

Revenue allocation had always been a controversial issue in Nigeria even before independence. From the Phillipson Commission in 1946 to the 2004 draft revenue formula by the Revenue Mobilization, Allocation and Fiscal Commission (NRAMF) – the issue of appropriate formula for the distribution of scarce but allocatable resources has always been controversial or crises ridden. Often, the problem is over the weight given to the various principles of distribution, such as derivation, population and national interest. Since 1999, the Niger-Delta (oil-producing states) has insisted on *resource control* – i.e controlling revenues which are derivable from their states. Attempts to get between 25% - 50% of revenues on mineral oil on the basis of derivation started at the National Political Reform Conference in 2005. Niger-Delta or South-South delegates had walked out of the Northern and other Southern states in order to convince the conference of their claims to resources.

c. Citizenship – Indigene/Settler Relations.

The Nigerian Constitutions from 1960-1999 recognize the citizenship of every Nigerian. All Nigerians supposedly have the right to settle down anywhere in the country, to pursue their legitimate businesses and are expected to have equal rights everywhere. But in practice, this is not true. Many states and communities recognize their indigenes and can easily isolate settlers. In the political process this has become very controversial and has generated many violent crises. In some cases, the spill-over or hang-over of this issue have led to electoral violence, because it becomes important who is elected – *indigene* or *settler.* The Jos North violence, the Wase Case, Jukun-Tiv and many similar other cases of violence illustrate the explosive nature of this issue in the polity and in the electoral process.

d. Local Conflicts Exacerbated by Actions of Government

At times, given the nature of societal cleavages, decisions of governments can generate violence. Illustrations are the cases of Ife-Modakeke, and Warri, in which the creation of Local Government Councils and the citing of local government headquarters, led to violent conflicts for over a long period of time. These local cleavages and conflicts can easily provide a conducive environment for electoral violence.

e. Aggressive Subnationalism and Ethnic Militias

Aggressive subnationalism in a competitive setting can provide an environment conducive to violence. The Niger-Delta case, with years of neglect of the oil-wealthy part of Nigeria has generated tension and violent conflicts over many years. Foreigners had been taken hostage, with demands for monetary rewards by militant groups, while some violent clashes with federal forces had led to the establishment of The Joint Task Force (JTF). The case of the Movement for the Actualization of the Sovereign State of Biafra (MASSOB) is similar. The *Boko Haram* Islamic sect has dealt a blow at the base of the country's security.In some other cases, the weakness of the police force in the maintenance of law and order, had led to emergence of ethnic militias such as the *Bakassi Boys,* the *O'Odua PeoplesCongress* (OPC), the *Egbesu boys* and others[16]. Initially serving as *vigilantés,* these militias often got out of hand, as Governors Obi of Anambra and Yuguda of Bauchi State found out[17]. Elections in this context are likely to be violent, if not adequately monitored.

f. Poverty, Unemployment and Economic Hardship

Massive poverty and unemployment in a depressed economy, provide a fertile environment for the recruitment of the young into the army of political thugs.Often, older persons accept bribes as they traded their votes and consciences for pittances – in some cases, literally, for mere

[16] For detailed account of this see, the chapter on "Ethnic Militia and Democracy in Nigeria" in J. Isawa Elaigwu, *Nigeria: Yesterday and Today for Tomorrow: Essays in Governance and Society.* (Jos: Aha Publishing House, 2005) pp 132-173.

[17] *ThisDay, (Abuja)* June 20, 2006; *Vanguard,* (Lagos)June 24, 2006, pp 13-14; *Daily Sun,* June 22, 2006, pp1& 4.

measures of salt and bread. It is ironic that in Nigeria, many political leaders seem to enjoy keeping the masses poor, as they steal public money to bribe their way back to office. Economic hardship often provides a conduscive environment for electoral violence and crimes.

2. *Institutional Sources of Electoral Violence.*

Inherent problems of institutions tasked with electoral matters, if not resolved, could lead to, or even generate electoral violence. Let us take a look at a few of those institutions.

a. *Political Parties*

Political parties have the functions of interest aggregation and articulation in a democracy. They also provide alternate leadership/go vernment. In 2011, Nigeria had over 60 political parties – some of which only existed by name.

Many of these political parties are weak, and have fluid internal structures. They also have the problem of democratizing their internal structures and processes. In some cases where the political party forms government, the political party depends on its government for its sustenance. Often the president and governors easily pocket these political parties. There is the story of the *Peoples' Democratic Party* whose chairman had been sacked by President Obasanjo and who had refused to vacate his office. The starving of the headquarters of money by government meant that the political party could not pay water and electricity bills. The reality of the situation dawned on the chairman, who had to vacate his office.

Electoral violence also emanates from within political parties as a result of democratic deficit in the parties' political processes. The imposition of candidates during party nominations and the crises arising therefrom have led to violence. In some cases, lives were even lost. (See Appendices)

Similarly, the weakness of the police force and other law-enforcement agencies has provided excuses for politicians to set up their own thugs. These thugs bear personal allegiance to individual politicians, rather than to the political party. In fact, it is alleged that the crises in the Niger-Delta, Borno, Bauchi, Gombe and Yobe States were compounded because some political leaders had set up contingents of thugs to deal with their opponents in the 2003, 2007 and 2011 elections and to help rig those elections. These politicians reportedly lost control of these groups which became rival groups, visiting violence on innocent civilians. Thus, the democratization of violence by politicians within and between political parties has become a source of perennial violence.

The *Yan daba, Yan kalare* and others took on their own dynamics after the elections. As politicians (who had no base before elections) tried to develop their bases after their 'elections' (in order to be independent of their *godfathers*) thuggery became a very lucrative business. Political thugs are essentially purveyors of violence – before, during and after elections.

Sensitive and inappropriate campaign and strategies among politicians have also generated conflicts among members of the political class (as the *Appendix A* shows).

Deliberate and blatant rigging of elections also have been known to be a major source of electoral violence. Often, incumbents mobilize their entire political arsenal for warfare during elections. The 2003 general elections and the 2004 local government elections were blatantly rigged. The 2007 and 2011 elections were also rigged, even though the 2011 elections were an improvement on earlier exercises. Sadly enough, the use or misuse of security agents in this process was so openly done that election observers and monitors reported these activities.[18] Convinced that political parties in government would rig elections in any case, many opposition groups get ready for any eventuality. Often the level of trust among politicians is low. Thus from the election of the Senate President in 1999 through the fraudulent activities of leaders in the process of passing the Electoral Bill of 2001 to the election of Adolphus Wabara as Senator and President of the Senate, the politics of self-interest, not statesmanship, dominated the polity.

In a political arena dominated by political contractors and thugs, politics is brutish and rough. There is no trust that cannot be broken, no confidence that cannot be betrayed, no deal that cannot be undone, and no promise that cannot be reneged. In essence, politics is not *a game* but *a battle*. In that battle, nothing succeeds as much as success and nothing fails as much as failure. Profit to the individual or group, not service, is the primary motive. All hope is not lost, as we continue

---

[18] Refer to the various *Reports of The Transition Monitoring Group and the Commonwealth Observers.*

to hope that political contractors would go legitimate and begin to care about what the people want, by transforming themselves into genuine politicians.

The point is that if "representatives" of the people, do not really represent the people, the authority of governors become questionable. In addition, if the representatives are in government to serve the ends of their mentors, then the people have been tragically hoodwinked—a clear case of *democratic deficit*. A variant of this is the Anambra case in which the list of candidates submitted by the Peoples Democratic Party (PDP) for the election, were replaced after the elections. Is this not substituting the people's will? Luckily, the judiciary came to the rescue of the original candidates.

b. Independent National Electoral Commission (INEC)

The role of INEC is very important, not only in determining who has the *right to rule* but also the credibility of the elections. An INEC that is only independent in name, but dependent on the Executive Branch, is not really independent. The integrity of the umpire is important in the legitimacy of the electoral process. In the 2003 elections, one accepts that the country is large and that not all the staff used for the elections belonged to INEC and they could not effectively control them in the field. But could INEC explain why it declared Ngige winner in the 2003 and yet wanted the elections nullified at the Appeal Court to enable the holding of a new election? The Appeal Court obviously did not find this funny. This sort of thing happened in many parts of the country.

The greater problem for the 2007 election was the low credibility of INEC. Not many Nigerians had confidence in INEC to carryout a 'free and fair elections', inspite of the pleas by its Chairman, Professor Maurice Iwu. Occasionally, INEC seemed to have been in a haste to make pronouncements on sensitive political issues without observing the setting to see the dynamics of events to the end. As an illustration when there was a declaration of a new faction of the PDP. INEC came out quickly to recognize the Ahmadu Ali – led faction. The legitimacy of the Ahmadu Ali faction had extracted court judgment earlier – a judgment the party refused to obey.The point here is that INEC can (and had been) a generator of election violence by its lack of neutrality. As people find their will apparently subverted by the umpire, they lose their confidence for redress in public institutions that are expected to be neutral, and often take laws into their hands.

With the appointment of Professor Attahiru Jega as chairman of INEC, there were high hopes for greater credibility in INEC's conduct of elections. Professor Maurice Iwu the former chairman was openly partisan. While the INEC under Jega has improved on past conduct of elections, there are still many protests. In fact, Election Tribunals, Appeal Courts and the Supreme Courts, have reversed and/or cancelled some of the results announced by INEC in 2011. Many observers feel that the centre of fraud in all elections since 2011 is the *collation centre*. Unfortunately, most of these collation centres at state levels were manned by academics, especially, Vice-Chancellors of universities.

c. *Security Agencies*

Security agencies are expected to maintain law and order in order to protect all – voters, contestants and election officials. They are expected to be neutral. However, in the past, the police force had been accused of complicity in electoral malpractices. In 2003 elections, all security agencies – military and para-military agencies were alleged to be openly partisan. In some cases, the personnel of these agencies were alleged to have fired gun shots in the air, and while the people scampered in different directions, ballot boxes were alleged to have been stolen. In addition, the use of security agencies to harass, intimidate, coerce political opponents by those in power can only generate reciprocal violence.

Candidly, we must insist on the *autonomy and neutrality of public institutions* in the election process. All Nigerians, through their tax, pay for the operation of public institutions. These do not belong to political leaders in government, but to the people. Public media houses at federal and state levels, exhibited nauseating biases in the electoral process. Public media houses became megaphones for the party or the individual in power at federal or state level. Nor should any public agency contribute to the campaign of any political candidate. Electoral tribunals are replete with allegations of how the military and other security forces were compromised as agents or officials of the party in government, to rig elections and intimidate people. This is a clear misuse of public institutions which belong to those in government as well as the opposition. It is a dangerous pattern of democratic deficit.

The use of the Armed Forces and security agencies for domestic politically partisan purposes can be very dangerous even to those in government. It is a misuse of authority given to the representatives to act on behalf of the people.

d. The Judiciary

The role of the judiciary in the electoral process is very crucial. Law-abiding Nigerians are expected to seek redress at the *Election Tribunals*, if they felt aggrieved by the results declared by INEC or the State Independent Electoral Commission (SIEC. Many election tribunal members were alleged to have taken bribe and had consequently given skewed judgements. The Anambra case involving Justice Nnaji over the Ngige case; the Akwa-Ibom case involving Justice Adamu, Senlong and others, illustrate the problems of impartiality on the bench.

It is to the credit of the *National Judicial Commission* that it carried out institutional self-purification by the sacking of Justices Egbo-Egbo, Adamu, Senlong, Nnaji and others. It is ironic that while some judges on the Akwa-Ibom electoral tribunal were dismissed or retired for unethical behaviour, there was no evidence that this really affected the judgment on the governorship election in that state. When those who thought that the judiciary would provide redress for their grievances became disgusted with the perceived injustice emanating from the courts, they took law into their hands.

Unfortunately, the judiciary has been forced by the ineptitude of INEC and other political institutions to engage in political rectitude of the adulterated electoral process. In the process, the judiciary, inspite of its good record, has not been immune from allegations of bribery and corruption.

3. Attitudinal Sources of Electoral Violence (Political Culture)

A number of attitudinal sources of violence would be discussed in this section.

Attitude to Democracy

With punctuations by long periods of military regimes, the political culture of our democratic polity is only inchoate. Nigerian politicians have not been able, in the short time available, to build a political culture which can cushion, regulate and moderate the political process.

Many politicians in Nigeria only use democracy in instrumental terms. They are not committed to democracy as end for which to fight. Often, many of those who become politicians do so make money. For them, as political contractors, politics is a battle. It is also a *zero-game* or a *winnertakes all.* In the circumstances, violence or threat of violence is accepted as a technique for enforcing their interests or protecting their investments. Thus violence transcends electoral period. It is not only useful for acquiring power, no matter how illegitimately, it is important to protect it and retain it, even after elections.

4. *Political Culture*

Many of our politicians have not yet imbibed the values that politics is a game, not a battle, and that your opponent is not necessarily an enemy. They have not learnt the *culture of tolerance, accommodation and participation of all* actors including those who hold different opinions. In addition, both electoral victors and losers do not know how to behave. It is hard to find gracious victors and gallant losers among our political elites. Similarly, politicians refuse to create open and plane field for all competitors. Thus nothing succeeds as much as success or fails as much as failure. Those who succeed will use political overkill to keep others out. Unlike the United States in which Nixon and Lincoln failed many times to achieve their political ambitions and yet came back to become Presidents, in Nigeria, once you fail, you are beaten by your successful opponent until you can get up no more. Thus driven to the wall, the apparently nationalistic Nigerian withdraws into his little cocoon utilizing ethnic, religious and other issues of primordial identity for mobilization of support. It is in the interest of politicians that they *are gracious in victory and gallant in defeat*. They must leave the political door open for erstwhile failures to enter, otherwise they will find it difficult to make graceful exit when they want to do so.

a. The Culture of Violence in Politics

The essence of democracy is freedom – and this includes freedom to hold opinions and to express these. Homogenized views and perspectives are anti-democratic to the extent that they recognize no dissent. Our political leaders and followers must learn that resort to violence in interaction with others of different opinion is anti-democratic. In fact, it is an acceptance of inability to convince the other party. Political parties should agree to co-exist and apply the rules which everyone accepted at the on-set. Violent interactions in legislative houses, political party congresses, at party headquarters, and in other areas of interaction are becoming part of our political culture. Lest we forget, violence leads to breakdown of law and order, and can provide a good excuse for military intervention. Politicians owe themselves and this country the obligation to ensure that political disagreements are handled decently without resorting to violence. A good politician is the one who seeks compromises as solution to problems. A rigid or inflexible politician often wallows in frustration. Unfortunately, many politicians seem to accept violence as part of the democratic political process. We must reverse this trend in Nigeria.

b. The Monetization of Politics

The excessive monetization of politics in Nigeria plays on the poverty of the people. The large army of unemployed youths becomes easy recruits into the platoons of political thugs of the individual politician. The inability of the state to monitor and stop this process is a pity. The easy access to firearms and the use of violence as a technique for settling the minutest of problems, store a rich legacy of instability. It does not always follow that the richest is the most popular among the people. Attempts to use money to subvert reverse or upturn the will of the people often leads to violence. In fact, in some cases, incumbent governments are involved. The violence over local government elections of March 28, 2004 in the Senatorial Zone a of Benue State was allegedly because opponents of PDP resisted attempts by government to rig elections. Each side had stories of how militias were setup to enforce each side's control of the local governments in this senatorial zone[19].

---

[19]*Daily Trust,* March 29, 2004; *ThisDay,* March 29, 2004.

Generally, the attitude of politicians has great impact on electoral violence. The fact that Nigerians have not yet developed a mutually acceptable political culture for regulating the dynamics of the electoral process further complicates the situation. On balance, therefore, the causes of electoral violence in Nigeria are multivariable. These, we have identified under three broad categories – Structural, Institutional and Attitudinal sources of electoral violence.

Manifestations of Electoral Violence

Electoral violence is manifestations of grossly unresolved grievances in the electoral process. They take different forms and dimensions – from boycott of elections through protest to violent reactions. Reactions to elections since independence have been varied. The 1959 elections conducted by the colonial authority did not elicit massive negative reactions. While there were complaints in some quarters, the general concern of Nigerian political leaders was the transition to independence. This was not the case of elections after independence.

In May 1961, the Northern Region held its regional elections which gave the NPC a victory of 94% of seats in the regional assembly. In reaction to this election, the opposition political parties – the *United Middle Belt Congress* (UMBC) and the *Northern Elements Progressive Union* (NEPU) protested the results. They alleged that the NPC used all forms of electoral manipulations, intimidation and even coercion, including the arrest and imprisonment of political opponents. While protests were the greatest manifestation of electoral fraud, there was post-election violence in Tivland.

The situation was no different in the Eastern Regional elections of 1961. The NCNC virtually made that region to have a uniparty assembly. Again, the election was marked by persecution of minority opposition parties, such as the Action Group (AG) operating within the region.

Similarly, with the creation of the Midwest Region, the NCNC and AG deployed men, money and material considered for winning in the regional election which followed. By 1963, it had become evident (after the Midwest elections and then the 1964 controversies over the 1962/63 census figures) that the NPC-NCNC coalition was going to break up. Disappointed from the census issue and afraid of the weight of Northern population, the NCNC teamed up with the AG and their Northern allies – the NEPU and the UMBC respectively – to form the

United Progressive Grand Alliance (UPGA). Okpara made it clear that the NNDP government in the West was a "baby of the NPC set-up in the West by the second Afonja of our time. It is a manoeuver of the NPC to stifle democracy in the West."[20]

On the other hand, by mid-1964, Sir Ahmadu Bello had declared that even if his party failed to "get the required majority in the next federal elections; it will definitely not enter into any agreements or coalition with NCNC." After all, he observed, "the Ibos have never been true friends of the North and will never be..."[21] The NPC, the NNDP, and the *Midwest Democratic Front* (MDF) formed an alliance resulting in a party: the *Nigerian National Alliance* (NNA.

The UPGA had started the 1964 electoral campaigns with every hope, through a consolidation of votes in the south and inroads into the discontented areas of the north (the Middle Belt and Kano areas), to be able to win the elections. However, this hope faded when 66 NPC members from the Northern constituencies were to be returned unopposed to the federal parliament. UPGA leaders were upset and complained about lack of freedom to campaign, and the prevention of its candidates from filing their nominations in the Northern Region. Allegations and counter-allegations from both the UPGA and NNA accentuated the tension of the campaign period.[22] Aggressive ethnicity escalated, and thuggery became an effective instrument of campaigning, especially by the *Sarduana and Okpara Youth Brigades.*

Dr. Okpara and the NCNC protested about the election machinery. The NNA and the Prime Minister, on the other hand, saw nothing wrong with the arrangements. UPGA therefore advised its members to boycott the elections. Only in the East was the boycott total, because the government refused to implement arrangements for the elections. Hence, NPC cleared the Northern seats, the NNDP won 36 out of 57 seats in the west and the NCNC won the belated elections in the Midwestern Region.[23] In Lagos, only a few people went to the polls.

---

[20]*Daily Express,*(8 June 1964), quoted in Mackintosh, *op. cit.* p. 564.
Afonja had called for Fulani help in his revolt in Yoruba land. This revolt was the beginning of the disintegration of the Yoruba Empire. That was how Ilorin and Kabba Provinces (later) became part of Northern Nigeria.

[21]*Daily Express,* (20 July, 1964), quoted in Mackintosh, *op. cit.*, p. 564.

[22] A good discussion of the tempo of the election is in J. O'Connell, "Politicsal Integration: The Nigerian Case", in Arthur Hazelwood (ed.), *African Integration and Disintegration* (London: Oxford University press, 1967), pp. 129-184.

[23] In the Midwestern Region, the NCNC government called off its election boycott.

Dissatisfied with the conduct of the elections, Azikiwe refused to ask Tafawa Balewa to form the government. He was accused by the north of being in league with the East.[24] His attempt to get the military to take over power temporarily was declined by the heads of the Armed Forces, who had been advised that they owed their allegiance to the Prime Minister for operational orders and not to the President.[25]

However, with the advice of the Federal Chief Justice, the Attorney-General, and the Chief Justice of the Eastern Region, an arrangement was worked out whereby Tafawa Balewa was to form a "broad-based" government comprising all major political parties, and elections were to be held in the Eastern Region.[26] Dissatisfied with the situation, the Eastern Regional leaders were said to have threatened to secede from the federation.[27] The UPGA boycott was a mistake it lived to regret. It could have done better than it eventually did in the Western Region, given the erosion of Akintola's legitimacy. One thing became clear; the fear of northern domination by population had become part of the southern political belief system, much as northern fears of southern domination by skills acquired through western education had encouraged its leaders to oppose any break-up of the north. The atmosphere of political corruption, violence and thuggery, and aggressive ethnoregionalism which had raised the political temperature of the federation beyond "normal" levels was further accentuated by the 1965 Western Regional elections.

In the Western Region, elections did not take place until October 1965. Given the Western crisis and the emergence of Akintola's *Nigerian National Democratic Party* (NNDP), the gulf between AG and the new party widened.The 1965 Western elections provided the

---

[24]Mackintosh, *op. cit.*, pp.603-146.

[25] N. J. Miners, *op. cit.*, pp. 139-146. While Azikiwe, as President, was nominally the Supreme Commander of the Armed Forces, the actual power to commit the forces to action laid with the Prime Minister. It took the election crisis to unveil how little power Zik had in the Constitution. He was reported to have threatened to resign rather than appoint Abubakar as the Prime Minister.

[27] Azikiwe's *State House Diary* had accused Okpara and his Eastern colleagues of threatening to secede on 26 December 1964 (see *Daily Times,* 13 January 1965). However, Mackintosh (p. 604) reported UPGA leaders as accusing only the President (Azikiwe) of having "contemplated breaking up the federation because he had felt that attacks on him and on the Ibos were becoming intolerable." Yet, Okpara was quoted on the same day as having said that "if this is how the NPC wants to run the election, then this country is finished, and that disintegration was inevitable if the NPC continued to act in ways that would undermine unity of Nigeria". *Daily Express* (22 December, 1964). It was reported that Ahmadu Bello welcomed the idea of Eastern Region's secession, if given the time to "divide our assets" *(Daily Express*, 30 December 1964), all on p. 604; Mackintosh, *op. cit.*,

Southern parties (AG - NCNC) the "last desperate attempt to challenge the hegemony of NPC," whose inroads into the south had threatened the security of many Southern politicians. They had thought that by "winning control of the West – a real possibility in view of the evident unpopularity of the Akintola regime – they would have the control of all three Southern Regions as well as Lagos."[28] This would then give UPGA members of the Senate a majority with which to frustrate legislation by the NPC majority in the House. The Senate then comprised of 8 members selected by each Regional House, four from Lagos and four by the President.

In the Western region election campaigns, accusations about the conduct of the 1965 elections were rampant. The opposition parties complained about difficulties in filing their nominations, while NNDP members were given easy access to filing their nominations. Among allegations against the Akintola government was the availability of ballot papers to NNDP members before polling, the violation of regulations in vote–counting and illegal announcement of results. The NNDP was eventually declared the winner. Violence, thuggery, arson and looting punctuated normal patterns of life in the Western Region. This was the era of *Operation Wetie,* in which thugs often threw petrol-wet tires around the neck of their opponents and set them on fire. Killings and intimidations of public officials drew repression from government, and more repression gave momentum to greater breakdown of law and order in the region. The military coup of 1966 only saved observers the speculations about the trend of Nigeria's political development.

The next election worth writing about, given the punctuation of the democratic process by military regimes, was the 1979 elections. While some political parties complained about the fairness of this election umpired by the military, the *National Party of Nigeria* was declared the victor. This led to court cases and the judgment that President Shagari had been duly elected President.

In the Second Republic, there were other manifestations of the 1979 elections. The 1979 elections had seen Alhaji Balarabe Musa as the Governor of Kaduna. However, the House of Assembly was dominated by the NPN, and not his *Peoples Redemption Party* (PRP members. He was easily impeached for matters which could have been resolved in other ways.

---

[28] Schwarz, *op. cit.,* p. 178.

The 1983 elections were also notorious for its history of electoral fraud. Before the elections, inter-party factional and ethnic rivalries had boiled over into political violence in many states. There were reports of rigging all over the country. In fact, if in 1964, pregnant women were going into polling booths and coming out unpregnant, by 1983, the technique of rigging had improved. Coffins were intercepted with thumbed ballot papers. Attempts to change the political landscape of Nigeria through the elections, by the ruling party generated reactions. In Oyo and Ondo States, there were protests and violent demonstrations as the NPN purportedly claimed victory in those states. Infact, one elected Governor could not operate in the State capital for a while. In Anambra, Gongola and Borno States, there were similar reactions to NPN 'landslide' victory. This 'landslide' victory of the NPN was quickly transformed into 'gunslide' as the military intervened in politics again.

The attempt by General Babangida to organize a Presidential election in 1992 was aborted. In June 1993, the Presidential election held was later annulled, even though many Nigerians considered it "freest and fairest" elections until then. The result of this annulment was heightened political tension, violence and insecurity of lives and property. Even though the acclaimed winner, Chief M.K.O. Abiola did not become President, this election sent reverberations into the polity which beclouded future attempts to restore democracy to Nigeria.

In 1999, elections were held which brought President Olusegun Obasanjo to power. Rigged as this election was, it was believed that on balance, the results were acceptable. The three major political parties – the *Alliance for Democracy* (AD); the *All Peoples Party* (APP) and the *Peoples Democratic Party* had control over a number of state governments, and also had members in the National Assembly. The PDP controlled the federal government.

In the 2003 elections, politicians seemed to have replayed the 1983 scenario. The PDP allegedly rigged its way into the South-West zones uprooting all AD - controlled states, except Lagos. Similarly, ANPP lost states such as Kogi and Kwara to PDP. The 2003 elections were blatantly rigged. Not only were ballot boxes stuffed, new techniques of elections fraud were used. Security agents fired shots in to the air while ballot boxes were carted away, in many places. In other places, there were amazing skills displayed in "voodoo mathematics" by adding zeros to figures. In some cases, the total figures allegedly counted were higher than the total registered population of the state. In other cases, candidates who had voted for themselves found that they had scored zero in their wards where they had voted.

Before, during and after elections there were various forms of electoral clashes. The AD suffered from factionalization, while the followers of Governor Bisi Akande of Osun and his Deputy, Iyiola Omisore clashed. Similarly, there were clashes between the followers of Senator Modu Sheriff and Malla Kachalla in Borno State. In Kwara State, Governor Mohammad Lawal and Senator Olusola Saraki had confrontations. In PDP, the followers of Governor Sam Egwu and Senate President Anyim had violent clashes, leading to loss of lives. The Nnamani–Nwobodo crisis in Enugu State followed the above pattern.

Political h omicides also was high. The assassination of Chief Bola Ige, the former Attorney-General of Nigeria, Honourable Tunde Olagbaju of Osun State House of Assembly, Ogbonnanya Uche, a commissioner in Imo State; Harry Marshall, Aminasoari Dikibo, PDP Chairman in Kogi; as well as the politically motivated political assassination of three gubernatorial aspirants in Plateau, Lagos and Ekiti (Mr. Jesse Aruku of ACD, and Engr. Funsho Williams and Dr. Ayodeji Daramola of PDP respectively) between July 1 to August 18, 2006– all point to some of the manifestations of electoral violence in Nigeria.

The 2004 local government elections conducted by the State Electoral Commissioners (SIEC) were even worse than the 2003 election. Each state government ensured rigging for its favourites – it was widespread across the country. Thus when election-time violence profusely dotted the Nigerian map in 2004, it was not surprising. From the violence in Esan West, Edo; Abudu, Edo; Malumeri, Borno; Zone A Senatorial District in Benue (Ukum, Katsina-Ala, Kwande, Ushongo, Koshisha and Vandeikya); Dadume in Katsina; Epe in Lagos; Oluji/Ike-Igbo in Ondo; to Jato Aka in Benue – all in March 2004 – we had violent reactions to perceived election frauds.

The April 2007 elections were even worse than the 2003 elections. Although, President Olusegun Obasanjo did not stand for elections (given constitutional provisions) he allegedly managed to turn himself into the 'de facto' chairman of INEC, virtually determining who won or lost in areas he was interested. The 2007 elections were probably the worst in the nation's history, and eroded the credibility of elected officials and institutions. The "do or die" politics espoused by

Obasanjo during these elections was a very negative contribution to Nigeria's electoral culture.

The 2011 elections were an improvement on the 2007 elections. While the judiciary reversed and/or cancelled some of the results, it is generally believed by observers that the 2011 election were better than those of 2007. However, while the 2011 elections were apparently free, they were adjudged 'unfair' given the numerous allegations of voting result tampering at the state collation centres.

In essence, reactions to perceived election fraud begin with voter registration exercise and the political party (during nominations) and continue well until after elections. They take the form of:

- Petitions to tribunals.
- Boycott of elections.
- Political intimidation/and reactions.
- Tension-charged and even violent campaigns.
- Violent clashes among different political groups.
- Insecurity of lives and property.
- Breakdown or near breakdown of law and order.
- Demonstrable recklessness–arson and wanton destruction.
- Failure of the police to cope with demands on their capacity.
- The adulteration of the political arena for all politicians, making life unsafe for political players and spectators.

Consequences of Electoral Violence

Electoral violence is like a *coup* or *war*. You know how and when it starts, but you never know when and how it ends. The most visible consequence of electoral violence is political instability. Every nation needs political stability for development and for the grafting of democratic values in the polity.

Nigeria's political history of elections and electoral violence has pointed to two factors. The first is that elections which are umpired by colonial and military governments seem to be, generally speaking, less fraudulent than those organized by civilian political incumbents – transiting from civilian to civilian democratic rule. Secondly, the politics of self-succession had been central to the level of electoral fraud and subsequent high level of intensity of electoral violence.

The fall of the First Republic was directly traceable to electoral fraud and violence, especially between 1964 and 65. The Second Republic also fell mainly as a result of the legitimacy of the 1983 electoral process and the violence arising therefrom. May be, if Nigerian politicians had been able to rein their mutual fears and suspicions, and had not bastardized the electoral process, we would not have had a civil war.

Are there direct consequences of electoral violence? Let us identify a few consequences:

a. ***Political Instability*** - caused by electoral violence can abort the democratic process and give way to authoritarian regimes, - thus robbing the people of their authority, since power belongs to them.
b. ***Loss of Lives and Property*** – create insecurity, thus threatening the fundamental basis of society. Law and order is an essential end of the state.
c. ***Increase in Fetish and Cult Activities***— electoral process is associated with increasing cases 'missing people' that are believed to be have been used for ritual purposes. Innocent citizens are believed to be used as 'sacrificial lambs' for the purpose of seeking power or winning elections. In some cases, political contractors are alleged to use occultic power to endorse political protégés in order to guarantee llegiance. Similarly, fetish oaths to political clients are also reportedly used as a means to secure loyalty.
d. ***Legitimacy*** -of governments gets eroded and their ability to perform becomes undermined; good governance becomes endangered.
e. ***Societal Consensus***- for purposive action is undermined by the various cleavages arising from electoral crises and violence.
f. ***Attenuation of Development***-programmes can directly result from the instability created by electoral violence. The destruction involved and the man-hours lost are incalculable, not to mention the advantage of such situations taken by criminals.
g. ***Expansion of Various Dimensions of Poverty*** – an issue which normally would have been tackled by good governance which is often lacking.
h. ***Deepening of Existing Structural Cleavages*** in the nation – ethnic, religious, geoethnic land and others – thus compounding the problems of nation-building.

i. ***Creation of Internally Displaced People*** – creating refugees in their own countries.

Candidly, one can go on listing possible consequences of electoral violence. To avoid unnecessary overlaps, we shall stop here. The consequences of electoral violence are so grave that the growth of a nation is dependent on how it responds appropriately to electoral grievances. All the consequences listed above have played themselves out in Nigeria. Where do we go from here?

Thus, there are challenges posed by democratic governance for security and peace in Nigeria. Nigerians must be honest and determined in dealing with these challenges in order to create a conducive environment for relatively stable process of national development.

CHAPTER FOUR

TOWARDS SECURITY AND PEACE FOR NATIONAL DEVELOPMENT

From the preceding chapters, it is clear that without peace and relative stability there can be no national development. The number of crises and conflicts which we have had is an indication of the need that political elites in Nigeria must device appropriate mechanism for managing conflicts. However, our records in conflict management have been poor. Often, we are incapable of predicting conflicts. Even when intelligence reports provide such warnings, we leave the matter unattended until conflicts escalate to a level in which we have to make *crises decisions*.[1] There is a pattern of government responding only after a violent conflict. As the *Institute for Peace and Conflict Resolution* (IPCR) report shows, government's responses are patterned and predictable.[2] First, government uses the option of demonstrable force to quell violent conflicts, with little effort to address the causes of the conflict. At times, it rushes to deal with symptoms of violent conflicts, rather than try to find the real causes and deal with them.

The usual second step by government is to provide relief materials. Appeals are also made to the National Emergency Management Agency (NEMA) to assist with relief materials. Thirdly, there is the establishment of *Commissions of Inquiry* into the violent conflict. Often, no one reads the report. Even when there is a *White Paper*, the recommendations are hardly implemented. Similarly where the perpetrators of conflicts are well known and are indicted by the reports, they are not punished. This shows lack of will to establish peace among belligerent groups.

---

[1] See editorial of the *Leadership Sunday*, August 2, 2009, p. 3. Also see J. Isawa Elaigwu, *The Shadow of Religion on Nigerian Federalism: 1960 – 93* (Abuja: NCIR Monograph Series, No. 2, 1993) for some crises decisions on Maitasine crises in the country.

[2] Institute of Peace and Conflict Resolution (IPCR, *Strategic Conflict Assessment: Consolidated and Zonal Reports, Nigeria* (Abuja: IPCR, 2003).

As IPCR report puts it

> The main thrust of government response is to use the military to suppress conflict. The problem is that this may stop the use of violence in the short term but it does not address genuine underlying problems Military responses often take place in isolation from other responses despite opportunities for joint activity and sharing of perspectives.[3]

In essence, our responses have been *ad hoc* and not organized. Force is no solution to communal and other conflicts. We must make efforts move on to identify how we can *prevent* conflicts, *manage* them and/or *resolve* or *cope* with them.

While inter-state collaborative effort among state governors and chairmen of local governments have been useful in inter-state conflicts, political, religious, traditional and ethnic leaders in most areas of conflict hardly sit together to discuss the causes of ethnoreligious violence and how to prevent future violent conflicts. Leaders hardly meet to build bridges of understanding and re-establish mutual confidence among feuding groups. These leaders also exhibit nauseating hypocrisy when violent conflict breaks out. Often these leaders make explosive and insensitive statements in favour of their various groups. Government must encourage the emergence of platforms for ethnoreligious and other leaders to establish a network for conflict prevention and management.

It is understood that at the federal, state and local levels, there are *Peace and Security Committees*. How effective are these committees? What support systems do they have? Or are they the usual structures established by governments after a violent conflict but left unequipped, under-funded and under-utilized?

In Nigeria, there seems to be a *large gap between the leaders and followers.* Amidst the *pervasive poverty* in the country, leaders exhibit blatantly conspicuous consumption. The army of unemployed graduates at all school levels tends to be on the rise. Except in a few states, there is no attempt by government to respond to this economic and social problem. The recruitment of the cheap labour from the market of the unemployed for the purposes of dispensing violence to political enemies or ethnoreligious opponents is a poor response to economic problems. It can even boomerang on the leader who hired the thugs.

---

[3]IPCR, *ibid* p.55.

The more frustrating part of the problem is that the most active actors in these cases of violence are very young people. These are people who at very young age have specialized in the wanton destruction of lives and property, as well as the reckless spillage of human blood. What kind of citizens are we building? Why are the elites not using their own children in these cases of violence? Why do they incite other people's children to engage in violence? Is it that their children can find jobs easily while those of the others cannot? We must, as leaders (in and out of government), be very sensitive to the demand for adequate socio-economic responses to conflicts.

There has been a *lack of political will* in the management of violent conflicts. Government should provide a regular platform for collaborative efforts by political, ethnic, religious and traditional leaders to meet with other stakeholders, such as Non-Governmental Organizations (NGOs), Civil Society Organizations, the media, business and labour. This may provide a broader basis for the effective prevention, control and resolution of conflicts.

It is sad that with so many violent communal conflicts in Nigeria over so many years, our management of these conflicts is so poor. Our inaction has destroyed lives and property, without a developing reservoir of skills in managing these conflicts. This is partly because some of the members of the elite benefit from these conflicts.

We must establish a collectively approved mechanism for managing communal conflicts. After all, violent conflicts are like bush fire, they respect no state or local government boundaries; they recognize no important man, and they even consume, at times, those who planned and helped to execute the violence.

As for *non-governmental actors*, there has been no evidence of coordinated efforts. Local NGOs are weak and donor agency fund-dependent. Traditional rulers, who had been useful in the process of peace-making, are losing their credibility in many parts of the country. Useful as the mass media are, they over-sensationalize news items. They need to exercise greater self-censorship on sensitive issues in order not to exacerbate conflicts.

As observed earlier, conflicts are inevitable. The important point is that the political elites at the centre of decision-making at all tiers of government, must make conscious efforts at reforms targeted to managing conflicts through - *prevention, control or containment, transformation and/or resolution.* It is often necessary that these reforms are targeted at:

a. ***Transcending Domestic Conflicts*** – when the issue of conflict at a point in time is transcended by time and exigencies. Issues which were contentious cease to be contentious because of new developments.
b. ***Limiting the Extent of Conflict*** – in this situation attempts are made to limit the actual spread of conflicts or its impact in order to enable decision-makers or even third parties to handle the situation. Efforts are then made to minimize the intensity and scope of conflicts.
c. ***Compartmentalizing Conflicts*** – in this situation, decision-makers reduce the scope of conflicts into smaller compartments in order to cope with arising conflicts. Some people argue that the creation of states was a way of compartmentalizing areas of conflicts into smaller units, in order to enable government manage ensuing conflicts; and
d. ***Cross-Cutting Conflicts*** – it is believed by experts that in a setting where people have cross-cutting loyalties, it is more difficult to mobilize total loyalty by any group for parochial actions.
e. These reforms can take many forms – from structural or institutional arrangements, through processual adjust-ments to constitutional amendments.

Conflict management is not a neat and unilinear affair. In fact, it may take place in such chaotic a setting; you would think that the state has failed. Ideally, there are professionally recognized techniques for conflict management. These include:

a. Bringing the conflicting parties together to "establish mutual agreement".
b. Intervention by third parties (governments or others) to directly intervene to "introduce or impose a decision".
c. Introduction of "new initiative, programmes, or institutional structures" (such as elections) to address the issue of conflict.
d. Compelling contending parties to utilize previously established agreements on means.

e. Using government or third party force to repress or "eliminate or instil fear among one or all those engaged in a given conflicts, leading to subsidence.[4]

Whatever technique or style is used to manage a conflict depends on the conflict situation. Governments must endeavour to have a data base for generating early warning signals to prevent conflicts. While conflict prevention may appear expensive, it is probably less costly in the long run for the society.

In the context of socio-economic, security and political challenges above, how do we proceed from here? Do we give up? This is not an option, because we owe our children a relatively stable polity within which development can take place. The only option available to us seems to be – taking up the challenges, facing these challenges collectively, with courage, discipline, and patriotism. We cannot afford to be overwhelmed by these challenges, rather, our resolve and actions should enable us to overcome these challenges.

Given the atmosphere of physical insecurity which currently envelops the country, especially Northern Nigeria, we need to take urgent actions to set up the machinery for the *prevention, management and resolution of conflicts.* Generally, we tend to treat security issues very lightly. Yet, without adequate security, nothing else can take place. Let us therefore, make recommendations on how to roll-back the c*arpet of violent conflicts* – ie. How to prevent, manage crises and conflicts in Nigeria, especially in Northern Nigeria.

We shall discuss our recommendations under four broad categories – 1) *Socio-economic issues;* 2) *Political (Democratic governance*); 3) *Security and 4) Others*. It is pertinent to note that these issues overlap and the categories used here are for analytic purposes.

1. Socio-Economic Issues

c. *The Development of Early Warning Signals*

Since political elites are not committed to resolving the problems of communal conflicts and violence, they are unprepared for future cases of violence. Having experienced these violent conflicts before, one would expect each state government to have a well-equipped and

[4] Christopher A. Miller, *A Glossary of Terms and Concepts In Peace and Conflict Studies* (Geneva: University of Peace, Education for Peace in Africa Programme) p. 8.

manned *Conflict Management Unit.* This unit should have data on conflicts, and the capability to analyze and provide an *early warning signal* to government. True, not all conflicts can be predicted because human behaviour can also be spontaneous or instinctive in reaction to external provocations. But such a Centre or Unit, which constantly liaises with IPCR, and holds regular seminars for the Federal, State and Local Government Security Committees, would be helpful. As the IPCR Report observed:

> The conclusion of this study is that an early warning does not exist yet in Nigeria and there is need to put one in place. An Early Warning Mechanism or system is not such until an early warning has been fed into the system and appropriate responses elicited as a result of such warning.[5]

Efforts have been made to establish an early warning system, but these are at initial stages and are not coordinated to have desirable impact.

Our governments must thus establish active *Conflict Management Units*, to help provide proper information, identification, and interpretation of conflicts and provide policy options, from which appropriate responses can be undertaken. This also involves training appropriate staff for these units. Many governments in Nigeria still operate as if they are in the 19thcentury. We must take advantage of the technological and communication revolution of the late 20thcentury, and operate efficient and effective governments.

d. Mutual Respect and Recognition of Claims of Others

Many of the conflicts we have witnessed emerged from the lack of mutual respect for one another. We cannot all be the same. We must realize that even within a single family, religious and ethnic group, there are differences in perspectives and opinions. Disdain and arrogance (bankrupt of content) are often marks of inferiority complex.

Similarly, as we mentioned earlier, we must be able to dialogue with one another, no matter how difficult. We should respect and recognize the claims of others in a competitive context even if we disagree with such claims. The non-recognition of claims of others generates major conflicts which often mobilizes total ethnic and

[5] IPCR, *op. cit.*, p. 61.

religious loyalties. The recognition of claims, while disputing the nature of claims, creates a basis for discussion. Here the quarrel is over shares; how much; and not the illegitimacy of claims. Governments can play helpful roles in mediating in some of these conflicting claims. It should not wait until the competitive process turns into violent interactions among claimants. So also can civil societies, NGOs and even the private sector contribute to the prevention of conflicts. We must accept the reality that while it is necessary to create "unity in diversity", we must identify and respect our differences – "diversity in unity"

e. Indigeneship And Settler Problems: Towards Residency Requirements

This has become a problem all over the country. In spite of the rhetorics about Nigerian *citizenship*, all Nigerians recognize that there is *indigeneship*. This problem cannot be solved by political hypocrisy and rhetoric. Yes, there have been patterns of migrations. But we all know the settlement patterns at this point in time. Even though the Hausa-Fulani have lived in Shagamu for over a hundred years, how many of them are in the local government councils or in the Ogun State House of Assembly? In Abia, Enugu and Anambra States, Hausa-Fulani people have lived there for a long time, how many are recognized as indigenes of even local government council areas? In Kano and Adamawa States, many Ibos have lived there for generations. How many of them are recognized as indigenes? Even the names of individuals immediately disqualify them. Similarly, in Jos and Kaduna, many Urhobo and Yoruba families have lived there for many generations. Have they been accepted as indigenes? One has been reliably informed that in Kaduna, Benue, Kano, Lagos and a few other states, there are non-indigenes in the various State Houses of Assembly or in the municipal councils. One hopes that this trend continues.

Yes, the constitution provides that every Nigerian can live anywhere in Nigeria, but do all Nigerians have the same indigeneship rights everywhere? No! Political hypocrisy will not help us resolve this problem. Let us be frank and realistic with ourselves. The 1999 Constitution, sections 25-32, and the Part I, provides in item 9, that "citizenship, naturalization and aliens" is an exclusive matter of the government of the federation. Thus, any Nigerian can live anywhere in the federation. Note that citizenship is not a concurrent matter as in the other federations of the world.

However, many activities of government, and the contents of the constitution still remind us that we need an identity called *indigeneship*. As an illustration, it does not matter how long a man has lived in Kaduna, his daughter who is admitted to the Federal Government College, is required to go to her local government to get a *certificate of indigeneship* even though she has never been there. Can you imagine Miss Ngozi Okoro going to Kafanchan or Yola to request for a certificate of indigeneship, even if she had been born there? Or Usman Sani getting a certificate of indigeneship from Shagamu? It is doubtful if she/he would ever get it unless she/he goes to her/his original local government, which she/he hardly knows or visits. In the light of these difficulties, State Liason Offices now issue certificates of indigenship, in Abuja but this is not really a solution to the problem.

In addition, in the employment into the federal or State Public Services, the principle of *Federal Characte*r is applied. The *Federal Character Commission* is expected to monitor these patterns of recruitment and call for corrections. In fact, recruitment into public services also requires an identification of one's religion and certificate of indigeneship.

As a federation, one believes that *citizenship should be a concurrent matter under the constitution.* Each state should have a residency requirement, given the laws of the state. A state could provide that if you have lived for 15 or 25 years in the state, or if you were born there and contributed to its development, you should be given a certificate of indigenship and entitled to all the privileges of an indigene. However, this means that you cannot carry your family in truckloads to your original village for census exercises or elections. You have a new base of territorial identity. This may be similar to provisions of residency requirements in most federal states.

Let us be honest with ourselves. We cannot eat our cake and have it. We cannot run a federal system and run away from issues of dual identities.

f. Depoliticization and De-Radicalization of Ethnic and Religious Groups

In the light of the cost of violent communal conflicts especially in the North, ethnic and religious groups need to be depoliticized and deradicalized. Politicians must halt the current trend of manipulating these two groups, with primordial identities, for political and selfish ends. Politics overly radicalizes religion and ethnicity as vehicles of violence. An elaborate process of depoliticizing and de-radicalizing ethnic and religious groups must be put in place. Government should seriously think of setting up a panel on this.[6]

g. Establishment of Framework for Constant Dialogue and Understanding

Perhaps one area of urgent action is the establishment of frameworks for constant dialogue and understanding among traditional leaders, religious groups and ethnic groups within each state, as a first step. This is important because violence can easy spill across borders of either local government of states. The second step is a national forum for dialogue. The current forum for religious leaders in Nigeria can be prodded to become more proactive, with branches at each state and local government level.

While the management of conflicts is important and continuous in the lives of nation-states, it is even more important to put in place *mechanisms for conflict prevention.* Conflict prevention, management and resolution are cardinal functions of government. The use of force is not the only way to deal with conflicts. There is a social limit to the use of force. Force only brings temporary order, not peace, because it does not tackle the sources of conflicts. One effective way of preventing and managing conflict is to invest resources on getting to the root of the problem, no matter how difficult these may be. Treating symptoms may cost the system dearly.

h. Education and the De-Almajarization of Violence

Educational institutions in the country have virtually collapsed – from primary through secondary schools to universities and other tertiary institutions. Education is the key to all forms of development. Northern Nigeria started with a lag in the educational sector, behind the South. The gap is growing wider everyday. Governments in the

[6] See, Bala Usman, *The Manipulation of Religion in Nigeria: 1977 – 1987* (Kaduna: Vanguard Publishers 1987). Bello Usman and others, "The Violent Politics of Religion and the Survival of Nigeria", *New Nigeria* (Kaduna) March 25, 1987; J. Isawa Elaigwu, *The Shadow of Religion on Federalism*, op. cit.; J. Isawa Elaigwu and Habu Galadima, "The Shadow of the Sharia Over Nigerian Federalism," *Publius: The Journal of Federalism*, 33.3 (Summer 2003).

North should declare an *Education Emergency* throughout Northern Nigeria. It should fund and encourage the improvement of the quality of education as well as increase the number of human capital developed through these institutions. All children of school-going age must go to school. Parents who default must face the legal music.

Our leaders, such as Generals Hassan Katsina and Muhammadu Buhari, had expressed their concern about the *Almajari* situation in the North. The Sultan had indicated the need for an urgent action in this area. Many northern leaders really did not take this issue very seriously until the *almajarization* of violence after the presidential election in 2011.

We must take urgent action to educate these young people so that they fend for themselves and derive self-dignity from the fruits of their labour. This is an urgent area of attention for all relevant state government in the North.

Related to the above issue is the fall in the quality of education. We destroyed the old Teacher Training System, and the primary schools are in shambles. Secondary Schools are no better. It was understandable for children in 1950s to study under trees, but there is no excuse for this in 2012. The proliferation of federal and state universities has further diluted the quality of education. The universities are currently producing many *graduates who are unemployable*. A situation in which a university lecturer shuttles between five to six universities (because of shortage in qualified lecturers) leaves no room for research, not to mention quality teaching. Often contact hours with students for purposes of advice and guidance are hardly available in tertiary institutions today. This does not augur well for development. All governments in Nigeria must *review their education programmes* urgently. Universities are not like industries to be distributed to political constituencies. They take time to grow and take on their dynamics, before they produce good fruits.

i. Delivery of Services

Most governments in the country have really become weak in the delivery of services. Take a look at our hospitals, and you will see how deplorable our health situation has become. The old Native Authority (NA health dispensaries, which served people, even in rural areas of the North have collapsed. The sanitary inspection system which was part of our primary healthcare system has disappeared. Government needs to totally revamp the health sector, because a healthy population is more likely to be a productive population, than an unhealthy one.

Governments must work hard to bring development to rural areas. Not only should rural roads be opened up, our people should drink water from clean sources. Good potable water, shelter, basic health services and roads are basic services that our people demand in the first half of the twenty-first century. These should help liberate the people from poverty. Many governments are weak in these areas, especially in the North. We must reverse the situation. Our mechanism for the delivery of services must be more efficient and effective.

j. Improving the Economy and Managing Unemployment

Candidly, unless those in government are in a country different from ours, they should realize that conditions of life are currently very hard for the average Nigerian. Eating poses a real problem, not to mention taking members of your family to hospitals. Many families can no longer pay school fees. There are no jobs for even those who have graduated from secondary schools, polytechnics and universities. There is a large army of the unemployed, ready to be used for odious jobs which bring in some income. Armed robbery, political thuggery, banditry, kidnapping and other forms of crimes have virtually been "legitimized" by the logic of the imperatives of survival.

The global economic meltdown has hit both industrialized and developing economies very hard. For an economy that largely relies on *petronaira,* it cannot be any harder. We seem sentenced to budget deficits as our foreign reserve dwindles. However we can turn around the current situation to fortune. We can make it a blessing in disguise. We need to diversify our monocultural economy. We must not forget that rural communities are the 'engine' of growth. They are the greens of the country, rich in land and labour even though they may have scarce capital and infrastructure. Our consumption pattern must be regulated, if we are to become a developed economic power by 2020. It is important, as part of our extractive and productive mechanism, that government funds agriculture, solid minerals and small and medium manufacturing sectors. Now is the time for the Government to wade into the crisis-ridden sectors of the economy as the erstwhile champions *of the free market* in the West are now sinking money into their productive economic activities. From deregulation, the apostles of the *free market* in the West have opted for *guided regulation*. What lessons do these experiences have for us?

With our abundant human and natural resources, we strongly believe that our poverty is related to the ineptitude and inefficiency in the governance of the country. Our governments at federal, state and local levels must summon the courage and will to fight this menace, which from all available indicators, is on the increase. Our deregulationand privatizationpolicies must be pursued with all sense of patriotism and sincerity, transparency and accountability. From available evidence (even in the media) the privatization exercise has been transformed into the personalization of our national assets, especially under the Obasanjo regime. Some cases of privatization should be revisited for justice and equity.

There can be no meaningful development today without energy (power). We have not been serious in this area. For an ambitions country which wants to be a world economic power, our epileptic power supply undercuts our industrialization efforts. We must effectively tackle corruption which has been a major source of decay and delay in the power sector.

k. Corruption

Corruption is probably the most dangerous cankerworm in Nigeria's process of development. It has devastating effect in all efforts at industrialization and modernization. Part of the problem is that many Nigerian leaders pay lip-service to anti-corruption crusades they launch. Often, anti-corruption laws apply to everyone else (especially the opponents of political leaders) but not to them. They live above the laws and wallow in conspicuous consumption to the chagrin of the masses.

In addition, Nigeria's anti-corruption laws place too much emphasis on the *punishment* of offenders, but are low on mechanisms for the prevention, control and management of corrupt practices. Mechanisms to check and/or prevent people from looting public treasury would perhaps save the country the collossal losses it has experienced. Putting in place auditing and effective inspectorate system may help to raise alarms before funds get stolen.

It must also be admitted that the Nigerian polity has little or no *reward* mechanism for honest and patriotic citizens. The National Honours awards have been so bastardised that it has lost its value as a token of reward or appreciation. Not many honest Nigerians are proud of receiving national honours these days. Something must be done urgently to reverse this perception. Other forms of rewards can also be established to appreciate the hardworking, honest and patriotic citizen. A country that only provides for punishing offenders, but has no appreciation for service, is likely to have problems of commitment from its citizens.

2. **Political/Democratic Governance Issues**

There are other issues of political importance that are relevant to our sustainable peace, security and stability for purposes of national development.

a. Government Sensitivity in Decisions and Policies

Our governments should be *sensitive, fair and just* in their decisions and policies. It is wrong for governments and/or their officials to be conflict-generators. Nor should government over-heat the polity through hurriedly reharshed and improperly thought-out policy because it suits the interest of a few people either in government or those who have influence over government. Good governance entails catering for the interests of the majority while protecting the interests of the minority. Nor should governors/politicians maintain their own *militia* for political purposes. The Federal Government should ban any existing ones. All extra-constitutional militia should be banned by law.

b. Political Maturity of Leaders

Leadership is not about privileges to loot public treasury or push personal interests to the disadvantage of the masses. Leadership is responsibility, an obligation to demonstrate co*mmitment, integrity, honesty* and *decency* in handling the affairs of a heterogeneous group which chose you as a leader. The speeches and utterances of our religious, ethnic, traditional and political leaders before, during and after communal conflicts clearly show that they do not have *patience, understanding, honesty, maturity and tolerance,* which are marks of good leadership. It is even worse when these leaders manipulate ethnic and religious identities[7] for their selfish ends. Mature leaders do treat their followers with respect and do not talk down to them. Our leaders must encourage mutual respect even in the context of vehement disagreements among groups. Perhaps even as important are such leadership qualities such as *Justice, Fairness and Equity* which are cardinal to the survival of any polity, not to mention a federal polity. Many of the demands for additional subnational states in Nigeria are results of feelings of injustices by those who feel deprived.

We need a National Conference of all ethnic and religious groups to jaw-jaw and also to learn the values of tolerance and accommodation. This takes a long time to achieve, but we must not underrate it. We must start now. We can start this at the state levels first, and then have delegations to a *National Conference on Conflict Management*. All State governments should host a State Conference on Communal conflicts (ie religious, ethnic etc).

c. ***Control of Electoral Malpractices and the Management of Polit ical Intolerance***

Leaders who are not genuinely *elected lack legitimacy*. These leaders know themselves. Driving in tinted glass cars with a retinue of scare-crows called security people is not leadership. A leader is usually close to the people. What should he be afraid of? Should he be afraid of his own shadows? I know some governors who drive with an entourage of three cars, and at times, they even drive themselves and stop to talk to the people along their way. Yet, I have also seen governor's entourage of between 10-20 vehicles intimidating other road users and deafening our ears with Nigeria's symptom of officialdom – sirens. Apart from share wastage, this latter group of governors demonstrates that it is wary of the very people whom it claims had elected it. This opinion is without prejudice to the security requirements of leaders. Even traditional leaders and their escorts stampede us off our roads. The nuisance of sirens has become an evidence of the reckless lifestyle of our leaders. In many other countries the sound of the siren reminds one of the police, medical ambulances, the fire-service and such others which deal with emergency situations.

---

[7] Politically mature leaders respect the religion of others. In a multicultural society such as Nigeria's, they exhort ecumenicalism – ie. the peaceful co-existence of multiple religious groups.

We must avoid electoral malpractices. It is an evidence of *democratic deficit* to rig elections – that is to replace the people's mandate. It is a way of telling the people – "you do not like me, but here I am in spite of you. Do your worst." Is it any wonder that people resort to doing their worst, especially when the judiciary does not always provide a fair avenue for redressing grievances?

The level of political intolerance among our leaders is amazing – even within the same political party. We must learn, as leaders, to interact and dialogue with one another, so that our followers can pick up the signal. One wonders where those official inter-state visits among governors during the Gowon and Shagari days have gone? Exchange of visits among political, religious and traditional leaders, inter-state sports, visits among youth groups, and cultural festivals and exchanges — may promote peace and harmony.

In addition, we must avoid the current *winner-takes-all* trend in our political terrain. At all tiers of government we must establish power-sharing arrangements to accommodate various groups. While our federal constitution provides for the interest of the majority, it also provides for the protection of minorities from eternal servitude and discrimination. However, it is doubtful if these are being implemented faithfully. We are high on constitution making but low on constitution alism.

d. ***Federalism***

Nigerians opted for federalism in terminal colonial period because of the compromises it offered in the relations among their heterogeneous groups. There are basically two issues which deserve urgent attention in order to enable the pendulum of the federation swing in favour of acceptable compromises and the sharing of power, statuses and resources among the component groups of Nigeria.

Two basic issues currently deserve urgent attention in order that Nigeria may avoid unnecessary conflicts.These issues are: - 1) the division of powers and responsibilities among tiers of government; and 2) the distribution of scarce but allocatable resources. Let us briefly discuss these.

The distribution of powers and responsibilities among tiers of government really deals with the vertical relationship between the Federal, State and Local governments. Over the years, military rule had centralised political power. By 1999 the federal government had become politically and financially *titanic*. There were complaints by political actors at subnational level that the grip of the federal centre was becoming suffocating. However, all attempts to revise the legislative lists have proved abortive. The 1995 Constitutional Draft (under the Abacha regime) which tried to address the issue, suffered abrupt death with the demise of General Sani Abacha. The 2010 -2011 Constitutional Amendments by the National Assembly cleverly avoided dealing with the legislative lists.

Candidly, the distribution of powers and responsibilities is currently in favour of the centre. The federal government is over-extending itself. It is not clear why the federal government should be directly involved in rural development, culture, tourism, water resources, agriculture and such others. These functions can be carried out by policy units in the federal government, for purposes of coordination and uniformity. These are functions that can best be handled by state governments.

The Concurrent Legislative List provides an excuse for adventurism by the federal government. This list contains functions which federal and state governments have concurrent jurisdiction. Of course, in cases of contradictions, federal laws prevail. It is necessary to review the list of the concurrent list in favour of states and local governments in order to check unnecessary centralization trends in the federation. As powers get transferred to lower tiers of government, it also involves the revision tax powers. Local and state governments should be given more tax powers to carry out their additional responsibilities.

The second area of concern is the distribution of scarce but allocatable resources, among the tiers or levels of government on the vertical level, and among states, and among local governments at the horizontal level. It is a pity that the chief executives of the component units of the federation are more concerned about sharing resources from oil, than they are about generating their own resources for development. There is complacency, if not docility, when it comes to internally generated revenues. Federal, state and local governments, except in few areas, tend to sit and wait for statutory allocation from the federation account.

The *Revenue Mobilisation, Allocation and Fiscal Commissions (RMAFC)* made internal revenue generation effort one on the principles for the sharing revenue from the federation account. Since no formula for revenue allocation has been approved over the last fifteen years, it has had on impact. In addition, the first quarter of 2012 was dominated by demands over the issue of derivation and the need for fiscal equalization, by geopolitical units. Candidly, one would recommend greater diversification of the economy in order to avoid the vagaries associated with a monocultural economy. Moreover, there should be greater efforts in revenue generation.

Let us briefly look at the issue of the distribution of mineral resources (oil and non-oil). It is suggested, as one has been done elsewhere[8], that the revenue issue should be revisited. The old dichotomy between *on-shore* and *off-shore* oil should be restored. It is recommended that:

a. ***On-Shore Revenues*** –i) 50% should go to the states of origin on the basis of derivation; ii) 50% should go to the Distributable Pool Account (DPA).
b. ***Off-Shore Revenues*** – 50% to a *Stabilization Account*, (of which 25% should be allocated for fiscal equalization among tiers of government; while 25% should go to the *Sovereign Wealth Fund* as savings for the future generation); for the remining 50%:

    - 10% for the rehabilitation of mining areas (solid minerals and oil);
    - 10% for social development (education, health and others) of the oil mineral producing areas; and
    - 30% should go to the Federation Account for the usual distribution.

One of the greatest dangers lurking in the dark is political instability as a consequence of wide disparities among geopolitical units in the federation. This is why the RMAFC should make recommendations for fiscal equalization among sub-national units as well as the revision of the vertical fiscal relations among levels of government.

---

[8] See Elaigwu, *Politics of Federalism, op cit.,* chapter 9.

3. Security

Security Agencies, Law and Order, and Peace

Nigeria finds itself in a very difficult security situation under our current experience in democracy. *Nigeria is operating a 'democracy' on military tenterhooks, propped up by bayonets.* We may not want to accept it, but it is the truth. The *Daily Trust*[9] Newspapers did a good investigative work on Nigeria's security situation for which they deserve commendation.

In the investigation, the newspaper showed that military troops have been deployed in an unprecedented fashion to at least 10 states "to contain sectarian violence in the North". The Niger-Delta has lived with Nigerian troops for up to 15 years. Given the rampant incidents of kidnapping in the South Eastern states of Nigeria, troops were also deployed there. In addition, many states have asked for assistance from the military to curb incidences of armed robbery. We see these military men at check-points between cities. Soldiers have been deployed to Plateau, Kaduna and Bauchi states, and at the borders between Benue and Nasarawa, and Benue and Taraba.

As an anonymous military officer was quoted to have observed;

> There are literally no soldiers in the barracks… There is an unprecedented deployment of troops in not less than 10 States to contain sectarian violence in the North, militancy in the Niger Delta and kidnappings in the South-East.[10]

In addition, state governments have established patrol units, some of which comprise officers from the military and the police. Examples of these include – *Operation Zenda* in Benue, *Operation Aradu* in Gombe, *Operation Mesa* in Lagos, and *Operation Rainbow* in Plateau States.

While the Constitution provides that the military should assist their civilian masters in matters of domestic crises, this is not their job. The military is trained to maim and kill in defense of the territorial integrity of the State. His country men are not his enemies. In essence, military training is the wrong training for domestic or civic unrest. The experience at Odi illustrates this very clearly. Killing one military

---

[9] *Daily Trust* (Abuja) September 20, 2011, p. 1.
[10] *ibid*;

officer often extracts drastic reprisals. The military should therefore be used sparingly for domestic duties of maintaining law and order.

Many politicians fail to understand that they are committing class suicide by generating violence. The military hates the breakdown of law and order and it gives them an excuse to intervene. Similarly, the regular use of the military for domestic duties politicizes them and gets them increasingly interested in the political process of their country. Many military coups are begotten in this process. More important is the fact that the regular use of the military to quell domestic riots and civic disturbances creates a dilemma for soldiers. Trained to kill enemies, not brothers, there comes a point when they begin to question why they should kill their brothers. Similarly, leaders should be careful enough to prevent cracks in the larger society from entering the barracks. Illustrations abound in the world of how this dilemma has led to coups. It is, therefore, not in the interest of politicians and the country's democracy, to regularly deploy soldiers to quell domestic violence.

Unfortunately, the Nigerian Police Force (NPF) seems overwhelmed by the scale of domestic violence. Inadequately kitted, irregularly trained, underfunded, and lacking in modern accoutrements for the maintenance of law and order, the police force finds itself grossly lacking the capacity for the maintenance of law and order. To make it worse, Nigeria has begun to experience *terrorism* with its *insurgency* techniques. The police force is trained to maintain law and order, and handle criminal activities. It is not usually equipped with skills to deal with cases of insurgency. Most countries set up special crack units to deal with insurgency.

If we must establish a durable, peaceful and democratic polity conducive to national development, politicians must stop being crises-generators. We need to take a serious look at our security situation. We, therefore, suggest.

1. ***The Armed Forces–***

   a. Needs reprofessionalization and more active and regular training and exercises; and deployment sparingly to deal with domestic violence, and even then, under clear rules of engagement;
   b. when deployed for such domestic duties, they must not be allowed to be out of the barracks for more than a period of three months, before being redeployed back to the barracks; and

c. The nation must use military capacity and capability more for development – such as using the military engineering corp to open up rural roads, or the use of the signals or medical corps to supplement civilian services where they are located.

2. ***The National Guard*** – (or call it by any name). Nigeria needs a force which is specially trained to deal with domestic or violent civil disobedience. This force should be properly equipped with modern gadgets for managing unruly crowds without shooting lethal bullets. The mobile police is not equipped or trained for this purpose.
3. ***Border Guards*** – Given Nigeria's extensive borders, we need a Border Guard, properly trained and equipped for the monitoring of our porous borders to ensure our security. It is interesting that continental Europe has extensive programmes of Border policing, yet their states have by far less extensive borders than Nigeria.
4. ***Crack Anti-Insurgency Squad*** should be established to deal with threats of insurgency. The skills required here go beyond those for chasing criminals and maintaining law and order.
5. ***A New Police Force*** – We must recreate our police force with new goals and strategies for maintaining law and order. We must:

a. Recruit and train far more policemen in addition to what we have.
b. Pay the police good salary regularly.
c. Train and retrain officers and men of the police force.
d. Equip and kit the police with modern wherewithals and skills to carry out their jobs efficiently.
e. Encourage greater interaction between the police and the civil populace – especially restoring the people's confidence in the police (and security agencies generally) in order to give useful information voluntarily.
f. Occasionally encourage joint training and exercise between the police and other para-military agencies.

6. ***The State Police*** - Inspite of concerns about the misuse of state police by state governors, it is probably time to allow for state police and its operation under clear guidelines, given Nigeria's status as a federation. Nigeria, is probably one of the very few, if not the only federal state, without a subnational police service.

Having listened to the debate on the State Police, there are genuine fears among different Nigerian groups. Let us summarize the case for and against state police.

The Case for State Police Service:

a. The Nigeria Police Force (NPF) is completely overwhelmed by the challenges posed by crime and the maintenance of law and order (useful as decentralization of NPF is, it is not a solution to the problems at hand).
b. The logic of federalism requires that subnational units should be able to enforce their laws, fight crime, and maintain law and order. (Governors are Chief Security Officers without any security outfit). This contradicts the basic principle of federalism.
c. The reality of our environment is that Nigeria is under-policed and the additional problems of insurgency and terrorism heighten the sense of anxiety and insecurity in the country. A state police service, with clearly defined roles, will fill the vacuum.
   - These are all facts of the Nigerian situation.

The Case against State Police Service:

a. Local and Native Authority Police services had been misused and abused in the past by politicians, and it may happen again.
b. Specifically, some state governors may use these police services for pursuing their political interests, hounding opposition political party members, rigging elections, and eroding the fundamental rights of citizens(especially non-indigenous groups) within the state;
c. That given our history, some over-ambitious governors of states may use these state police services as bases for challenging the security and territorial integrity of Nigeria.
   - These fears are based on genuine concerns for the smooth operation and survival of the Nigerian federation.

The Problem:

a. We have a problem of maintaining law and order, securing the lives and property of Nigerians, and creating an enabling environment for development.
b. Some have argued that the time is not **ripe** to have state police. When will the time be ripe? We had local police in late 1950s to 1966. Agreed they were misused by our leaders? Is that an excuse not to try again in 2012?
c. Let us face the problem and tackle it – we need state police and other security agencies. **How do we prevent their being misused by our leaders** (bearing in mind that the NPF has been misused by various leaders). This seems to be the main challenge. People seem to have forgotten that there was a time in this country when we had the *Railway Police* (even within the NPF), just as India today has all kinds of police for different purposes.

Recommendations:

State Police Service

a. There shall be a State Police Service for states which so desire. (Remember that for historical reasons, while the Northern Region had Native Authority Police (i.e N. A. Police); the Western Region had Local Police; the Eastern Region did not have local police, but relied on the NPF. It is therefore, not mandatory in a federation that all states must have state police service). This is a state matter, not aregional matter, and we should not play politics with our security.
b. This therefore needs an amendment of section 214 – 216 of the Constitution.
    - The National Assembly shall provide for the **establishment, structure** and **powersof the** State Police Service.
c. For any State which desires to have a state police:

    - The Governor of that State shall send a bill to the State House of Assembly for the establishment of a State Police Force, and the Police Service Commission;

- For the Bill to become a law, the State House of Assembly shall pass the bill by a two-third majority of the House;
- The State Police Service Commission shall derive its powers, mandate and act in accordance with the act of the National Assembly as mentioned above.

Operational Issues:

a. The Chief Commissioner of State Police shall be **nominated by theGovernor of the State** to the State House of Assembly for **confirmation.**

b. The Chief Commissioner of State Police shall be removed from office only by a vote by two-thirds majority of the members of State House Assembly.

c. The Chief Commissioner shall be directly responsible to the Governor for policy and to the Police Service Commission for operational orders; and shall brief the State House of Assembly twice a year on the state of law and order.

d. No member of the state police shall bear lethalarms (but may use batons rubber bullets, tear gas, carbonated water etc) for our crowd control.

e. The State Police shall not be used for any electoral purposes; nor shall it be used for political or other purposes, except as specified by National Assembly.

f. The State House of Assembly shall make laws for the upkeep of the State Police, as are in consonance with all laws of the National Assembly on this matter.

Functions of State Police:

a. Shall have powers of investigation, arrest and prosecution (depending on the court) in accordance with the directive of the office of State Attorney-General.

b. Shall have powers to check crime and maintain law and order in accordance with the constitutionally delineated areas of operation of the state – ie State laws.

c. In situations which require use of arms, shall interface (synergize) with the NPF for efficacy of law enforcement.

d. Shall not be armed, with weapons of violence under any guise, by the state government; this is without prejudice to communication technology equipment.
e. Shall protect the rights of the populace, and shall not be used by any public officer to infringe the fundamental human rights of any citizen.
f. No state police service shall have the right to relate directly with any foreign country (even neighboring countries) without the express permission of the government of the Federation.

Security and Territorial Integrity of Nigeria:

a. The President of the Federal Republic of Nigeria, when he is convinced of any threats to the security and territorial integrity of Nigeria from a State Police Service, or of gross misuse of the State Police, and/or gross violations of the guidelines for a State Police established by National Assembly, shall:

   - Send a bill to the National Assembly for the dissolution of such State Police Service.
   - The National Assembly shall treat this request as a matter of national importance.
   - Once the National Assembly passes the bill by two–thirds majority in each Chamber, and the president signs the bill into the law; the State Police Service shall cease to exist.
   - In situations of national emergency, and/or national catastrophe the president shall dissolve such State Police Service, and
   - Inform the National Assembly for ratification.

b. The dissolution of State Police Service shall also mean the dissolution of the State Police Service Commission and its employees.
c. *These recommendations are designed to address the concerns of Nigerians raised about the State Police. We need to experiment with the State police first, before thinking about the Local Police.
d. For the successful operation of the State Police Service, we need an independent, strong and *impartial judiciary*, committed to dispensing justice and protecting the rights of individuals and groups.

7. ***Other Intelligence and Security Agencies***, such as the State Security Service (SSS) and others from the military and para-military units should be adequately and regularly funded, while their staff is regularly trained. The State Security Service has proven that, if adequately funded and professionalized, it is capable of dealing with Nigeria's main security concerns. However, there is a need for synergy of effort of all security agencies, for desirable results.
8. ***Coordination of Security Agencies*** –It is important that government creates an effective coordination structure for the suggested new and old outfits. This will reduce communication gaps and institutional rivalry, while encouraging regular and effective sharing of information and collaboration in the field.
9. ***Security Emergency Fund***: At this point in time, it is necessary to see the security situation as an **emergency**. We therefore suggest a Five-Year *Security Emergency Fund.* Security is the responsibility of all of us. We suggest therefore that this Fund should be based on money/ resources collected from Federal, State and Local Governments, the private sector and well-meaning individuals and groups. Government alone may not be able to fund security. It is expected that the money from this Fund shall be used to *establish, train*, and *equip* the various new security outfits suggested above. It is also expected that within five years, these outfits shall all be in place and be fully operational.

To ensure accountability and transparency, this Fund should have a *Board ofTrustees* comprising honest and credible Nigerians, responsible to the President, but accountable also to the National and State Assemblies, State Governors, as well as the private sector and the civil society.We must genuinely spend on security if we are to be ready for dangers. As George Washington once observed:

> Avoiding occasions of expense by cultivating peace, we should remember also that timely disbursements to prepare for danger frequently prevent greater disbursements to repel it.[11]

10. ***Neutrality of Security Agencies*** – Security Agencies must be allowed to carryout their functions in a neutral manner – without fear or favour. Politicians must always remember that security

[11]George Washington in *55000 Amazing Quotes* No. 3854.

agents swore to defend the nation security, not regime or personal security of political incumbents. They are paid and maintained by funds from public treasury and their neutrality must be respected. Using security agencies to rig elections as Nigeria had witnessed in the past only creates crises of loyalty for these security agents. It could also lead to other forms of violent conflicts. Politicians must therefore learn to leave security agencies alone and respect their neutrality. Security agencies must inoculcate in their members the value of loyalty to Nigeria, and their communiment to defend **national security, not personal or regime security.**

4. Others

There are other variables relevant to ensuring security and peace in Nigeria. Some of these include:- a) the *Sovereign Wealth Fund*; b) *The Judiciary*; c) *the removal of petroleum subsidy*; d) The political will of the leadership e) *Security and the media*; and, f) the *National Anthem and symbolism.*

a. ***The Sovereign Wealth Fund (SWF):*** While we are concerned about our current state of security, we must think about our future generation. We do not want to store a legacy of instability for our future generations. Many countries which have oil and non-renewable resources make efforts to save for the future. As the former President of Botswana, Hon. Sir QKI Masire put it:

> ...We intend to conserve our resources wisely and not destroy them. Those of us who happen to live in Botswana in the 20th century are no more important than our descendants in centuries to come.[12]

It is high time that we stopped our generation ofits selfishness and start saving for the future. Most countries with oil or other lucrative natural resources save for the future. Examples of countries which have successfully established Futures fund (insulated from political interference), include – Norway, Chile, Kuwait, and Alaska (in the United States of America). Even non-resource producing countries

[12] Sir Masire, former President of Botswana, quoted in Maria Sarrat and Moortaza Jiwanji, *Beating the Resource Curse* (Washington: The World Bank, Environmental Services, Paper No. 3, 2001); also quoted in Chinedum Nwoko, "How Should Nigeria Manage Oil Windfalls?".

such as Hong Kong, Singapore, and Mauritania have copied this policy of savings which have given them budget surpluses.

The opposition to the SWF by state governors is understandable in terms of the logic of federal autonomy of states, but not rational in terms of our realities. The SWF can be worked out in ways which allay the fears of states. We suggest that the SWF be disentangled – separating the Futures Fund from the Infrastructure Fund. A *stabilization fund* can be established for infrastructure. The SWF should have a *Board of Trustees* comprising an honest former Head of State or responsible and credible Nigerian, with credible and patriotic representatives from each geopolitical zone. The Board should be non-political and should have the mandate to invest funds outside the country. It must report to the National Assembly annually, copies of such report shall be sent to the president, governors of states and Houses of Assembly, and chairman of local governments. No fund can be withdrawn without the consent of 2/3rds of the two chambers of National Assembly, and simple majority votes in 2/3rds of the number of states making the federation. This will protect the SWF from political interferences as witnessed in Venezuela and Papua New Guinea. All funds from excess crude oil sales, 25% from off-shore oil revenue, and 5% of all accruals to the Federation Account annually should be the basis of the SWF funding.

b. ***The Judiciary: Towards Institutional Political Hygiene:*** Since May 1999, the Nigerian Judiciary, with all its problems, has contributed to the survival of our fledgling democracy. It has tried to carry out institutional hygiene by purging itself of some 'bad eggs'. Unfortunately it has been laden with so many political/electoral issues which had been mishandled by the relevant state agencies, such as INEC. It has, over these years, therefore carried out political rectitude. Illustrations of these abound in the number of court judgments on election petitions. One is glad about the current attempts at judicial reforms. Candidly, all attempts at creating effective security structure will not guarantee peace, unless the people develop confidence in the judiciary as the last hope for securing justice. This institutionalization of the **rule of law** is cardinal to security and peace in our democratic polity.

c. ***Petroleum Subsidy Removal:*** One can understand the economic concern of some Nigerians that there is too much leakage in the oil sector because of apparently huge subsidy in that sector. They are probably correct. From a social/security point of view, may be government needs to be more cautious. Subsidy removal should come into being after certain conditions have been met. These include: i) that oil refineries in Nigeria work to full capacity; ii) there is no importation of refined fuel (or PMS) and other petroleum products; iii) there is effective checking of smuggling and; iv) the plugging of leakages even under the current subsidized system. These will prove to Nigerians that government has done all it can to protect their interests. This issue is a potential security threat to the nation and should be handled with care – through discussions and demonstrable actions as recommended above. What is economically neat and proper may not be politically prudent, at a point in time. We must always remember that economics without politics is tidiness in stagnation; and politics without economics is an invitation to chaos. Nigerians expect some form of endowment from its resources. This may come in form of some form of subsidy.

One indication that Nigerians are tired of corrupt governments passing on to them the burden of their wasteful lifestyle, was the near-unanimity with which Nigerians responded to the call out for strike against the January 2012 oil subsidy removal. While government (through advertisements on radio, TV and newspapers) maintained that it would use the proceeds of the subsidy removal for infrastructure and development, nobody believed it. In fact, questions were raised about government's lack of accountability and transparency with regard to the proceeds of the removal of subsidy on diesel or gas (much earlier). The Nigerian public had been united by what it saw as the dispensation of equal quantums misery among the various groups.

This was why all attempts to break the eight-day strike failed. Attempts to use geopolitical differences among Nigerians to break the strike up failed. Even the attempt to use religion as a divisive variable did not succeed. In Lagos, Kano, Abuja and Kaduna, Muslims prayed while Christians formed a cordon around them. The situation was the same when Christians prayed. In essence Nigerians were tired of burdensome levies by an apparently sybaritic and selfish class of political leaders who wallowed in conspicuous consumption amidst the abject poverty of the people. Governments must be sensitive to the yearnings of the people. Communications or consultations with people involve a two-way track – from government to the people and from the people to the government. The oil subsidy removal strike demonstrated clearly that government had made up its mind on a policy and was not interested in a feedback from the people. It did cost the government and President Jonathan plenty of goodwill. The nation also lost heavily in economic and financial terms.

d. ***The Political Will of the Leadership:*** The leadership especially, the political elite or class must demonstrate that they have political will and sense of resolve in their decisions. Often, political and other considerations dilute the will to take firm actions in the interest of the Nation. This is vividly illustrated by the Editorial of *Leadership Newspaper o*n "2011: The Danger Signals":

> The Director-General of the State Security Service (SSS) Afakriya Gadzama, last week expressly indicted the federal government for the sectarian uprising in parts of the North that has led to the death of many civilians and members of the armed forces. Gadzama exonerated the SSS noting that the operatives were not taken unawaresby the rising profile of the Boko Haram sect. Rather, he said, the federal government has shirked its role and has tactically condoned the growth of sects in the land. According to him, the SSS had notified government of the insidious dangers lurking in parts of the North since 1995. He said that the leaders of the movement were shielded from prosecution and that the nation's **Political Leadership lacked the will to deal with the situation.** He added that there was nothing the SSS could have done apart from collating intelligence reports which the outfit dutifully did. These reports were handed to government which either ignored them or never bothered to complete any action taken. The result is the avoidable bloodletting that is currently rocking the nation.[13]

It is clear that government officials and other members of the political class, through acts of omission and commission, contributed in no small measure to our current high level of insecurity. Leaders must be impartial and firm in the execution of their duties. There should be no 'sacred cows', otherwise the rule of law is profusely eroded and corroded. Everybody's rights become jeopardized as people take laws into their hands. Thus, the first step in restoring order and sanity to the Nigerian polity is for

[13] *Leadership Sunday* (Abuja), August 2, 2009, P. 3. The bold features are mine for emphasis.

our Leaders to be resolute and demonstrate clearly that they respect the laws of the land.

e. ***Security and the Media:*** The mass media is a very powerful instrument for the dissemination of information; for the education of the masses, and for the articulation of their perceived interests of the masses. It thus acts, at times, as the social conscience of the people. While the media is a powerful weapon for *nation-building*, it is also a potent source of *nation-destruction*. The way the media reports events, the level of sensationalism, the manipulation of data to achieve particular objectives, and the level of self-censorship are directly relevant to the escalation or dampening of conflict. I am opposed to government clamping down and unnecessarily regulating the operation of the mass media. Our collective sense of responsibility, however, should make the media more sensitive to national security issues. The media can impose on itself restraint and self-censorship in the light of the possible consequences of their reports. It is suggested therefore, that journalists specializing in *security matters* should be trained. These journalists should interact with, and be regularly briefed by, the security agencies, to avoid communication gaps and the peddling of unfounded rumours.

f. ***National Anthem and The Symbolism:*** Finally, it is important to **revisit our National Anthem**. At a point in time when we need our old National Anthem to affirm our efforts in nation-building (our *unity in diversity*), we do not have the embedded inspirations of the old National Anthem. We reproduce it below:

Nigeria, we hail thee,
Our own dear native land,
Though tribe and tongue may differ,
In brotherhood we stand,
Nigerians all are proud to serve
Our sovereign motherland.

Our flag shall be a symbol,
That truth and justice reign,
In peace or battle honoured,
And this we count as gain.

To hand on to our children
A banner without stain.

O Lord of all creation,
Grant this our one request
Help us to build a nation
Where no man is oppressed;
And so, with peace and plenty,
Nigeria may be blessed.[14]

The current National Anthem while ascriptive in values does not reflect the reality of our daily lives. I believe that the argument that it was written by a foreigner is frivolous. Why have we not changed our country's name – NIGERIA? It was given by a foreigner.

Perhaps, our leaders (after 1975) thought that the civil war had sufficiently united us and that a new Nigerian nation had been born. So the call to duty and other ascriptive values which transcended ethnic and other parochial values looked appropriate. But alas! In 2012, we are still grappling with problems arising from differences in "tribe and tongue", the issues of "justice", accepting the flag as our "symbol" and building a land "where no man is oppressed", blessed with "peace and plenty".We may have to rethink the possible reversion to the old National Anthem to provide our young people some **inspiration and hope** for the future.

[14] The original Nigeria National Anthem adopted at her Independence in 1960. The bold features are mine, for emphasis.

CHAPTER FIVE

CONCLUSION

In this book, we have argued that **Security** is the first order or priority of every State, because all other forms of development depend on a secure and relatively peaceful environment. However, we observed that since May 1999, there have been greater challenges of security than at any point in our history, thus rendering our political stability fragile, democratic institutions and processes weak and fluid, and our economy debilitated.

It is our contention, that governments, political leaders and followers, and all of us, must summon the courage and honesty to get to the root causes of our current state of insecurity, underpinned by criminality and terrorism. We also suggested that government should take immediate and long term steps to respond to our current threats, by architectonically designing and building a security system which would produce a stable and peaceful environment for national development in the twenty-first century.

It is our belief that all Nigerians (leaders and followers) must rise up now to:

1. Create an ecumenical society in which all religious groups can peacefully co-habit.
2. Establish a civil, federal and democratic society which accommodates our ethnic and lingo-cultural differences, in the context of **Justice, Equality and Fairness**.
3. Put pressure on our governments to take emergency measures to drastically reduce the poverty level among our populace.
4. Establish mechanisms for enforcing the rules guaranteeing the promotion of a democratic polity in which no man is oppressed by hunger or by the violent pangs of sectarianism, and the dictates of authoritarianism.

Unless we make haste to take all the above actions now, we shall be handing over to our children an unenviable and unstable society with an incurable propensity for undermining its own development.

Finally, we argued that Security is the duty of all Nigerians, and we must, therefore, take our destiny in our hands, determined to face the future with confidence, discipline, patriotism and demonstrable honesty. The violence visited on the system by the *Boko Haram* sect is probably the highest source of anxiety today. While I supported the idea of amnesty for the Niger-Delta militants by late President Umaru Yar'adua, I was very worried about how this was carried out. Today, amnesty for the Niger-Delta has generated calls for the federalization of amnesty for criminals. Some Nigerians have called for amnesty for kidnappers because their actions were supposedly precipitated by poverty. Similarly, others have called for amnesty for members of the *Boko Haram*, because their actions were also the result of the "failure of leadership" which had led to massive unemployment of youths and pervasive poverty among the people. Now we have opened the *Pandora's Box*. It does seem that the signal which we are giving members of the future generation is that i) unless you take up arms against your motherland, your grievances would not be adhered; and ii) that it pays to rebel against the state. The big question is – unless we do something to change this perception, would *Boko Haram* be the last violent rebellion against the State?

Candidly, no matter what the source of "*angst*" or *pain* is, if one commits crime, he should be punished by law. Not only have our leaders failed in their duty to provide for the welfare of the people, the rule of law has broken down. Yesterday, we had Niger-Delta militants (some of whom were criminals); then we have kidnappers, and now we have *Boko Haram*. Which group will take arms against the State tomorrow, hoping that in the end, there would be dialogue with them, followed by the grant of amnesty on a platter of gold?

We have driven ourselves to a corner from which it is becoming difficult to get out, without generating new waves of aggressive ethnicity in the polity. Maybe, we can correct the process of granting amnesty to aggrieved and violent groups. It does not make sense to offer amnesty to people who take arms against the State without engaging in dialogue to review the issues at stake for both parties. Given where we are, in the context of internal security in Nigeria, let us engage in DIALOGUE with the *Boko Haram* sect first. Other steps to be taken would depend on the nature of the dialogue. It must be clearly demonstrated that government has the monopoly of the legitimate use of instruments of violence and that any other use of violence is illegitimate. However, since government has a responsibilit y for the welfare of the people, it must patiently listen to the grievances of its people, and respond appropriately, in a responsible manner. But the declaration of blanket amnesty for people who take arms against the State, before dialogue, is a call for instability in the future. We must not give the signal that it pays to take arm against the State. There are other legitimate ways of making our cases.

On the *Boko Haram issue*, it is difficult to make recommendations, when the actual demands of the aggrieved have not been put forward beyond ideological issues. However, given the little one knows, we make the following recommendations:-

1. **GOVERNMENTS** should:

    a. Address the issue of **education**; they must go beyond special *Almajiri* schools, and integrate these schools into the formal secular school systems in which Islamic and Charistian religious teachings take place.
    b. (Together with religious and traditional leaders) emphasize the role of the parents in the upbringing of children.
    c. Grow the ECONOMY.
    d. Drastically reduce unemployment.
    e. Urgently manage and control the level of corruption among public officers, and their conspicuous consumption amidst the abject poverty of the people.
    f. Check the level of electoral malpractices and actions which amount to *democratic deficit*.
    g. Have a functional Early Warning System at all tiers of government.
    h. Carryout drastic overhaul of the security system as recommend ed above; encourage inter-service collaboration.
    i. Dialogue with representatives of the *Boko Haram*, even if it means doing so, initially through third parties.
    j. Charge all those arrested in the *Boko Haram* cases to court, pending negotiations.
    k. Ensure serious considerations for intelligence reports, and allow the law to take its course.
    l. Stop public officers from making inflammatory statements.
    m. Regulate the use of force.

n. Then consider AMNESTY as an option, but under what conditions, bearing in mind the demonstration effect on future 'rebels' in the system.
o. Set up Early Warning Systems at each State and Local Government level, while creating a network of Research Institutes for purposes of data collection and analysis.

2. **POLITICAL ELITES**, must :

   a. Respect the' rules of **the game'** of politics – politics is not a **battle**.
   b. Respect the electoral process – play gallant losers and gracious victors.
   c. Demonstrate faith in our democratic Constitution, through constitutionalism.
   d. Be sensitive to the yearning of the people.
   e. Shun corruption and conspicuous life-style.
   f. Help to reach out to members of the *Boko Haram*, even if it implies mediating between government and the sect.
   g. Not build illegal constabularies or recruit young unemployed people as thugs.
   h. Not politicize and manipulate religious and ethnic differences for selfish ends.
   i. Always remember that national interests supercede our parochial concerns.

3. **RELIGIOUS LEADERS** should:

   a. Demonstrate maturity, patriotism and patience inspite of any provocations by the violent actions of the *Boko Haram* sect.
   b. Be sincere in encouraging ecumenicalism (religious tolerance) among their followers.
   c. Extend the hand of fellowship to the other side (including *Boko Haram*), difficult as this may humanly be, in order to initiate discourse at individual and group levels.
   d. Work with government and civil society organizations to prevent the manipulation of religion for selfish ends.
   e. Encourage all young people to go to school, and help in the career development of the youth.

4. **TRADITIONAL LEADERS** should:

a. Be Fathers to all, and provide a wide umbrage for various religious practices and tolerance.
b. Be frank and serve as moderating influences on contending interests.
c. Tower above politics and corruption, and thus generate the respect of all.
d. Help to find ways of reaching out to individual and group members of the *Boko Haram*, with the objective of assessing the consequences of the current insecurity in the land and seeking a way out of the situation.
e. Be honest in advising government, even though governments pay their salaries.

5. **SECURITY AGENCIES**

While many have lost their lives, and we all appreciate their sacrifices; they should:

a. Depend more on human intelligence, which means making the people to cooperate with them.
b. Try to professionally regulate the use of force to achieve targets, even though the contexts may be very fluid.
c. Avoid the temptation to carryout extra-judicial killings inspite of their losses.
d. Cooperate with one another in the security arena, and eschew rivalry; each service taking credit for particular actions pales out in the light of the costs of such actions.
e. Adequately kit all operational staff, to reduce the effect of surprise attacks. Proper situation alert may save lives.
f. Identify and find opportunities for talks in the course of investigations and interrogations.
g. Always remain loyal to the Nigerian State, not to regimes or political incumbents.

6. **BOKO HARAM** should:

   a. Review where it started and where it is going? Has it steadily been losing sympathy? If so, should the sect find new paths to trod and new techniques (beyond violence) for achieving its goals?
   b. Reassess the use of violence and cost in human lives, and socio-economic instability, and evaluate if Nigeria's disintegration is in its own interest.
   c. Stop the violence and seek ways of engaging government and sincere members of the political elite, with regard to finding a solution.
   d. Realize that all wars end at the negotiation table, and therefore stop more damage that would make negotiations more difficult.
   e. Remember the initial desires of the sect for *justice*; and assess whether the families of innocent souls who died as a result *Boko Haram* violence, also deserve *Justice.*
   f. Negotiate with government, even if initially, through third parties.

All the above roles assigned to the various groups are appeals to all actors in the current imbroglio to make efforts to enable us transcend the current level of insecurity. This country, and especially the Northern part of this country, has lost so many lives; and experienced other forms of socio-economic losses, it would take many years to recover.

Let us establish durable and impartial institutions and processes for adequately addressing the grievances of the people. Let us diminish the huge shadow of personality in our operations, because lack of strong institutions create opportunities for nepotists, corrupt people, mischief makers, champions of parochial interests, and professional conflict-generators, who benefit from perennial crises.

As the venerable Mahatma Ghandi aptly observed, "An eye for an eye would make the whole world blind". Let us strive to arrest the cycle of violence grafted on revenge. In fact, let us create a strong society with resilient institutions which provide individuals and groups gentler means of seeking redress. Samuel Johnson captured the essence of our point here:

> As peace is the end of war, it is the end, likewise, of preparations for war; and he may be justly hunted down, as the enemy of mankind, that can choose to snatch, by violence and bloodshed, what gentler means can equally obtain.

Let us create gentler means for collectively obtaining our goals in the future, through **Justice, Fairness and Equality**.

God Help us All. Long live the Federal Republic of Nigeria!

Appendix A

SELECTED CASES OF ELECTION-RELATED CONFLICTS IN NIGERIA (MAY 1999 TO SEPTEMBER2012)

S/N	CONFLICT	**CAUSE(S)**	MANIFESTATIO N	CONSEQUENCES
1	Politically Motivated Assassination; September, 1999	▪ Perceived political threat	▪ Gruesome murder	▪ Loss of life, mistaken for Hon. Nwabueze ▪ Threat to opponents/ Tension
2	Political mob action, Delta; February 4, 2001	▪ Inter-party rivalry between ANPP and PDP	• Violent attack on Governor Ibori	▪ Provoked security agency's reaction ▪ Increased tension
3	Inter-party conflict, Okene, Kogi; March 5, 2001	▪ Inter-party rivalry between ANPP and PDP	▪ Gruesome murder	▪ Loss of life ▪ Increased tension
4	Intra-party squabble in Abakaliki, Ebonyi; August 24, 2001	▪ Alleged interference in Ebonyi State's affairs by the Senate President, Anyim Pius Anyim	▪ Protest by women and youths ▪ 4 killed ▪ Open violence as supporters of the Senate President clash with that of the Gov. Sam Egwu	▪ Loss of lives ▪ Insecurity of opponent
5	Politically motivated assassination, Osun; December 21, 2001	▪ Perceived political crises – mostly intra-party	▪ Gruesome murder	▪ Insecurity of opponents ▪ Loss of life, Hon. Odunayo Olagbaju, member State House of Assembly ▪ Tension
6	Politically motivated assassination in Ibadan, Oyo State; December 23, 2001	▪ Perceived political threat	▪ Gruesome murder	▪ Loss of life, Minister of Justice, Chief Bola Ige ▪ Shock and tension in the Nation ▪ Insecurity of political opponents
7	Political mob action, Effurun, Delta; March 7, 2002	▪ Inter-party rivalry	▪ Protest by students ▪ Snowballed into violent clash after PDP	▪ Security agency's reaction ▪ Loss of lives, students ▪ Heightened

			rally	restiveness
8	Election-time, Jos, Plateau; May 2, 2002	▪ PDP local congress	▪ large-scale violence ▪ communal violence with ethno-religious colouration	▪ Loss of lives ▪ Destruction of property ▪ Suppression of all electoral exercises ▪ Tension
9	Politically-motivated assassination, Odigbo LGA, Ondo State; August 13, 2002.	▪ Perceived political threat	▪ Gruesome murder	▪ Loss of life, Janet Olapede, PDP leader ▪ Insecurity of opponents
10	Inter-party conflict in Enugu, Enugu State; August 13, 2002	▪ Preventing the pasting of a candidate's posters ▪ Inter-party-rivalry	▪ Violent attack	▪ Loss of life ▪ Increased tension
11	Politically motivated assassination, Kwara; August 15, 2002	▪ Perceived political threat ▪ Intra-party squabbles / crises	▪ Gruesome murder	▪ Loss of life, Kwara State PDP chairman, Alh. Ahmed Pategi ▪ Insecurity of opponents
12	Inter-party conflict, Wannune, Benue; August 18-20, 2002	▪ Struggle for control of local government between PDP and UNPP	▪ Violent attack	▪ Injuries sustained ▪ Wanton destruction of property ▪ tension heightened ▪
13	Politically motivated assassination in Onitsha, Anambra State; September 1, 2002	▪ Perceived political threat	▪ Gruesome murder	▪ Loss of life, Barr. Barnabas Igwe and wife ▪ Insecurity of opponents/tension
14	Politically-motivated assassination, December, 2002	▪ Perceived political threat	▪ Gruesome murder	▪ Loss of life, National Vice-Chairman, UNPP North-West, Alh. Isyaku Mohammed ▪ Insecurity of opponents/tension
15	Inter-party conflict, Ilorin, Kwara State; November 15, 2002.	▪ Battle for supremacy and political control between ANPP and PDP	▪ Bomb blast at the National Pilot Newspaper building, Ilorin , Kwara;	▪ Destruction of property ▪ Increased tension.
16	Politically-motivated assassination, Lagos;	▪ Perceived political threat	▪ Gruesome murder	▪ Loss of life, Lagos State PDP gubernatorial aspirant, Dele

	November 25, 2002			Arojo ▪ Insecurity of opponents
17	Inter-party conflict, Yobe; January 13, 2003	▪ Inter-party rivalry between PDP and ANPP	▪ Violent attack	▪ Intimidation of opponents ▪ Insecurity ▪ Destruction of property
18	Intra-party squabble, Ibadan, Oyo State; January 13, 2003	▪ Battle for local control of party between different factions of ANPP	▪ Violent clash	▪ Loss of lives ▪ Increased tension
19	Intra-party squabble, Warri, Delta State; January 18, 2003	▪ Intra-party rivalry between different factions of PDP during primaries	▪ Violent clash	▪ Loss of life ▪ Disrupted electoral exercise
20	Inter-party conflict, Buhari/Bulafara/ DOkiri, Yobe; January 18, 2003	▪ Inter-party rivalry between supporters of PDP and ANPP	▪ Violent clash	▪ Loss of lives ▪ Destruction of property ▪ Increased tension
21	Intra-party aquabble, Owo, Ondo State, February 2003	▪ Battle for local control between different factions of AD	▪ Bloody clash	▪ Loss of life ▪ Heightening tension
22	Inter-party rift, Jato-Aka, BenueState; February 18, 2003	▪ Inter-party violent clash between ANPP and PDP	▪ Gruesome murder of about 7 persons ▪ Open-violence	▪ Loss of lives ▪ Heightened of tension ▪ Destruction of property
23	Politically-motivated assassination, Owerri, Imo State; February 10,2003	▪ Perceived political threat	▪ Gruesome murder	▪ Loss of life, Chief Ogbonanya Uche, ANPP Senatorial candidate ▪ Insecurity of opponents
24	Politically-motivated assassination, Owerri Imo State, February, 22, 2003	▪ Perceived political threat	▪ Gruesome murder	▪ Loss of life, Mr. Theodore Agwatu, Principal Aide to Imo State Governor
25	Politically-motivated assassination, Abuja FCT; March 5, 2003	▪ Perceived political threat ▪ Inter-party rivalry	▪ Gruesome murder	▪ Loss of life, Chief Harry Marshall, Campaign Coordinator of the ANPP presidential candidate ▪ Insecurity of opponents ▪ Development of alternative security—thugs or vigilante
26	Politically-motivated	▪ Perceived political	▪ Gruesome murder	▪ Loss of life, Hon. Uche Nwole,

	assassination, Owerri Imo State; March 6, 2003	assassination		ANPP chieftain
27	Intra-party squabble, Abuja, FCT; March 7, 2003	▪ Rivalry between different factions of the PDP	▪ Invasion of party's national secretariat by thugs	▪ Intimidation and charged-atmosphere
28	Political mob action, Minna NigerState; March 2003	▪ Inter-party rivalry between PRP and PDP	▪ Attack on governor's convoy	▪ Destruction of property ▪ Provoked security agent's reaction ▪ Increased restiveness
29	Political mob action, Adamawa State; March 13, 2003	▪ Inter-party rivalry	▪ Attack on ANPP presidential campaign train	▪ Destruction of property ▪ Intimidation and insecurity of opponents
30	Inter-party clash, Benue State; March 2003	▪ Scuttling of ANPP's presidential candidate's rally ▪ Inter-party rivalry	▪ Gruesome murder ▪ Retaliatory attack and large-scale violence ▪ Communal violence with destruction of opponents' local strong holds	▪ Loss of lives ▪ Increased tension ▪ Emasculation of opponents
31	Political mob action, Ekiti State; March 2003	▪ Perceived political threat	▪ Attack on NCP's presidential candidate	▪ Insecurity and intimidation of opponents
32	Politically motivated assassination, Yamaltu-Deba, Dida LGA, Niger State; March 2003	▪ Perceived political threat	▪ Gruesome murder	▪ Loss of life, PDP LGC chairman ▪ Insecurity of opponents
33	Inter-party rivalry, Urhonigbe, Edo State; March 2003	▪ Battle for supremacy between ANPP and PDP	▪ Attack on campaign train ▪ Security agent's reaction	▪ Loss of life, school pupil ▪ Heightened restiveness
34	Communal violence with electoral calculations, Wase-Lantang crisis, Plateau State, April 9. 2003	▪ Indigene/settler conflicts	▪ Violent attack	▪ Believed to be timed during elections to disrupt and depopulate perceived political opponents
35	Oke-Oyi, Kwara State; April 10, 2003	▪ Inter-party rivalry between ANPP and PDP ▪ Campaign for	▪ Violent clash between party supporters	▪ Loss of life ▪ Suspicion and tension-charged elections

		elections		
36	Election-time violence, Diobu, Rivers State; April 19, 2003	▪ Inter-party rivalry between ANPP and PDP	▪ Harassment of voters ▪ Physical assault	▪ Disruption of electoral exercise and disenfranchisement ▪ Electoral malpractice ▪ Questionable legitimacy ▪ no-election cases ▪ Apathy in subsequent elections
37	Electoral violence, Effrurun, Delta State; April 19 2003	▪ Inter-party rivalry between PDP and AD	▪ Violent attacks	▪ Disruption of electoral exercise and disenfranchisement of the people ▪ Electoral malpractice ▪ Questionable legitimacy ▪ no-election cases ▪ Apathy in subsequent elections
38	Election-time violence, Irua, Edo State; April 19 2003	▪ Allegations of electoral irregularities ▪ Inter-party rivalry	▪ Seizure of ballot boxes ▪ Violent attacks	▪ Disruption of electoral exercise and disenfranchisement ▪ Malpractices ▪ Questionable legitimacy ▪ Apathy in subsequent elections
39	Election-time violence, Pankshin, Plateau State; April 19 2003	▪ Dissatisfaction with electoral results released by INEC ▪ Inter-party rivalry between AD and PDP	▪ Revolt by supporters	▪ Loss of lives ▪ Questionable legitimacy ▪ Apathy in subsequent elections
40	Election-time violence, Ahiazu-Mbaise, Imo State; April 19 2003	▪ Allegations of irregularities ▪ Inter-party clash between APGA and PDP	▪ Protest ▪ Open-violence	▪ Destruction of LGC Secretariat ▪ Questionable legitimacy ▪ Apathy in subsequent elections
41	Election-time violence, Abo-Mbaise, Imo State; April 19 2003	▪ Allegations of electoral irregularities ▪ Inter-party rivalry	▪ Violent Protests	▪ Destruction of INEC office ▪ Loss of lives ▪ Questionable legitimacy ▪ Apathy in subsequent

				elections
42	Election-time violence, Nkwogwu Nguru, Imo State; April 19 2003	▪ Allegations of electoral irregularities ▪ Inter-party rivalry	▪ Violent Protests ▪ Ballots papers destroyed ▪ Violent attacks	▪ Disruption of electoral exercise and disenfranchiseme nt ▪ Loss of lives ▪ Questionable legitimacy ▪ Apathy in subsequent elections
43	Election-time violence, Bassambiri, Bayelsa State; April 19 2003	▪ Allegations of irregularities ▪ Inter-party rivalry between PDP and UNPP	▪ Violent attacks	▪ Loss of lives ▪ Questionable legitimacy ▪ Apathy in subsequent elections
44	Election-time violence, Oponoma, Bayelsa State; April 2003	▪ Allegations of electoral malpractice ▪ Inter-party rivalry between supporters of ANPP and PDP	▪ Violent clashes during the distribution of materials to various polling centres ▪ Free-for-all-fight	▪ Loss of lives ▪ Alleged electoral malpractices and no-election cases ▪ Questionable legitimacy ▪ Apathy in subsequent elections
45	Election-time violence, Katsin-Ala, Benue State; April 2003	▪ Inter-party rivalry—ANPP and PDP ▪ Allegations of malpractices	▪ Raiding of polling centres ▪ Intimidation ▪ Open violence	▪ Disruption of electoral exercise and disenfranchiseme nt ▪ Contestable results ▪ Questionable legitimacy ▪ Apathy in subsequent elections
46	Election-time violence in Okowba, Bayelsa State; April 2003	▪ Inter-party rivalry rivalry—ANPP and PDP ▪ Suspected malpractices	▪ Protests by aggrieved youths ▪ Violent attacks at polling centres ▪ Soldiers opened fire on youths	▪ Disruption of electoral exercise and disenfranchiseme nt ▪ Alleged malpractices ▪ Contestable results ▪ Questionable legitimacy
47	Inter-party conflicts in Ilorin, Kwara State; April 2003	▪ Dissatisfaction with election result ▪ Inter-party rivalry between ANPP and PDP	▪ Violent attacks on crowd celebrating victory ▪ Police reaction	▪ Loss of lives ▪ Increased inter-party rivalry
48	Intra-party squabble in Awka, Anambra	▪ Intra-party squabble between PDP leaders	▪ Abduction of State governor ▪ Intimidation to	▪ Restiveness ▪ Development of militia and

	State; July 10, 2003	▪ Godfatherism – 'patron-client' relations gone sour ▪ Alleged electoral malpractice	resign	political thugs ▪ Removal of Governor's security aides ▪ Legal battles and absurdities
49	Inter-party rivalry, Takum, Taraba State; February 2004	▪ Local government elections ▪ Inter-party rivalry between NDP and PDP supporters	▪ Violent clashes	▪ Loss of lives ▪ Disruption of electoral exercise ▪ Malpractices
50	Politically-motivated assassination, high-way attack in Delta State; February 6, 2004.	▪ Perceived political threat ▪ Intra-party rivalry	▪ Gruesome murder	▪ Loss of life, Chief Aminasoari Dokubo, PDP South-South Vice-chairman ▪ Insecurity of opponents
51	Politically-motivated assassination, high-way attack; March 2004	▪ Perceived political threat	▪ Attack on Governor Akume's official car in convoy ▪ Gruesome murder	▪ Loss of life, political strategist of the Governor, Mr. Andrew Agom ▪ Increased tension
52	Politically-motivated killing, Kwara State; March 27, 2004	▪ Political witch-hunt	▪ gruesome murder	▪ loss of life, INEC commissioner in Kwara State
53	Election-time violence in Esan West, Edo State; March 28, 2004	▪ Allegations of planned electoral malpractices ▪ Inter-party rivalry between ANPP and PDP	▪ Violent attacks on electoral officials ▪ Dispossession of electoral materials	▪ Delay in polling ▪ Electoral malpractices ▪ Questionable legitimacy
54	Election-time violence in Abudu Edo State; March 28, 2004	▪ Inter-party rivalry ANPP and PDP ▪ Allegations of malpractices—already thumb-printed ballots	▪ Violent attacks by fake policemen ▪ Reaction of mobile policemen ▪ Injuries sustained	▪ Electoral malpractices ▪ Questionable legitimacy
55	Election-time violence in Magumeri, BornoState; March 28, 2004	▪ Dissatisfaction with conduct of polls ▪ Inter-party rivalry	▪ Violent attacks ▪ Destruction of government and opponents buildings	▪ Loss of lives ▪ Questionable legitimacy
56	Election-time violence in Zone A senatorial zone—Ukum, Katsina-Ala. Kwande, Ushongo, Kwoshishi and	▪ Allegations of malpractices – ▪ Inherent inter-party rivals between ANPP, UNPP and PDP	▪ Violent attacks on electoral security agents, officials, politicians and supporters—affected areas besieged for	▪ Disruption of electoral exercise ▪ Alleged malpractices ▪ Contestable election results ▪ Questionable legitimacy

	Vandekiya all in Benue State; March 28, 2004		more than 24 hours ▪ The development of armed militias ▪ Communal violence based on political persuasions ▪ Security agents reaction	▪ Virtual breakdown of law an order
57	Election-time violence, Dandume, Katsina State; March 28, 2004	▪ Inter-party rivalry ▪ Dissatisfaction with results of election	▪ Violent protests ▪ Mob action ▪ Destruction of property	▪ Contestable results ▪ Questionable legitimacy ▪ Tension-charged society
58	Election-time violence in Epe, Lagos State; March 28, 2004	▪ Inter-party rivalry between AD and ANPP ▪ Snatching of ballot boxes	▪ Mob action against students involved in alleged electoral offences	▪ Loss of lives ▪ Electoral exercise disrupted
59	Election-time violence, Ile-Oluji/Ike-Igbo, Ondo; March 28, 2004	▪ Alleged malpractices ▪ Inter-party conflict---ANPP and AD	▪ kidnap of returning officer, SSS agent and police officer	▪ tense political atmosphere ▪ acceptance of victorious candidate
60	Inter-party rivalry, Jato-Aka, Benue State; March 2004	▪ Inter-party rivalry between ANPP and UNPP	▪ Violent clashes	▪ Loss of lives ▪ Increased restiveness
61	Inter-party rivalry, Jato-Aka, Benue State; May 20, 2004	▪ Inter-party rivalry between ANPP, UNPP and PDP	▪ Violent clashes	▪ Loss of lives ▪ Increased restiveness
62	Intra-party clash, Awka and Onitsha, Anambra State; November 8, 2004	▪ Intra-party squabbles ▪ Godfatherism – soured patron-client relations	▪ violent attacks ▪ pandemonium to provoke declaration of state of emergency	▪ loss of lives ▪ destruction public property including governor's office, INEC office and State Broadcasting Service office ▪ infiltration of the Judiciary
63	Anambra Political Crisis in Awka, Anambra State, November 10,2004	▪ Intra-party squabbles	▪ Hundreds of armed youth stormed the State capital destroying government properties.	• Seven people were killed. • Lost of properties.
64	Inter-party conflict, Funtua, Katsina State;	▪ Battle for local control ▪ Inter-party rivalry	▪ Violence	▪ Injuries sustained ▪ Tension heightens

	August 2005	between ANPP and PDP supporters		
65	Intra-party conflict, Bauchi, Bauchi State; December 2005	▪ Clash between factions of PDP for control of campaign office ▪ Battle for supremacy	▪ Violence	▪ Injuries sustained ▪ Tension heightens
66	Intra-party clash, Ibadan, Oyo State; February 2006	▪ Political godfatherism ▪ Battle for supremacy between supporters of impeached governor and those of his erstwhile political father	▪ Violence	▪ Loss of life ▪ Increased tension
67	Politically-motivated assassination in Gwaram, Jigawa State; February 2006	▪ Perceived political threat	▪ Gruesome murder	▪ Loss of lives ▪ Insecurity of opponents
68	Security agent's actions in Katsina State; February 19 & 20, 2006	▪ Opposition to self-succession	▪ Violent protest ▪ Securityagent's reaction	▪ Loss of life
69	Political mob action, Lagos; April 8, 2006	▪ Self-succession ▪ Intra-party (PDP) squabbles	▪ Harassment of Vice-President	▪ Intimidation ▪ Threat to security of opponents
70	Political mob action, Kano State; April 24, 2006	▪ Opposition to self-succession ▪ Inter-party rivalry between ANPP and PDP supporters	▪ Violent protest ▪ Open violence	▪ Reaction of security agents
71	Politically-Motivated attack, Port Harcourt, Rivers State; May 20, 2006	▪ Support for self-succession, Third-Term Agenda ▪ Misrepresentation of constituency's popular view.	▪ Gun shots	▪ Loss of life, PA to Senator Lee Maeba. The senator was the actual target.
72	Inter-party conflict, Borno State; June 2006	▪ Inter-party rivalry between ANPP and PDP supporters	▪ Open violence of all kinds	▪ Loss of lives ▪ Security threat to opponents
73	Intra-party clash; Osogbo, Osun State; June 19 2006	▪ Conflict of interest between PDP incumbents and other interested aspirants	▪ Free-for-all fight between supporters of different aspirants	▪ Injuries sustained ▪ Tension heightened
74	Intra-party fracas, Lau and	▪ Alleged imposition of	▪ Violent protest ▪ Free-for-all	▪ Loss of lives ▪ Destruction of

	Ardo-Kola LGCs, Taraba State, June 21, 2006	candidates during PDP ward primaries ▪ Intra-party rivalry	fight	property ▪ Increased tension
75	Politically-motivated assassination, Jos, Plateau State, July 1, 2006	▪ Perceived political threat ▪ Inter-party rivalry between ACN and PDP	▪ Violent attack ▪ Brutal murder	▪ Loss of life, Chief Jesse Aruku, ACN gubernatorial aspirant
76	Intra-party clash, Lafia, Nasarawa State; July 7, 2006.	▪ Struggle for local control by two factions of PDP	▪ Free-for-all-fight	▪ Loss of lives ▪ Tension heightened
77	Intra-party clash, Lau, Taraba State; July 9, 2006.	▪ Appointment of caretaker chairman of local council ▪ Grievances among supporters of different (PDP) aspirants.	▪ Open violence	▪ Loss of lives ▪ Increased tension
78	Politically motivated attack in Port-Harcourt, Rivers State; July 9, 2006.	▪ Allegation of poor performance of elected officers ▪ Crisis of legitimacy	▪ Bomb attack	▪ Destruction of houses of Deputy Speaker, House of Representatives; State governor's in-law; and State Commissioner of Finance ▪ Legitimacy question ▪ Disregard of law and order.
79	Politically-motivated attack, Enugu, Enugu State; July 23, 2006.	▪ Perceived political threat	▪ Gun shots on ACD National Chairman	▪ Insecurity of opponents ▪ Breach of trust
80	Politically-motivated attack, Makurdi, Benue State; July 24 July, 2006.	▪ Perceived political threat	▪ Thugs attack ANPP gubernatorial candidate	▪ Insecurity of opponents ▪ Breach of trust
81	Politically-motivated assassination, Lagos, Lagos State; July 27, 2006.	▪ Perceived political threat	▪ Gruesome murder	▪ Loss of life, PDP gubernatorial aspirant— Engr. Funsho Williams ▪ Insecurity of aspirants
82	Intra-party clash, Marte, Borno State; July 30, 2006.	▪ Distribution of ANPP member ship cards and registration of supporters ▪ Factional vendetta	▪ Violent attack ▪ Free-for-all fight	▪ Loss of lives ▪ Increased tension
83	Inter-party clash, Osogbo, Osun	▪ Clash between supporters of	▪ Bloody clash	▪ Loss of life ▪ Tension

	State; August 5, 2006.	gubernatorial aspirant of AD and incumbent PDP governor		heightened
84	Inter-Party clash in Osogbo,Osun State; August 7, 2006	▪ Between supporters of Governor Olagunsoye Oyinlola and AD Mr. Rauf Aregbosola	▪ Bloody clash	▪ Loss of life of a 17 year old student
85	Politically-motivated assassination, Ado-Ekiti, Ekiti State; August 18, 2006.	▪ Perceived political threat ▪ Intra-party rivalry (PDP)	▪ Gruesome murder ▪ Public disorder	▪ Loss of life, Ekiti State gubernatorial aspirant—Dr. Ayodeji Daramola ▪ Insecurity of aspirants ▪ Destruction of public properties.
86	Intra-party conflict in Oyo, Osun, Imo, Bayelsa, and other states across the federation,Nov.4, 2006	▪ PDP Ward Congresses	▪ Three people killed and several others injured	▪ Loss of lives ▪ Two civilians killed ▪ One policeman killed
87	Intra-party conflict in Imo State, Nov.4,2006	▪ PDP Ward Congress	▪ Thugs numbering 63 arrested	▪ Political thugs on increase ▪ Legitimacy crises
88	Intra-party conflict in Akwa Ibom State, Nov.4,2006	▪ PDP Ward elections resulted in Protest over doctored list of delegates	▪ Five people wounded. ▪ Sporadic shooting by the police in attempt quell protest	▪ Violence in elections on increase ▪ Need to equip police to cope with crises situations
89	Election primaries in Onitsha North and South, Anambra State, Nov 4, 2006	▪ Election into House of Assembly flagbears ▪ Use of illegal delegate lists	▪ Protest	▪ Elections not legitimate
90	Inter-party violence in Maiduguri, Borno State, Nov.19, 2006	▪ Clash between ANPP and PDP supporters over removal of posters by ANPP supporters	▪ Commotion in the city ▪ Police intervened before normalcy could return	▪ The visiting Gov. Duke convoy was attacked by ANPP thugs ▪ Political intimidation
91	Intra- party violence in Rivers State, Nov.19,2006	▪ PDP Local Govt. congresses	▪ Eight people killed	▪ Legitimacy question ▪ Violent elections ▪ Loss of lives
92	Intra-Party Violence in Imo State, Nov. 23,	▪ In a rescheduled primary for Imo House of	▪ Shooting at the party secretariat	▪ The election marred by Violence

	2007	Assembly		▪ Rampant use of dangerous weapons during election
93	Intra-party violence in Yenagoa, Bayelsa State, December 2, 2006	▪ PDP primary election for elective positions	▪ A storey building bombed ▪ Furniture, office equipment destroyed	▪ Elections more violent
94	Politically motivated Violence in Asaba, Delta State; December 11, 2006	▪ In a rescheduled primary election in Delta governorship candidate	▪ Unidentified hoodlums set Delta State PDP Secretariat ablaze	▪ Loss of PDP Secretariat
95	Politically motivated assassination in Agborho, Ughelli South Local Govt Area, Delta State. Feb. 3, 2007	▪ Perceived political threat	▪ Suspected assassins killed Mr. Lawson Onokpasa of PDP	▪ Loss of Prominent Urhobo and PDP leader.
96	Demonstration in Ebonyi by people of Onicha Igboeze community Feb. 4, 2007	▪ Against total neglect of their community by Ebonyi state government	▪ 4 people were killed and 60 others injured	▪ Loss of lives and properties ▪ Break down of law and order.
97	Intra-Party violence in Ibadan, Oyo state; February 3, 2007	▪ Protracted conflict between Gov. Ladoja and his Deputy, Chief Adebayo Akala	▪ Three people were killed and many others injured	▪ Loss of life ▪ Military deployed to the state
98	Inter-Party clash in Bichi Local Govt. Area, Kano State;March 2007	▪ Between supporters of ANPP and PDP ▪ Attack on the convoy of Kano state governor Ibrahim Shekarau	▪ Bloody Clash ▪ Use of Political thugs with weapons including locally made pistols and 300 live ammunition	▪ Several Vehicles destroyed ▪ Police state command introduced 24 hour stop and search order
99	Inter-Party clash in Botsari Local Govt. in Katsina state, March 2007	▪ Between ANPP and PDP supporters over removal of campaign posters.	▪ Violent clash	▪ Three people arrested
100	Politically Motivated attack in Gombe, Gombe State; March 2007	▪ Political thuggery	▪ Gunshot t at the personal assistant to the governor, Alhaji Kawaji Barwa	▪ Increasing violence
101	Politically motivated	▪ DPP governorship	▪ DPP governorship	▪ Many people injured.

	assassination attempt in Oro, Kwara state, March 2007	candidate attacked. ▪ The State Govt. was accused of the attempt on his life	candidate escaped assassination attempt.	▪ Vehicles and properties damaged.
102	Assassination of councilor in Giwa Local Govt. Area of Kaduna state March 10, 2007	▪ Killed by unknown persons on his way to a council meeting	▪ Alhaji Abdullahi Saidu killed	▪ Loss of life
103	Political motivated attack in Sokoto state, March, 2007	▪ Private security guards clashed with hoodlums	▪ The National Campaign secretariat of PDP burn's down	▪ Two people killed ▪ Further polarization of PDP and DPP ▪ Police ban on political rallies.
104	Politically motivate attack on Segun Oni at Irepodun Ekiti State, March 21 2007	▪ Governorship candidate for PDP was shot by suspected hoodlums while coming from campaign meeting.	▪ Gunshot, Attempted assassination	▪ Increasing cases of political hoodlums and assassins
105	A mass protest in Awka Anambra state; March 28, 2007	▪ INEC purported disqualification of the former Gov. Chris Ngige from contesting 2007 on AC plat form	▪ Threatened INEC to rescind its decision or else no election in Anambra state	▪ No loss of life ▪ Threat to disrupt the April election
106	Inter-Party conflict in Keffi, Nasarawa State, March 20, 2007	▪ ANPP Supporters attacked Abdullahi Adamu of Nassarawa state.	▪ Attack on the convoy of the State Governor while returning from campaign tour	▪ Increasing violence in the state
107	Politically Motivated Violence in Balanga LGA, Gombe State, March 29, 2007	▪ Protracted political violence	▪ The killing of Mr. Ayuba Tella, the PDP youth leader in Balanga local govt. area.	▪ Loss of life ▪ Police ban on political rallies in the state
108	Politically motivated violence in Lafia and Assakio councils of Nasarawa state April1 & 2, 2007	▪ Clashes between supporters of PDP and ANPP	▪ Many people lost their life, and property destroyed (number unconfirmed)	▪ Increasing political violence in the state ▪ Loss of lives and properties
109	Inter-Party conflict in Gusoro villege, Shiroro Local Govt. Area, Niger state,	▪ Clash between ANPP and PDP as a group of supporters removed Bill Board of the rival	▪ Two people killed	▪ Loss of lives ▪ Campaigns characterized with violence

	April 1st, 2007	party		
110	Inter-Party conflict in Ibadan, Oyo state, April 2, 2007	▪ Clash between PDP and AC, Inter-Party rivalry	▪ Three People Killed ▪ Some vehicle vandalized	▪ Loss of lives and properties
111	Inter-Party conflict in Yola, Adamawa state April 2, 2007	▪ Clash between PDP and ANPP, inter-party rivalry over pasting of posters	▪ 12 people hospitalized	▪ Loss of valuables
112	Inter-Party violence at Gate way, Ogun state, April 3, 2007	▪ Clash of the supporters of PDP and ANPP at Ogun state Governorship debate	▪ The commissioner for Agriculture, Ogun state, Hon. Samuel Akindele Elegbede was machetted, two others received gunshot wounds	▪ Increase in Political motivated violence
113	Governorship And State House of Assembly elections across the country, April 14, 2007	▪ The general election into various Government Houses and State Houses of Assembly	▪ Vandalization ▪ thuggery, ▪ Electoral mal practices. ▪ 44 persons killed and 250 arrested	▪ Loss of lives ▪ Legitimacy question ▪ Intimidation ▪ Fraud in our electoral process ▪ Poor image of election in Nigeria abroad. ▪ Widespread protests ▪ Both local and international condemnation ▪ Dusk-to-dawn curfew imposed in some states
114	Politically related clashes between AC supporters and PDP supporters in Lagos Island, Lagos State on April 14, 2007	▪ Nothing specific	▪ The free for-all fight led to killing of three people in Lagos Island	▪ Loss of lives
115	Governorship Election to Imo state Government House, April 14, 2007	▪ Cases of electioneering violence and irregularities in some local govt ▪ Expulsion of Ifeanyi Araruume from PDP	▪ Number of deaths in Aboh Mbaise (5), Mbaitoli, Oguta, Njaba, Owerri North, Nwangele etc ▪ Electoral materials were hijacked. ▪ Multiple voting	▪ Election cancelled by INEC. ▪ To be conducted on a future date ▪ Loss of lives

116	Governorship and House of Assembly elections in Idima Ohaeke Abam in Arochukwu LGA, Imo state, April 14 2007	▪ Politically motivate murder ▪ Snowballed into further tension	▪ Murdering of a 27year old Okorukwu Ogbaegbu, a staff of Arochukwu LGA	▪ Increasing wave of insecurity ▪ Youths threatened to destabilize the elections
117	Governorship and House of Assembly elections in Enugu, Enugu State; April 14,2007	▪ Thuggery and intimidation during the elections	▪ 36 persons arrested ▪ 3 soldiers also arrested ▪ 40 cutlasses, charms, live cartridges and locally made pistols	▪ Increasing cases of violence
118	Governorship election in Oyo State, April 14, 2007	▪ Hoodlums hijacked the election materials	▪ Voting materials were snatched at various locations in Ibadan South-west LGA ▪ Indiscriminate shooting by hoodlums at various polling stations at about 1.20 pm ▪ Ballot boxes burnt by hoodlums at Popoye Moja in Ibadan South- west LGA ▪ Many did not vote, including former governor of Oyo state, Lam Adesina due to the activities of hoodlums ▪ Mobile police deployed to strategic roads, including Molate, Iwo Rd. areas to quell crises	▪ Disenfranchised eligible voters in various voting locations ▪ Increasing number of hoodlums ▪ Election adjudged fraudulent
119	Violence that followed the announcement of the result in Ondo	▪ Declaration of Agagu as winner of the election. ▪ Rioters challenging the	▪ Women went on street demonstrating, ▪ houses and vehicles of	▪ Legitimacy question of the incumbent ▪ Most people were beaten up by

	governorship election on April 15, 2007	result as false.	PDP stalwarts destroyed ▪ Police gunshots quelled the riots.	thugs ▪ Soldiers, Mopol drafted to quell riot
120	Violence as INEC announced the Edo governorship election result, April 15, 2007	▪ Declaration of Osarheimen Osunbor as winner, ▪ AC supporters went to the streets, protesting the result	▪ Thousands of irate youths, market women, and motorcyclists protested in the streets.	▪ Legitimacy question to the incumbent governor
121	Governorship result in Osun state, April 15, 2007	▪ Rivalry between Gov. Oyinlola (PDP) and Action Congress gov. candidate Rauf Aregbesola ▪ Declaration of Oyinlola winner triggered off protest from AC supporters	▪ Bloody battle between supporters of the two parties ▪ A carryover of what happened previously at Ila and Atakumosa local govt. areas during voting proper ▪ 20 ballot boxes were recorded snatched ▪ Weapons and charms were used ▪ Protests by AC supporters over the result ▪	▪ 6 persons killed ▪ Many houses burnt ▪ Legitimate question ▪ Increasing cases of electoral violence ▪ Police ordered shoot- on- sight to arsonist ▪ Curfew imposed
122	Political motivate violence in Obio/Akpor LGA, Rivers state; April 2007	▪ A Gang of unsuspected militants invaded police station on the eve of the election and burnt it down	▪ Killing seven policemen at Obio/Akpor local govt. area of the state.	▪ Loss of life and property ▪ General insecurity ▪ Intimidation of political opponents.
123	The announcement of result of governorship election in Kaduna state; April 2007	▪ Opposition parties alleged rigging of the election by PDP	▪ Irate youths in Sabon Gari local govt. area burnt down the local govt. secretariat	▪ Police deployed to the area ▪ ANPP Governorship candidate Alhaji Sani Shaban was arrested by the police.
124	The announcement of the governorship result in Ekiti state; April 17, 2007	▪ The declaration of Segun Oni (PDP) winner by INEC triggered protest ▪ Opposition alleged rigging	▪ Youths and women in Ado- Ekiti and Ikere areas trooped the streets in thousands protesting the	▪ Major roads were barricaded by protesters ▪ Legitimacy question

			▪ announcement of Oni as the governor elect ▪ Demanding for justice	
125	Protest that trailed the results of the governorship and houseof Assembly elections in Funtua, Katsina State; April 17, 2007	▪ Protests against the result of the governorship and House Assembly of election	▪ The Funtua Council secretariat was set ablaze	▪ Loss of government property
126	Attempted bomb of INEC Headquarter on the eve of Presidential and National Assembly elections; Abuja April 21, 2007	▪ A petrol tanker, fully loaded with dangerous substance attempted to burn down INEC Headquarters	▪ No driver was found in the vehicle directed to the INEC office	▪ Orgy of violence and vandalization in the country.
127	In presidential election in Jigawa state, April 21, 2007	▪ A clash between PDP and ANPP during voting	▪ About five persons were killed ▪ Eight houses including a commissioner's house burnt	▪ Electoral violence ▪ Loss of lives and properties
128	Presidential election in Ibadan, Oyo state, April 21, 2007	▪ Violent and fraudulent elections dominated by hoodlums	▪ Illegal possessions of arms ▪ Hijacking of ballot boxes ▪ Army GOC arrested over 100 suspects ▪ Some INEC officials were also arrested	▪ Electoral violence on increase ▪ Election adjudged to be massively rigged
129	Presidential Election in Makera ward Minna, Niger state, April 21, 2007	▪ Perceived political violence by unidentified gunmen	▪ 9 policemen gunned down	▪ Violence ▪ Assassination
130	Presidential Election in Osun state, April 21, 2007	▪ Ballot bags were snatched in Obokun and Oriade local government areas	▪ Soldiers were deployed to the area	▪ Opposition said security agents are in compliance ▪ Low turn out of voters ▪ Dusk-to-dawn curfew
131	Presidential Election in Gbagada, Lagos state, April 21,	▪ Election rigging by AC members. ▪ Thumb printing on ballot papers	▪ 12 people were arrested ▪ People nabbed with ballot	▪ Election not free and fair.

	2007		papers ▪ Police was deployed to stop their activities	
132	Presidential Election in Ondo town, Ondo state, April 21, 2007	▪ An unidentified electoral officer was abducted and taken away with voting materials from INEC office	▪ Abductees dressed in Army and Police uniforms ▪ Thugs intimidated and arrested political opponents. ▪ Dangerous weapons were used	▪ Electoral violence ▪ Thugs in elections, ▪ Legitimacy of our elected candidates ▪ Insecurity of life and property ▪ Dusk-to-dawn curfew imposed
133	A Clash between supporters of PDP and ANPP at Hadejia, Jigawa state, April 24, 2007	▪ Supporters of Alh. Abdulazeez Usman Turabo (PDP) ambushed the former Deputy Gov. and senatorial candidate for ANPP	▪ Five people were killed ▪ Many houses, a filling station and cars including that of the Commissioner for Political Affairs were burnt down	▪ Loss of lives and properties ▪ Several people were turned into refuges
134	In a re-scheduled governorship election in Bende, Abia state, April 28, 2007	▪ Snatching of ballot boxes and other electoral materials ▪ Other electoral offences were recorded	▪ A policeman and four others were arrested over snatching of ballot boxes including other electoral offences by Orji Uzor Kalu's security men	▪ Legitimacy question
135	Inter-party rivalry in Ihima, Kogi state, May, 2007	▪ The fallout of April 14 and 21 general elections ▪ Remote cause, Dec. 2005 and July 2006 communal clashes ▪ Rivalry between PDP and AC in the state.	▪ 20 people were killed, 400 houses destroyed in Ihima community in a full scale crisis	▪ Heightening of ethnic rivalry ▪ Endangering the life in the community ▪ Dusk-to-dawn curfew imposed
136	The assassination of Assistant commissioner of Police, the Chief Security Officer to Gov Agagu in Akure, Ondo	▪ Politically motivated assassination ▪ The government and opposition traded blames over the killer	▪ Gunmen killed CSO to Gov. Agagu, Mr Tunde Awanebi barely eight hours after he was relieved of	▪ Loss of lives ▪ Increasing wave of insecurity after general election

	state ,May 30, 2007		his position ▪ Another member of PDP killed by unidentified gunmen	
137	At the House of Assembly inauguration in Ibadan, Oyo state, June 4, 2007	▪ Politically motivated attack ▪ Beating and embarrassment of a newly elected House member	▪ Hon. Kayode Animasaun (ANPP) representing Ona- Are state constituency was beaten by thugs said to be loyal to Alh Lamidi Adedibu for alleged being disloyal to their boss	▪ Loss of valuables ▪ Increasing waves of insecurity ▪ Political intimidation
138	Bomb blast at Oshogbo and Ilesha, Osun State, June 14, 2007	▪ Politically motivated violence ▪ Aftermath of contentious April 14 and 21 elections	▪ Explosion in the State secretariat killing one person and injuring another ▪ At Ilesha, similar bomb explosion ▪ Assassination attempt on the life of the state Chairman of PDP,Alh. Ademola Rasaq ▪ Rasaq's two orderlies lost their lives	▪ Loss of lives ▪ Destruction of properties ▪ Insecurity of life in the state
139	Electoral Tribunal sitting in Ibadan, Oyo state, June 15, 2007	▪ Unknown people planted bomb in the court	▪ The sitting of the tribunal was transferred to another court. ▪ The security operative alerted the court.	▪ High level of insecurity ▪ The use of clandestine means even in the law courts.
140	Attack on AC Candidate for House of Assembly in Ibadan, Oyo State, June, 17,2007	▪ Politically motivated assassination attempt on Mr.Babatunde Falola (AC) House of Assembly candidate	▪ 40 minutes shooting at Falola's house ▪ Police confirmed samples of cartridges	▪ High level of insecurity of life
141	Council	▪ Politically	▪ Alh.	▪ Loss of life

	chairman killed in Minjibir LGA, Kano State, June 19,2007	motivated assassination by a gang of armed bandits	Muhammed Abdu Kaya, Chairman Minjibir local government area was murdered	
142	The National strike over the hike on fuel price and VAT by President Obasanjo few days before he handed over, in some areas in Lagos (Fadayi, Jibowu, Mushin, Oshodi, Ikotun and Iyanoba), June 20, 2007	▪ Hoodlums hijacked the process and vitriolic attack on innocent citizens	▪ Raping and maiming residents and commuters ▪ Breakdown of law and order	▪ Violence and extortion ▪ Lawlessness
143	Assassination attempt on Afe Babalola and Mr. Sola Omolayo, former speaker of Ekiti H/A, Ekiti State, June, 24, 2007	▪ Politically motivated assassination attempt on prominent citizens of the State Afe Babalola (a foremost Lawyer) and Sola Omolayo(a former Speaker)	▪ Afe Babalola house was attacked by assassins	▪ Threat to lives of prominent citizens ▪ Increasing violence
144	Assassination of a former councilor from Ikot Essien in Mkpst Enin LGA, Akwa Ibom State, July 31, 2007	▪ Suspected assassins	▪ The murder of Mrs Marie Ata Udo in her home town	▪ Loss of life
145	Assassination of Police Inspector in Uyo, Akwa Ibom State, August 13, 2007	▪ Suspected assassins	▪ Inspector Patrick Etim of the Police Anti Robbery Squad was murdered by gunmen in his home in Uyo	▪ Loss of life
146	Assassination of a Member of the House of Rep. at Ejioku village Lagelu LGA, Oyo State, September 15,2007	▪ Politically motivated assassination by unknown gunmen	▪ Hon. Moses Olusegun Oladimeji was shot dead	▪ Loss of life
147	Two people were killed in intra-	▪ The ward primary election for the	▪ Ikechukwu Eze; a student	▪ Loss of lives and property

	party conflict between rival PDP supporters in Ugwuagu in Afrikpo LGA, Ebonyi State, September, 19, 2007	forthcoming local govt. election	was killed ▪ Another Youth was lynched ▪ Looting and burning of houses	▪ Breakdown of law and order
148	Two people killed in intra-party clash b/w PDP groups rivalry in Sagamu LGA, Ogun State, October 12,2007	▪ No concrete reason was given	▪ Two people were killed ▪ Fifteen others sustain serious injuries ▪ Seven people were arrested	▪ Loss of lives and property
149	Local Govt. election in Ugep in Yakur Local Govt. area of Cross River State; Nov. 4, 2007	▪ The violence was triggered off by members of the PDP who opted to support the Action Congress in protest against the choice of Mr Itam Eta as the candidate for PDP	▪ Itam Eta was taken hostage by the people ▪ Police attempt at freeing him led to shootout that lasted for hours ▪ An electoral officer was manhandled and his money destroyed ▪ Similar cases were reported in Odukpani and Calabar, where electoral materials were reported diverted by CROSIEC	▪ Low voters turn-out ▪ Violence
150	Electoral violence between PDP and ANPP in Local Govt. election in Gwarzo, Kaura and Kwankwanso towns in Kano state; Nov. 17, 2007	▪ in inter-party conflict over the result of local Govt. polls ▪ thugs hijacked the exercise	▪ 6 people were killed and several others wounded ▪ 3 local Govt. secretariats were burnt down	▪ Several people lost their lives ▪ Top politicians including the former Minister of Defence Rabiu Musa Kwankwanso were attacked ▪ Soldiers deployed to the area ▪ Over 300 suspects arrested
151	Intra-party conflict between PDP members over Local govt. primary elections in Benue state; Nov. 27,2007	▪ Intra-party rivalry among PDP members which claim five lives and properties in Mbatya, Ado, Katsina-Ala, Tor-Donga,	▪ 5 people were killed, among them were; a female councillorship, Aze Wanye and Mr. Mzenda Iho	▪ Loss of lives and property ▪ Increasing cases of violence

		Okpokwu, Guma and Jato –Aka	▪ Several properties were burnt ▪ Electoral materials snatched by hoodlums	
152	Special Asst. to Jigawa State Gov. was assassinated in Naibawa, Kano state, Dec.1,2007	▪ Unknown assassins	▪ Alhaji Alkasim A Gwaram the Special Asst. was found in pool of blood in his compound	▪ Loss of life
153	Inter- party conflict between supporters PDP and Labour Party in Igboeze South Local Govt, Enugu State, December 15, 2007	▪ Local Govt. in Igboeze South political thugs clashed and people were killed	▪ 2 people lost their lives ▪ Buses were burnt ▪ 22 thugs arrested ▪ Dangerous weapons discovered	▪ Increasing violence
154	Local Govt. election in Edo State, Dec. 2007	▪ Politically motivated violence after the Local Govt. election	▪ EDSIEC Secretariat burnt down ▪ Electoral Officers beaten-up ▪	▪ increasing violence during election
155	Aftermath of Local Govt. election in Benue State, Dec. 29, 2007	▪ wide complaints of rigging and electoral manipulation by PDP	▪ Several cases deaths and violence ▪ Dangerous weapons used by irate Youths	▪ Breakdown of Law and Order as result of increased violence
156	Intra- party conflict between PDP members in Ibiono Ibom LGA, Akwa Ibom State, Jan. 21&22, 2008	▪ Clash over primary election of the party at Ward congress	▪ Hijack of election materials	▪ One person killed
157	Inter-party conflict between PDP and AC in Lalupon Lagelu Local Govt. Oyo State, Jan. 22, 2008	▪ Campaign for bye- election	▪ Dangerous weapons were used ▪ Many people injured	. 10 people injured . Use of political thugs
158	Inter-party conflict between PDP and Action Congress in Okene Local Govt. Kogi State, Jan. 23,2008	▪ A politically-motivated conflict, over the appointment of a Caretakers Chairman of Okene Local Govt.	▪ Guns and dangerous weapons were used	▪ Over 20 people killed ▪ More than 120 houses burnt

159	Assassination in Agharho, Ughelli North LGA,Delta State, Jan. 2008	▪ Politically motivated assassination	▪ Mr. Imere, a retired Navy Captain and a politician was assassinated	▪ Increasing insecurity of lives and property
160	Communal violence in Okene, Kogi state Feb.27 2008	▪ Police reprisal attack	▪ 20 killed ▪ 15 others bodies discovered after the attack ▪ Over 5,000 people rendered homeless	▪ Increasing violence
161	Assassination of Alh.Alih Ayegba, PDP Chairman in Ankpa LGA, Kogi state, March 2008	▪ A by-election of gubernatorial led to the politically motivated killing of PDP Chieftain including other series of killing in Okene	▪ Alh. Alih Ayegba killed few meters from his house ▪ Other series of killing in Okene, Ayigba, Dekina and Ankpa	▪ Increasing cases of violence during elections
162	Assassination of a Commissioner in Edo state, March 28, 2008	▪ Politically motivated assassination	▪ Mr. Calus Enoma, a Commissioner for Information and Orientation was allegedly murdered in cold blood. Police report claimed that he died of cardiac arrest.	▪ Insecurity of life
163	Local Govt Election in Rivers state, March 29, 2008	▪ Thugs, hoodlums attacked and set ablaze properties in Koroma, Nonwa-Gbam in Tai LGA, ▪ Similar electoral violence occurred in Abua/Odual LGA, Etche LGA where ten AC members were shot; in Eleme one person was kille; in Andoni LGA PDP was accused of hijacking of electoral materials in ward 10 &11, in the same Opobo/Nkoro	▪ 4 persons received injuries from machete cuts ▪ Several people lost their lives ▪ Properties worth millions destroyed	▪ Serious implications to legitimacy of leaders at grassroots ▪ Disenfranchising of citizens

		council and Gokana voting materials were diverted, other places within the State were affected in similar manner		
164	Local Govt Election in Niger State, March 29, 2008	▪ Election in various council areas were marred by violence and lack of provision of voting materials ▪ Affected areas include Kagara, Rafi, Muyan, Suleija LGA, old Minna Park and Anguwar Gayain polling stations ▪ In Gbako and Bida LGAs were cases of late starting of elections and intra-party clashes respectively	▪ One person was stabbed to death ▪ Three policemen injured	▪ Serious legitimacy crises to grassroots democracy
165	Intra-party conflict between ANPP in Bauchi state, April 12,2008	▪ ANPP primary for local govt election scheduled for May 17, 2008	▪ Two people killed including a Police Inspector, Mr. Kadiri Ahmed ▪ 45 persons arrested for encouraging violence ▪ Violence in Toro, Misau, Bogoro, Alkaleri, Giade and Ningi LGAs	▪ Increasing violence ▪ Threat to democracy at local level
166	Inter-party clash between PDP and DPP in Sokoto State, April 13,2008	▪ The nullification of the election of Gov. Aliyu Wamako's election by the Tribunal	▪ 4 people killed ▪ 35 vehicles burnt ▪ Several other casualties ▪ Free use of dangerous weapons by thugs	▪ Breakdown of law and order ▪ Increasing violence
167	Intra-party clash between PDP in Gombe State, April 19, 2008	▪ Politically-motivated violence between PDP groups	▪ Mohammed Ibrahim was killed; the 25 years old	▪ Increasing violence ▪ Threat to lives of citizens

		(Yankalare) and another called the Gandu Quarters	Ibrahim was an undergraduate student of the College of Administration and Business Studies, Kumo, Gombe State	
168	Explosion rocks Tribunal Chairman's house in Benin City, Edo State; October 6, 2008.	▪ Genocide attempt on the Chairman of Edo State Local Government Election Tribunal	▪ Justice Rowland Amaize lost almost all his property to fire triggered by explosion ▪ Some people had earlier threatened his life ▪ He and his family narrowly escaped death	▪ Threat to lives and property
169	Local government election in Jos North, Plateau State November 27, 2008	▪ Election-inspired violence degenerated into ethno-religious violence	▪ About 400 people killed (figure unconfirmed) ▪ Hundreds of thousands of people displaced ▪ Property worth billions of naira destroyed ▪ Joint Military, Police and other Security outfits deployed to quell riot ▪ 6 pm – 8am Curfew imposed in Jos, while 24 hour curfew imposed in the worst affected areas ▪ Shoot-on-sight order issued by the Gov. ▪ It took five days to restore order	▪ Threat to lives and property
170	Political killing in Ekiti State; Jan. 3, 2009	▪ Politically motivated killing by unknown assassins	▪ Kehinde Fasuba, A General Manager Of	▪ Insecurity of life

			PHCN, Kaduna zone who was nursing an ambition of vying for the Ekiti Central Senatorial seatin 2011	
171	Assassination attempt on AC member of Ekiti State House of Assembly; Jan. 18, 2009	▪ Inter-party rivalry	▪ Hon. Biola Olowokere narrowly escaped assassination ▪ His house was ransacked	▪ Insecurity of life
172	Assassination attempts on lives of Politicians in Ekiti State; Jan. 25, 2009	▪ politically motivated assassination attempts at political figures	▪ Funminiyi Afuye (AC leader representing Ikere1 constituency) ▪ David Taiwo (AC , representing Ado-Ekiti 11constitency in the House of Assembly) were attacked	▪ Insecurity of life In the State
173	Assassination of the South-East zone PDP leader in Umuahia, Abia State, Feb. 19, 2009	▪ Gruesome murder of Chief Rex Ebo	▪ Chief Ebo, a member of South East Disciplinary Committee of PDP murdered few hours after the inauguration of the Committee	▪ Fear and insecurity of persons.
174	Attack on opposition leader in Zamfara	▪ Hoodlums attack an opposition politician.	▪ House of Ex-Commissioner and his neighbourswer e vandalized by hoodlums.	▪ Fear and insecurity of persons.
175	Ekiti Re-Run Election in 10 LGA of Ekiti State; April 25 – May 5, 2009	▪ the re-run of 2007 governorship election between Oni(PDP) and Fayemi (AC)	▪ Horrendous electoral malpractices in various wards ▪ Violence and intimidations of people ▪ Snatching of ballot boxes and illegal thump printing ▪ Delay in announcing the	▪ Threat to survival of our democracy

			result ▪ Thugs and the use of weapons	
176	Politically-motivated attack on an opponent, Abuja; June 2009.	▪ Attack on National Assembly Clerk, Special Duties, one of the contestants of the Clerk to the National Assembly.	▪ Alh. Maikasuwa attacked by gunmen	▪ Injuries sustained.
177	Intra-party conflict in Bayelsa; November 20, 2009.	▪ Struggle for control of party and state between state governor and his deputy.	▪ Violent attacks	▪ Injuries sustained.
178	Political Assassination of Dapo Dina in Sango Ota, Ogun State; January 9, 2010.	▪ Political rivalry	▪ Assassination of AC Gubernatorial candidate in 2007 elections.	▪ Loss of life
179	Inter-party (ANPP-PDP) clash in Ibadan, January 19, 2010	▪ Contested election ▪ Inter-party rivalry	▪ Clash between supporters of ANPP gubernatorial candidate in 2007 election and that of serving PDP governor in Ogun State.	▪ Loss of life ▪ Destruction of property
180	Inter-party clash in Edo House of Assembly, Edo state; February 2010.	▪ Political rivalry ▪ Change of power as a result of annulment of the 2007 elections that led to the replacement of PDP governor by AC candidate. ▪ Change in leadership in the State House of Assembly.	▪ Some Members of the House of Assembly sustained injuries. ▪ Use of armed thugs by politicians.	▪ Political tension
181	Inter-party clash in Oye-Ekiti, Ekiti State; March 8, 2010.	▪ Inter-party rivalry ▪ Election campaigns	▪ Attack on AC gubernatorial candidate by suspected PDP supporters.	▪ Loss of life ▪ Injuries sustained ▪ Tensed atmosphere for election.
182	Politically-motivated killing in Birinin Kebbi, Kebbi State; April 13, 2010.	▪ Ibrahim Dan-Ilela, a PDP chieftain and others were crushed to death by a political thug driver over	▪ Political rivalry ▪ 7 persons including Ibrahim Dan-Ilela loss their lives	▪ Loss of lives

		ran them with high speed car.		
183	Clash between LP and PDP supporters in Irele, Ondo State; April 2010	▪ Inter-party rivalry ▪ Discontent over replacement of PDP governor with LP gubernatorial candidate in 2007 election following court ruling	▪ Attack on party supporters ▪ Patronage of thugs	▪ Injuries sustained ▪ Property destroyed
184	PDP-ANPP clash in Jakuso, Yobe State; April 2010	▪ Inter-party rivalry	▪ Attack on party supporters following the visit of the Deputy Governor	▪ Injuries sustained ▪ Loss of property
185	Intra-party squabble in Oyo State House of Assembly; June 2010.	▪ Intra-party rivalry ▪ Attempt to change speaker of House of Assembly.	▪ Attack on members of House of Assembly	▪ Injuries sustained ▪ Disruption of legislative activities.
186	Politically motivated assassination; Akwa Ibom State; June 20, 2010.	▪ Perceived political threat	▪ Gruesome murder of PDP chieftain in Akwa Ibom, Chief Paul Inyang	▪ Loss of life
187	Kidnap, attempted murder; Ilaje constituency, Ondo state; July 31, 2010.	• Electioneering irregularities ▪ Thuggery and intimidation during the elections	• Kidnap of 2 electoral staff ▪ Attempted murder of INEC officials	• Panic among voters and INEC staff ▪ Kidnap of 2 INEC staff
188	Politically motivated assassination in Benin, Edo state; August 8, 2010.	• Perceived political threat	• Gruesome murder of the AC House of Representative s aspirant, Engineer Ayo Oghogho	• Loss of life • Fear and panic among other aspirants in the state.
189	Inter-party clash, Gusau, Zamfara State; August 9, 2010.	• Inter-party rivalry between PDP and ANPP supporters	• Free-for-all fight • Destruction of property worth thousands of naira	• 3 persons killed, 11 injured • Property destroyed
190	Politically motivated assassination. Maiduguri, Borno State; October 5, 2010.	• Inter-party rivalry • Perceived political threat	• Gruesome murder of ANPP national Vice-chairman (North east), Alhaji Awana Ngala	• 8 lives lost • Panic among residents of Maiduguri
191		•	•	•
192	Intra-party rivalry, Osogbo and Ede south	• Rivalry between supporters of various PDP	• Violent clash between the various	• Panic among residents of the area

	local governments, Osun state; October, 2010.	chairmanship candidates in the primary elections.	factions leaving about 25 persons injured.	
193	Intra-party squabble; Akko, Gombe State; December 3, 2010	• Clash between rival PDP groups over the candidacy of a gubernatorial aspirant	• Violent confrontations • Gruesome murder	• Loss of lives • Tension and heightened restiveness
194	Politically-motivated assassination in Mubi, Adamawa State; December 15, 2010	• Perceived political threat	• Gruesome murder of Alhaji Tafida Umar, chairman, PDP Mubi North L.G.A	• Loss of life, • Increased tension
195	Explosion at Political rally in Yenagoa, Bayelsa State; December 29, 2010	• Perceived political threat	• Dynamite explosion at PDP gubernatorial campaign rally	• Panic and heightened tension • Scores of supporters injured
196	Intra-party squabble in Ago-Iwoye, Ogun State; December 29, 2010	• Clash between rival PDP groups over ward congresses	• Violent confrontations	• Loss of life • tension
197	Intra-party squabble in Oyo State December 30, 2010	• Clash between rival PDP groups at the state congress elections	• Violence • Gruesome murder of Alhaji Lateef Salako, the factional leader of NURTW and party delegate	• Loss of life • Panic • Restiveness
198	Inter-party clash in Ughelli, Delta January 3, 2011	• Inter-party rivalry	• Clash between PDP and PRN supporters over Delta re-run election	• Loss of life • Destruction of property
199	Intra-party clash, following disagreements among CPC members at the Party congress; Jan. 2011	• Intra-party clash	• No fewer than 10 people killed following disagreements among CPC members at the party congress.	• Lost of life

200	Intra-party squabble in Akure, Ondo State; January 9, 2011	• Clash between rival Labour party groups at the party primaries	• Open violence	• Tension • Restiveness
201	Intra-party squabble in Benin, Edo State January 12, 2011	• Clash between rival ACN groups at the party primaries	• Open violence • Gruesome murder	• Loss of lives • Panic and tension
202	Politically-motivated assassination in Maiduguri, Borno State January 28, 2011	• Perceived political threat	• Gruesome murder of Alhaji Fanami Gubio, an ANPP gubernatorial candidate; and six others	• Loss of life, • Increased tension
203	Political violence in Lafia, Nassarawa State February 9, 2011	• Violent clash between CPC supporters and police over the arrest of their gubernatorial candidate, Alhaji Tanko Almakura	• Open violence • Gruesome murder of 2 party supporters	• Loss of lives • Tension and heightened restiveness
204	Presidential rally stampede in Port-Harcourt, Rivers State February 12, 2011	• Gunshot fired by a policeman in an attempt to disperse the mammoth crowd	• Loss of no fewer than 20 lives • Lots of supporters injured	• Loss of lives • Panic and tension
205	Inter-party clash in Idanre, Ondo State; February 12, 2011	• Clash between LP and ACN supporters	• Violent clash	• 7 persons seriously injured • Increased tension
206	Political violence in Aniocha, Delta State February 18, 2011	• Clash between rival political groups	• Open violence • Attack on Charles Odiaka, PDP chieftain	• Panic and tension
207	Inter-party clash in Afikpo, Ebonyi State; February 19, 2011	• Clash Between PDP and APGA supporters	• Attack on APGA governorship candidate, Franklin Ogbuewu by suspected PDP thugs • Destruction of property	• Tension • Heightened restiveness
208	Inter-party violence in Abakiliki, Ebonyi State;	• Attack on APGA supporters by suspected PDP thugs	• 4 APGA supporters shot by suspected PDP thugs	• Panic and tension • Heightened restiveness

	February 19, 2011			
209	Inter-party clash in Awka, Anambra State; February 23, 2011	• Clash between APGA and ACN supporters	• Violence	• Injuries sustained by supporters • Loss of property
210	Attack on ACN chairman in Makurdi, Benue State; February 23, 2011	• Perceived political threat	• Attempted murder of Benue state ACN chairman, comrade Abba Yaro, and publicity secretary of the party, Mr Okpe Andrew Onoja by unknown gunmen	• Panic and tension
211	Inter-party clash in Dandagoro, Katsina State March 1, 2011	• Clash between PDP and CPC supporters	• Violence • Loss of life	• Loss of life • Heightened restiveness
212	Bomb blast at political rally in Suleija, Niger State; March 3, 2011	• Bombs planted by unknown persons at the venue of PDP campaign rally	• Bombs exploded at the venue of PDP zonal campaign rally killing no fewer than 10 persons with several others severely injured	• Loss of lives • Destruction of property • Panic and tension
213	Inter-party clash in Babura, Jigawa State; March 6, 2011	• Clash between PDP and ACN supporters	• Open violence resulting in the death of 1 person with several others injured	• Loss of life • Heightened restiveness
214	Ambush on ACN senatorial candidate in Otukpo, Benue State; March 8, 2011	• Perceived political threat	• Ambush on General Lawrence Onoja and his entourage while traveling for a political function	• General Onoja was allegedly shot • Panic and tension • Opposition PDP disputed claims by ACN
215	President's convoy pelted in Gombe State March 10, 2011	• Political differences	• Restive youths armed with stones and other objects pelted president Jonathan's convoy as he went to address a presidential	• Heightened restiveness

			campaign rally	
216	Inter-party clash in Etim Ekpo, Akwa Ibom State March 13, 2011	• Clash between PDP and ACN supporters at ACN rally	• Violence • Destruction of property • Injury sustained by supporters	• Heightened restiveness
217	Inter-party clash; Ose LGA, Ondo State; March14, 2011	• Clash between LP and ACN supporters	• Violence leading to the death of 1 person	• Loss of life • Panic and tension
218	Inter-party clash in Ekiti West, Ekiti State; March 16, 2011	• Clash between PDP and ACN supporters	• Violence leaving a policeman shot with several others injured	• Panic and tension • Heightened restiveness
219	Thugs disrupted political rally in Kogi State; March 16, 2011	• Political differences	• Armed thugs invaded ANPP gubernatorial campaign rally causing mayhem	• Panic and tension
220	Political violence in Giade, Bauchi State; March 20, 2011	• Perceived political threat	• Armed thugs attacked the campaign team of senator Baba Tela, ACN gubernatorial candidate, killing 1 person and leaving several others injured	• Loss of life • Panic and tension
221	Party supporters shot at presidential campaign rally in Jos, Plateau State March 21, 2011	• Indiscriminate shooting by policemen	• Police shot at hundreds of CPC supporters as they welcomed their presidential flag-bearer, Gen. Buhari. 4 supporters were killed, several others severely injured	• Loss of lives • Heightened restiveness • Political differences
222	Attempted assassination of party candidate in Benin, Edo State March 21, 2011	• Perceived political threat	• ACN senatorial candidate, Senator Ehigie Umazere's convoy was attacked by a 4-man gang attempting to assassinate him, killing his	• Loss of life • Panic and tension

			police orderly in the process	
223	Political violence; Anambra State, March 22, 2011	• Political differences	• Series of political violence leadind to the attack of Chris Ngige's campaign team	• Panic and tension • Heightened restiveness
224	Inter-party clash in Awka, Anambra State; March 22, 2011	• Clash between APGA and Accord party supporters	• Violence leading to the death of 1 person	• Loss of life • Heightened restiveness
225	Inter-party clash in Makurdi, Benue State; March 22, 2011	• Clash between PDP and ACN supporters	• Violence claiming a life and destruction of property worth millions of naira	• Loss of life and property • Heightened restiveness
226	Inter-party violence in Akwa Ibom State; March 22, 2011	• Violent clash between ACN and PDP supporters	• Violence leading to the death of over 20 persons with property worth millions of naira destroyed	• Loss of lives and property • Heightened restiveness
227	Assassination attempt on party candidate in Dakingari, Kebbi State; March 22, 2011	• Perceived political threat	• Hired thugs attacked a CPC campaign rally, attempting to assassinate the governorship candidate, Alhaji Abubakar Mallam and a senatorial candidate, Muhammad Adamu Aliero	• Destruction of property • Heightened restiveness • Panic and tension
228	Inter-party clash in Maigatari, Jigawa State; March 28, 2011	• Clash between PDP and ACN supporters	• Violence leaving 1 person shot	• Heightened restiveness
229	Gunmen disrupt party rally in Oji, Enugu State; March 29, 2011	• Political differences	• Gunmen suspected to be political thugs disrupted a Labour party rally	• Panic and tension
230	Inter-party clash in Warji, Bauchi State; March 29, 2011	• Clash between PDP and ACN supporters	• Violence resulting in the death of 2 persons	• Loss of lives • Panic and tension • Heightened restiveness
231	Party chieftain kidnapped in Onitsha,	• Perceived political threat	• APGA chieftain, prince Emeka	• Panic and tension

	Anambra March 29, 2011		Asoanya kidnapped by unknown persons	
232	Electoral violence in Ekeremor, Bayelsa State; April 2, 2011	• Political violence	• 3 lives lost as JTF soldiers clashed with restive youths over electoral issues	• Loss of lives • Heightened restiveness
233	Politically-motivated murder in Ogbomoso, Oyo State; April 2, 2011	• Perceived political threat	• ACN member, Mr Isiaka Ademola, killed by suspected PDP supporters	• Loss of life • Heightened restiveness
234	Inter-party clash in Ofu/ Ejule LGAs, Kogi State; April 4, 2011	• Clash between rival political thugs	• Violence leading to the death of 2 persons	• Loss of life • Panic and tension
235	Bomb explosion at INEC office in Suleija, Niger State; April 8, 2011	• Political violence	• Bomb blast at INEC office ahead of elections leaving no fewer than 13 persons dead and several others severely injured	• Loss of lives • Heightened restiveness • Panic and tension
236	Bomb explosion at polling unit in Maiduguri, Borno state; April 9, 2011	• Political violence	• Bomb blast at polling unit leaving a police woman dead and about 10 persons critically injured	• Panic and tension • Heightened restiveness • Loss of life
237	Politically-motivated murder in Maiduguri, Borno State; April 9, 2011	• Perceived political threat	• ANPP chairman in Jere Local Government, Alhaji Fannami Garnam, assassinated by unknown gunmen	• Loss of life
238	Political violence in Ile-Ife, Osun State; April 9, 2011	• Perceived political threat	• 5 persons killed as hoodlums attacked the residence of ACN house of reps candidate	• Loss of lives • Heightened restiveness
239	Electoral violence in Ndokwa West, Delta State;	• Attempt to disrupt electoral process	• 3 persons killed as they attempted to disrupt	• Loss of lives • Heightened restiveness

	April 9, 2011		peaceful election process	
240	Hoodlums invade politician's home in Kaduna April 9, 2011	• Alleged attempt to snatch a ballot box	• Hoodlums invaded Ambassador Sule Baba's residence, Director General of Governor Patrick Yakowa's campaign organization, for allegedly sending one of his aides to snatch a ballot box	• Panic and tension • Heightened restiveness
241	Politically-motivated murders in Nwangele, Imo State; April 9, 2011	• Perceived political threats	• Suspected hired assasins invaded the country home of Mr Ezekiel Chukwukere, local council chairman, leaving 5 PDP loyalists dead and several others injured	• Loss of lives • Heightened restiveness
242	Electoral mayhem in Brass, Bayelsa State; April 9, 2011	• Clash between PDP and Labour party supporters	• Violent clash between PDP and Labour party supporters over electoral issues leaving 1 person dead	• Loss of life • Heightened restiveness
243	Ballot papers snatched in Ughelli, Delta State; April 9, 2011	• Ballot papers snatched by political thugs	• Ballot papers were intercepted and snatched by unknown political thugs, who also held the INEC officials and 2 police orderlies hostage	• Heightened restiveness • Panic and tension
244	Election materials thrown into the sea in Warri, Delta State; April 9, 2011	• Clash between PDP and DPP supporters	• Election materials meant for National Assembly polls were thrown into the Escravos sea as	• Panic and tension

			PDP and DPP supporters clashed	
245	Electoral violence in Bagudo, Kebbi State; April 9, 2011	• Violent clash between PDP and CPC supporters	• Violent clash between PDP and CPC supporters leading to the postponement of elections	• Loss of life
246	Ballot boxes stolen in Bayelsa and other states April 9, 2011	• Attempt to rig elections	• 117 ballot boxes reported stolen from INEC in National Assembly polls, with Bayelsa having a total of 23 cases	• Disruption of electoral process
247	Irate youths mob commissioners, others in Kano April 10, 2011	• Party failure at National Assembly polls	• Angry ANPP supporters attacked party chieftains at the state house over their inability to rake in votes at the just concluded polls	• Panic and tension • Heightened restiveness
248	Gunmen went after returning officer in Awka, Anambra State; April 12, 2011	• Aftermath of election results	• Unknown gunmen invaded Nnamdi Azikiwe University in search of the returning officer in the National Assembly polls, Mr. Alex Anene	• Threat to life
249	Post election bomb explosion in Kabala, Kaduna State; April 16, 2011	• Post election violence	• Bomb explosion rocked Kabala west, leaving 2 people injured	• Panic and tension • Heightened restiveness
250	Election day bombings in Maiduguri, Borno State; April 16, 2011	• Attempt to disrupt peaceful elections	• 2 bomb explosions rocked Maiduguri metropolis causing panic among residents	• Panic and tension • Heightened restiveness
251	Post election	• Outcome of	• Irate youths	• Loss of lives and

	violence in Bauchi, Bauchi State; April 17, 2011	Presidential polls	believed to be CPC supporters attacked rival party supporters, corps members and set buildings on fire	property • Heightened restiveness
252	Post election violence in Adamawa State; April 17, 2011	• Outcome of presidential polls	• Mayhem as irate youths protested the outcome of the presidential polls	• Loss of lives and property
253	Post election violence in Gombe State April 17, 2011	• Outcome of presidential polls	• Irate youths took to the streets protesting the outcome of presidential polls	• Loss of lives and property • Heightened restiveness
254	Post election violence in Kaduna State; April 17, 2011	• Outcome of presidential polls	• Attacks on opposition members and churches, burning of properties belonging to prominent PDP members	• Loss of lives and property; • Panic and tension
255	Post election violence in Kano State; ;April 17, 2011	• Outcome of presidential polls	• Violent riots as youths took to streets protesting the outcome of presidential polls, burning properties belonging to PDP supporters	• Loss of lives and property; • Heightened restiveness
256	Post election violence in Minna, Niger State; April 18, 2011	• Outcome of presidential polls	• Angry youths protesting the outcome of presidential polls stormed a corpers lodge, locked the corps members inside and set the building on fire	• Loss of property • Corps members sustained severe burns • Panic and tension
257	Post election violence in Bida, Niger State; April 19, 2011	• Outcome of presidential polls	• 2 persons killed as irate youths protesting the Etsu Nupe's support for the	• Loss of lives • Heightened restiveness

			PDP, stormed his palace	
258	Electoral violence; in Akwa Ibom State; April 26, 2011	• Attempt to disrupt free and fair elections	• Sporadic shooting as unknown gunmen stormed various polling units carting away ballot boxes and other electoral materials	• Loss of lives • Panic and tension • Heightened restiveness
259	Electoral violence; in Ogbomosho, Oyo State; April 26, 2011	• Attempt to disrupt elections	• 2 persons killed as people believed to be PDP thugs attempted to scare other party agents away from polling centres	• Loss of lives • Heightened restiveness
260	Returning Officer abducted in Bungudu, Zamfara State;April 26, 2011	• Attempt to rig election	• INEC returning officer Mr. Mainasara Nasiru was abducted by armed policemen and threatened at gunpoint to alter electoral results in favor of the PDP	• Heightened restiveness
261	ACN guber candidate's convoy attacked along Lafia-Makurdi road, Nassarawa State; May 13, 2011	• Perceived political threat	• Unknown gunmen attacked the Benue ACN governorship candidate's convoy, killing his aide, Charles Ayede	• Loss of life • Heightened restiveness
262	ACN candidate kidnapped in Asari Toru, Rivers State; May 21, 2011	• Perceived political threat	• ACN chairmanship candidate, Mr. Sobibu Horsfall, abducted during the local government election in the state	• Threat to life • Heightened restiveness
263	Man arrested with ballot box in Rafi, Niger	• Attempt to rig election	• Ibrahim Seidu, who claimed to be an INEC official, caught	• Heightened restiveness

	State; May 22, 2011		with a ballot box used for the House of Assembly polls	
264	Bomb blast in Zuba near Abuja; 29 May, 2011	• Politically perceived	• Two persons died • 11 sustained injuries	• Loss of lives and properties • Growing insecurity and tension
265	Post election violence in Niger and Kaduna; States, May 2011	• Politically motivated protests on the outcome of 2011 general election	• 514 civilians killed • 6 policemen died • 75 others injured • 165 churches destroyed • 53 mosques destroyed • 444 vehicles destroyed • 1442 houses destroyed	• Loss of lives and properties
266	Post election violence in Niger State, June 10, 2011	• Aftermath of 2011 general election in Niger State	• 25 Churches burnt down	• Loss of lives and property;
267	Post election violence in Kaduna; June 20, 2011	• Politically motivated and aftermath of 2011 electoral violence	• 33,000 persons displaced	• Growing insecurity of lives and property in Nigeria
268	Tinubu and Mimiko crisis in Ado Ekiti, Ekiti State; August 11, 2011	• Politically motivated	• Many people were injured including 2 prominent members of Labour Party	• Heat the polity
269	Assassination of ACN Chieftain in Abeokuta, Ogun State, August 27,2011	• politically motivated assassination	• murder of Chief Yomi Bamgbose	• Threat to lives and property
270	LG Boss killed in Borno; state, August 29,2011	Politically motivated	• 1 person killed	• A local government boss was killed in Borno;
271	Clash among ACN supporters, August 29, 2011	• Intra- party conflict	• Many sustained injuries	• Heightened restiveness among supporters.
272	killing in Kafanchan, Kaduna State; state,August 31, 2011	• Politically motivated	• 4 people died	• As government imposed curfew as a result of continued tension in the area
273	ACN and PDP Supporter's clash in Ibadan, September 2,	• Inter-party conflict	• 10 persons seriously injured	• Disturbance of public peace

	2011			
274	PDP chieftain murdered in Enugu State; October 5, 2011	• Politically motivated assassination	• The Chairman, PDP Enugu South LGA, Mr. Steven Ani was assassinated by a suspected assassins on his way to his country home	• Loss of life
275	Crisis over LG poll in Niger State; October 8, 2011	• Aftermath of LG election results	• 3 persons died	• Loss of lives and property;
276	ACN, PDP clash in Benue State. October 17, 2011.	• Politically motivated	• There is no agreement on the number killed as various Newspapers reported that between 6-15 persons.	• Loss of lives and property;
277	Crises over LG Poll in Mushim and Ikoyi, Lagos State; October22, 2011.	• Aftermath of LG election results	• Two people were feared dead • And 20 others arrested in Mushin and Ikoyi, following a clash between rival groups of the political parties contesting for Local government elections in Lagos.	• Loss of lives.
278	Clashes between supporters of two governorship aspirants of the People's Democratic Party in Sokoto; October 23, 2011.	• Politically motivated	• One Vehicle burnt and, • Six others vandalized, when supporter of two governorship aspirants of People's Democratic Party (PDP) clashed.	• Loss of properties.
279	Unknown gunmen killed former NLC Boss in Osun state. October 24, 2011	• Politically perceived violence	• The late unionist was attacked in his Cyber Café' along Osogbo/Ilorin	• Loss of life

			Express road	
280	Assassins killed Edo State's Hope Democratic Party Chairman, November 21, 2011.	• Politically perceived	• The late Chairman was shot, at residence.	• Loss of life
281	Suspected thugs attacked the Campaign train of Action Congress of Nigeria (ACN) Governorship Candidate in Kogi State, November, 24, 2011.	• Politically perceived	• Attack on campaign train of ACN, Governorship Candidate in Kogi State.	• Destruction of properties.
282	The shooting of CPP governorship candidate by the police in Delta State; December 2,2011	• Politically perceived	• The killing of Chief Ogbe Onokpite gubernatorial candidate of Citizens Popular Party, CPP, Delta State.	• Loss of life.
283	Bauchi PDP crisis, January 3,2011	• Politically perceived	• Bauchi PDP crisis: • Mu'azu's supporters clash with Dr.Abdullahi Umar Ganduji supporters.	• Destruction of properties
284	Benue ACN, PDP, crisis, January 15, 2012.	• Politically perceived	• One killed, • Market set ablaze in Benue as CAN, PDP Youths clash.	• Loss of life and Destruction of properties.
285	Clash between supporters of PDP at a Rally in Oporoma Southern IjawLocal Government in Bayelsa State; February 7, 2012.	• Politically motivated	• 3 killed, • Several injured as Sylva, Dickson supporters clash at PDP rally.	• Loss of lives.
286	Attack on ACN Members in Ose local government Area, Ondo State; February	• Politically motivated	• Gunmen attack ACN members in Ondo	• Destruction of properties.

	12, 2012.			
287	Police stop Anambra PDP Congress, March 17, 2012.	• Politically motivated	• PDP Congress turned violent	• No loss of life
288	Oshiomhole's aide killed in Benin, Edo State; May 4, 2012.	• Political motivated	• Oshiomhole's aide murdered in Benin.	• Loss of live,
289	Gunmen shoot Benue law maker's brother, May 14, 2012.	• Politically motivated	• Unknown gunmen shot Benue Law maker's brother.	• Loss of life.
290	Gunmen kill PRP chairman in Maiduguri, Borno State; May 25, 2012.	• Politically motivated.	• Unknown Gunmen killed Mr. Amodu Gombe, the PRP Chairman.	• Loss of life.
291	Edo PDP,ACN trade allegations, May 30,2012	• Inter-party conflict.	• PDP, ACN trade allegations.	• No loss of life.
292	Abduction of the PDP chieftain in Kogi State in Kabba/Bunu LGA, Kogi State, June 16, 2012.	• Politically motivated	• Gunmen abducted Alu Raphael Olorunpomi, thePDP chieftain in Kabba/Bunu LGA, Kogi State.	• No loss of life.
293	Inter-party clash between ACN and LP in Akoko Southwest, Ondo State; September 19, 2012	• At a weekly constituency meeting of Action Congress of Nigeria	• Suspected labour Party(LP) hoodlums violently attacked ACN members • 5 ACN members seriously injured and several property destroyed	• Insecurity of opposition parties • Destruction of property
294	Inter-party violence in Akungba Akoko, Ondo State October 5, 2012	• Fight over the sharing of campaign money by Labour Party thugs	• Gruesome killings, number not confirmed	• Loss of lives

Sources: *News Watch*, April 28, 2003, August 4, 2004; *Daily Sun,* March 24 & 27, 2004, February 22, 2006, June 21, 2006, August 7, 2006; *Daily Trust,* March 7, 11 & 14 2003, March 29, 2004, March 25, 2005, August 28, 2005, April 25, 2006, July 3, 12, 26 & 28, 2006, August 2 & 9, 2006 ; *Weekly Trust,* March 15-21, 2003, December 3-9, 2003; *This Day,* May 5, 2002, March 22, 2003, March 4, 28 and 29, 2004, February & 19, 2006, April 9, 2006, July 11, 2006; *Vanguard,* April 29, 2004, May 2 & 26, 2004, April 26, 2006, *Vanguard,* August 20, 2006; *The Guardian,* March 13, 21 & 22, 2003April 9, 2006; *Tell,* March 10, 2003; *Leadership,* July 3, 2006; *Punch,* May 21, 2006., July 11, 2006.;*WeeklyTrust*, April 7, 2007; *Newswatch* Magazine, April 30, 2007.*Leadership* April 15, 2007,*Daily Trus*t April 24, 2007 *Sunday Trust*, Nov.25,2007, *Vanguard*; Dec.4, 2008, *Punch,* March 10 and 12, 2009; *Vanguard* April 27, 2009; *DailyTrust* April 27, 2009; *Leadership*, May 5,,2009; *The Sun,* November 30, 2009; *Vanguard,* Jan.2010, p.1, *Daily Trust,* April 13, 2010, p.1.; *Daily Trust,* June 9, 2010, p.9; *Daily Trust,* February 10, 2009, p. 6.; *The Nation,* January 10, 2010; *Daily Independent,* February 24, 2010; *punch,* April 6, 2010; *The Compass,* April 8, 2010; *Peoples Daily*, May 20, 2010; *Daily Champion,* May 27, 2010; *Daily Trust,* Tuesday May 31,2011 p4; *The Nation*, Wednesday June 1, 2011 p6; *The Nation*, Thursday June 2, 2011 p2& 9; *The Nation*, Friday June10, 2011 ; *Nation Mirrow*, Friday August 12, 2011; *The Nation*, Monday June 20, 2011; *Vanguard*, Tuesday June 28, 2011; *Vanguard,* Monday August 29,2011; *Vanguard,* August 30,2011 p.5; *The Nation,* Tuesday August 30,2011 p.53; *Vanguard*, Thursday September 1,2011 p.16; *TheNation*, Saturday Sept.3,2011 p.5; *Weekly Trust* Saturday October 8,2011 p.5; *Leadership*, Monday Oct.10, 2011 p.47; *Vanguard,* Monday August 29,2011 p.13 ;*The Nation*, Tuesday October 18, 2011 p9 ,*Vangard,*Tuesday,October18,2011 p6,*Leadership,*Tuesday,Oct ober 18,2011 p5,*Daily Trust*,Tuesday,October18,2011 p2 ,*The Nation* Sunday, October 23,2011,p.8,*The Nation* Tuesday, October 25,2011,p.6, *Leadership* , October 26, 2011 p43 ,*Leadership*, November 22,2011,p.46,*The Nation*, November 25,2011,p.5,*Vangard*,December2,2011,p.10,*Leadership*,January4,2012,p.8;*TheNatio n*, January 15,2012,p.6,*DailySun* ,February8,2012,p.9,*TheNation*, February 13, 2012,p.8,*Vanguard*,February 15,2012, *Leadership* Sunday, March 18,2012,p.9.,*Lead ership*weekend, May 5,2012,p.5,*TheNation*, May 17,2012,p.58., *DailyTrust*, May 17,2012,p.5;Sunday Sun,May27,2012,p.12.,*TheNation*, May 31,2012,p.12.,*Leadersh ip*,June 18,2012,p.6.; *The Nation*, Oct. 5, 2012, p.5

Appendix B

SELECTED CASES OF ETHNO-RELIGIOUS CONFLICTS IN NIGERIA
(MAY 1999 TO SEPTEMBER2012)

S/N	DATE	LOCATION	NATURE OF CONFLICTS AND PRINCIPAL ACTORS
1	May 31, 1999	Warri, Delta	Violent clash between the Ijaw and Iteskiri communities which has it roots in the grievances harboured by the *Olu* of Warri and his subjects over the recognition of new Kings in Warri by the Military Administration.
2	July 2, 1999	Sagamu, Ogun	A violent ethnic clash between Yorubas and the Hausa/Fulani residents. *The News* magazine attributed the crisis to the O'odua Peoples Congress (OPC).
3	July 22, 1999	Kano, Kano	Hausa/Fulani youth took vengeance on the killing of their kith and kin in Sagamu. Their target was the Yoruba community.
4	August 4, 1999	Arobo, Ondo	A violent clash between two feuding communities, the Ijaw and Ilaje communities of Arobo, Ondo State.
5	October 5, 1999	Port Harcourt Rivers	Violent clash between the Eleme and Okrika communities over traditional and legal titles to the stretch of land where Port Harcourt refinery is located.
6	October 19, 1999	Ajegunle, Lagos	It was reported to be an extension of the Arobo-Ijaw/Ilaje crisis, which started with kidnap of an Ijaw man. It later became a fracas between the Ijaws and OPC.
7	October 21, 1999	Aguleri-Umuleri, Anambra	A violent communal clash between two neighbouring communities of Aguleri and Umuleri. Whichlinkedto the April 4, clash as a result of an orgy of hatred and vengeance.
8	Nov. 8, 1999	Odi Killing (Bayelsa)	Youth group associated with *Egbesu* youth kidnapped and killed policemen in revenge of the killing of their members. The Ajegunle Ijaw/OPC crisis also heightened the restive situation in Ijaw community. The town received a shelling and bombardment with artillery from soldiers.
9	Nov. 16, 1999	Isoko, Delta	A bloody communal clash between Oleh and Olomuro communities over sharing of used pipes from Oleh-Olomuro flow station.
10	Nov. 26, 1999	Port Harcourt Rivers	An extension of hostility between the two neighbouring communities of Eleme and Okrika.
11	Feb. 28, 2000	Kaduna, Kaduna	Kaduna city exploded in violence as Muslim and Christian extremists and other hoodlums clashed over the proposal to introduce the Sharia.
12	Feb. 28, 2000	Aba, Abia	The riot which began in Aba, as a reprisal to that of Kaduna, later spread to other Eastern states.
13	March 10, 2000	Ife-Modakeke, Osun	Communal killings between Ife and Modakeke communities of Ijesha. This was a fresh hostility after a long truce. It is believed to have a history of ancestral rivalry, which became heightened by local Government Council creation and the tussle over the location of the Headquarters of the new LGC.

14	March 18, 2000	Port Harcourt, Rivers	A communal hostility between the Eleme and the Okrika communities which degenerated into violence, claiming several lives.
15	April 12,2000	Gokana, Rivers	A bloody encounter involving six communities in Gokana LGA of Rivers state.
16	April 14, 2000	Agyragu, Nasarawa	Communal clash that started with a protest against the location of Local Government Council Headquarters. The militant youth group rioted took to the streets killing and destroying.
17	May 4, 2000	Ife-Modakeke, Osun	Another round of hostility between the two warring communities.
18	May 16, 2000	Akaasa-Igwama, Bayelsa	A bloody ethnic encounter between the Akaasa and Igwama communities.
19	June 5, 2000.	Olowo, Ondo	A violent clash between supporters of two lineage groups over the succession of the *Owo* Stool. The tomb of Pa Ajasin (a respected Yoruba leader and former Governor) was destroyed in the conflict.
20	July 15,2000.	Tsagari, Kwara	Clash between Tsagari and Share communities of Kwara state, which claimed several lives.
21	September 8, 2000.	Kaltungo, Gombe	A religious violence that was sparked off by the presence of the state's Sharia implementation committee.
22	October 17, 2000.	Ilorin, Kwara	A face off between the militant members of OPC and Hausa/Fulani community over supremacy of Emirate system in the state.
23	October 18, 2000	Lagos	Violent clashes between the militant OPC and Hausa residents in Ajegunle, which escalated and spread to other parts of the city recording heavy casualties. It was gathered that the clash might have been a spill over of Ilorin crisis.
24	October 21, 2000	Minna, Niger	Violent ethnic crisis erupted after the OPC assaults in Kwara and Lagos states.
25	October 22, 2000	Owaale-Olukare, Ondo	Hostilities between Owaale and Olukare of Ikare over Obaship.
26	December 2, 2000	Hadejia, Jigawa	A sectarian disturbance that was caused by a debate between Muslims and Christians in Hadejia (Jigawa). There was wanton destruction of worship places.
27	June 28, 2001	Azara, Nasarawa	An ethnic conflict between the Tiv and the Azara indigenes. It started with gruesome killing of an Azara traditional leader, and later spread to the Tiv villages, with the Tiv community on the defense.
28	September 7, 2001	Jos, Plateau	A violent ethno-religious crisis between the Muslim/Hausa-Fulani and Christian/indigenes. The subject of discord between the Jasawa Development Association and Plateau Youth Council was over political appointment in Jos North LGC.
29	September 15, 2001	Onitsha, Anambra	A reprisal killing of Northerners in Onitsha after the Jos crisis in which several Igbos were victims.
30	October 13, 2001	Rivers	A chieftaincy crisis, which snowballed into (clan) violence that claimed several lives and destruction of properties.

31	October 12, 2001	Kano, Kano	A peaceful anti-American protest over the bombing of Afghanistan turned violent, taking ethnic and religious tone. It degenerated into uncontrollable violence, which claimed lives and damaged properties and places of worship.
32	October 29, 2001	Taraba, Benue and Nasarawa	Ethnic clashes between Tivs and Jukun/Fulani, which was extension of the May 2001 clash and could be linked with the protracted dispute between both sides. *Newswatch* reported that 16 soldiers were killed which later led to the gruesome revenge on the Tivs in Zaki Biamby the Nigeria Army.
33	November 2, 2001	Gwantu, Kaduna	A clash that started on a political ground (over the relocation of LGC Headquarters) later took on ethno-religious dimension. Several places of worship were destroyed.
34	December 30, 2001	Barikin Ladi, Plateau	A violent communal conflict in Vwang district between the indigenes and non-indigenes exploded at the backdrop of the September 7, 2001 Jos crisis. It started when an illegal group of 40 men attacked the District Head of Vwang. It also had religious colouring.
35	Jan. 18, 2002	Awe, Nasarawa	A renewed communal clash between two indigenous communities in Awe LGC of Nasarawa State. The cause was not certain but two people were killed and several others injured.
36	February 12, 2002	Idi-Araba, Lagos	An inter-ethnic violence between the Hausa resident community and the Yoruba in Idi-Araba. It started on the trivial accusation of a Yoruba man being manhandled but later escalated and took on ethnic line.
37	March 25, 2002	Ikom, Cross River	Hostility erupted at Ikom when Ofara Natives launched a revenge attack against their Nselle neighbours, killing ten people in the process.
38	March 2002	Ika, Akwa-Ibom	*The Punch* reported an inter-communal war in Ika LGC. Hundreds of lives were said to be lost.
39	May 2, 2002	Jos, Plateau	Another mayhem that followed PDP Wards Congress but later took an ethno-religious colour.
40	May 13, 2002	Bori, Bayelsa	A communal clash in Ogoni land over the ownership of Bori town between the Yeghe people and the Zappa community.
41	May 27, 2002	Bassa, Plateau	An ethnic clash between the Hausa/Fulani and the Irigwe Indigenes, which was said to be a reprisal attack.
42	June 2002	Isoko, Delta	A clash between youth of Ozoro and Okpaile communities in Isoko. *The Punch* reported that five people were found dead and more injured.
43	June 26, 2002	Yelwa-Shendam, Plateau	A religious/ethnic fracas between the native people (predominantly Christians) and Hausa settlers (predominantly Muslims). This violence extended to about 14 LGCs in Southern Plateau.
44	July 3-6, 2002	Wase, Plateau	The Yelwa-Shendam riots spilled over to Wase.
45	January 2003	Abotse, Edo	Conflict over land ownership: irate youths protested against strangers taking over their lands.
46	January 31, 2003	Warri, Delta	Renewed hostilities between the two feuding communities-Urhobo and Itsekiri. Several lives were lost including police officers.
47	March 2003	Langtang North, Wase and Kanam LGC of Plateau	Fresh ethno-religious conflicts in the three neihbouring LGCs which is an extension of the crisis in southern Plateau.
48	March 17, 2003	Warri, Delta	Continued hostilities that led to the death of over 100 people and the sacking of 20 towns by suspected Ijaw militia.
49	May 7, 2003	Inyimagu/Agbaja, Ebonyi	Communal clash between rival cult groups. About 13 persons were reported dead and property worth millions od naira destroyed.

50	May 2003	Warri, Delta	Ethnic clashes between Ijaw and Itsekiri over the former's agitation for political autonomy. Five Itsekiri towns were razed, over 40 persons were feared dead
51	July 2003	Edo/Kogi	Communal clashes between border communities in Edo and Kogi states-Ekepedo and Ogori over land ownership.
52	July 10, 2003	Andoni, Rivers	Communal clashes over lingering chieftancy tussle in Ataba community.
53	July 14, 2003	Epen, Delta	Communal clash in Epen, a community in war ravaged Uvwie LGC. The conflict is connected to political rivalry in the area.
54	August 14, 2003	Delta	Renewed hostilities between Ijaw and Itshekiri.
55	August 14, 2003	Warri, Delta	Extended Ijaw Itsekiri crisis.
56	October 26, 2003	Owo, Ondo	Violent clashes over chieftancy tussle, which led to the killing of several people including a high chief.
57	November 12, 2003	Ebokiti, Delta	Attack by suspected Ijaw militants, on Itsekiri communities on the Benin River. The attack is connected to the alleged kidnapping and killing of Ijaw youth in Iyara.
58	November 23, 2003	Burutu, Delta	Ijaw youths in a new assault abducted oil workers and soldiers in Burutu LG.
59	November 23, 2003	Rivers	A reprisal attack by Debam community on Npolu-Oroworukwu community, which was believed to have launched attack on Debam community.
60	November 24, 2003	Lagos Island	Violent clash between rival groups of *Area Boys* over sharing of money paid by businessman for clearance of his imported goods.
61	December 9, 2003	Bayelsa	Communal clashes between Ijaw and Epie communities following the killing of an Ijaw youth.
62	January 19, 2004	Irawo, Oyo	Communal rivalry among feuding clans in Irawo, Atisbo LGC, which claimed 25 lives.
63	January 9, 2004	Ganye, Adamawa	Clash between Fulani herdsmen and farmers over grazing land.
64	January 9, 2004	Warri, Delta	Attack on Ijaw communities by suspected Itsekiri militia.
65	January 12, 2004	Diebu, Bayelsa	Violent clash in the riverine communities of southern Ijaw LGC following attempts to dethrone the traditional ruler of the community. Five people were feared dead.
66	January 12,2004	Yobe	Militant Islamic group operating under the name of *Muhajirun* launched a Taliban-like attack on police. Men of the Nigeria Army killed five and arrested several others.
67	January 16, 2004	Gbukuma, Rivers	Communal clash between riverine communities, which claimed several lives and the kidnapping of a traditional ruler.
68	January 17, 2004	Delta	Bloody clash between Ugbukuru and Obotie communities over land dispute. Over 25 lives were killed.
69	January 18, 2004	Rivers	Gun battle between Bush Boys and Niger Delta Vigilante in Okrika kingdom. This was believed to be a renewed hostility between the rival groups, which was characterised by attacks and counter-attacks.
70	January 20, 2004	Sapele, Delta	Fierce fighting between Urhobo and Itsekiri, which is believed to be the spill over of the Obotie/Ugbukueusu clash. Not fewer than 10 persons were killed.
71	February 21, 2004	Wase/Kanam, Plateau	Violent clash between Mavo and Taroh communities, which claimed 11 lives. Suspected Taroh youth were alleged to raid Mavo villages.
72	February 21, 2004	Makurdi, Benue	Communal clash over land ownership between Minda and Kparev groups. Several lives were lost.
73	March 11, 2004	Okitipupa, Ondo	Clash between supporters of claimants of *Jegun* of Idepe chieftancy tittle.
74	March 23, 2004	Epebu, Bayelsa	Bloody clash between oil communities in a coastal town over disagreements in the sharing of royalties given by an oil company. At least 14 lives were lost.

75	April 3, 2004	Makarfi, Kaduna	Religious protest in Makarfi town over desecration of the Qur'an by a Christian teenager.
76	April 11, 2004	Langtang South, Plateau	Continued clashes that led to the sacking of Taroh villages in Langtang South LGC by suspected Hausa-Fulani insurgents.
77	April 26, 2004	Bakin Chiyawa, Plateau	Renewed hostilities launched by suspected displaced Fulani herdsmen. The conflict was believed to be spill over of the ethno-religious crisis that has been bedevilling southern Plateau LGCs of Langtang South and North, Wase, Kanam and Shendam.
78	May 1, 2004	Yelwan Shendam, Plateau	A fresh ethno-religious mayhem that claimed over 650 lives and over 250 women abducted by suspected Taroh militia.
79	May 12, 2004	Kano	Kano mayhem following the Yelwan Shendam ethno-religious crisis in Plateau. Non-Muslims were attacked in reprisal of the Plateau crisis. Over 200 lives were feared dead.
80	June 5, 2004	Konshisha/Gwer, Benue	Boundary disputes between neighbouring Konshisha and Gwer communities. Thirteen lives were lost.
81	June 8, 2004	Numan, Adamawa	Ethno-religious crisis in Numan over the construction of a mosque's minaret over the Hamman Bachama's palace. Over 50 people were feared killed and the traditional ruler of the area deposed.
82	June 12, 2004	Iko Nyo Ndem/Efut Esighi, Cross River	Communal clash between Iko-Nyo Nde and Efut-Esighi communities over the ownership of oil palm plantation.
83	July 14, 2004	Port-Harcourt Rivers	Gun battle between rival militant groups over struggle for control of territory within the metropolis.
84	August 3, 2004	QuanPan, Plateau	Fresh outbreak of violence in Lankaka village. Suspected armed militia from a neighbouring state allegedly stormed the village community killing two and razing twenty houses.
85	August 14, 2004	Andoni, Rivers	Bloody clash between '*Biafrans*' and '*Federal troops*' in Ataba, Andoni LG. Government claimed that the conflict was over lingering chieftaincy dispute.
86	August 14,2004	Yenagoa, Bayelsa	Clash between two factions of Ijaw Youth Council over leadership tussle. Not fewer than 6 lives were lost.
87	August 29, 2004	Port-Harcourt Rivers	Clash between youth groups believed to be cultit groups operating along canals and waterways. Not fewer than 500 lives were lost between February and August 2004 in cult-related killings in the state.
88	September 27, 2004	Rivers	The leader of Niger Delta Volunteer Force declared an all time war against Nigeria after claiming to have successfully cleansed Rivers state of cult groups. He claimed to have liberated the Ijaw nation and the Niger Delta. The group had been involved in fierce fire exchange with the police and military.
89	September 27, 2004	Limankara, Borno	A self-styled Taliban group hiding on the Goza hills and Mandara mountains on the north eastern boarder with Cameron raided police station killing officers and stealing ammunition.
90	November 11, 2004	Iyuku, Edo	Chieftaincy tussle, which claimed 33 lives and property worth millions, destroyed.
91	December 9, 2004	Yamaltu-Deba, Gombe	Clash between farmers and cattle herdsmen over grazing land and alleged destruction of farm produce.
92	December 9,2004	Adikpo, Benue	Fresh violence in Adikpo, Kwande LGC connected with the protracted conflict trailing the March 2004 local elections.
93	January 16, 2005	Ipakodo, Lagos State	A religious mayhem between OPC and Muslims over the erection of Ogun Shrine in a Muslim praying ground. Over 50 lives were lost.

94	February 5, 2005	Odioma, Bayelsa	Communal clash heightened by the drilling of Crude oil wells in a disputed land between Nembe and Odioma communities. Twelve people were reported killed including four elected councilors, who were on a peace mission to feuding communities.
95	February 6, 2005	Bidoma, Adamawa	Clash between farmers and herdsmen over accusation of destruction of farm produce.
96	February 12, 2005	Wase, Plateau	A group of Tash men suspected to be from Langtang LGC set a complete Fulani settlement ablaze leaving two persons dead.
97	February 12, 2005	Ringim, Jigawa	Clash between normads and farmers over claims of invasion of farmlands and destruction of crops. Six people were feared dead.
98	February 21, 2005	Odioma, Bayelsa	Blood bath caused by invasion of Ibidi and Odioma communities by armed men in military uniform. Over 30 people lost their lives. The crisis has its origin in the ownership of Owukubu oil field, which is claimed by Bassambali community.
99	February 21, 2005	Den-One, Plateau	A group of armed men suspected to be Taroh attacked and Killed a Fulani herdsman at Den-One, WaseLGC.
100	February 22, 2005	Taura, Jigawa	A bloody clash between farmers and Fulani, which claimed ten lives and five villages were destroyed by, suspected invading Fulani from Niger Republic.
101	February 2005	Sokoto, Sokoto	Sectarian violence between Sunni and Shiites in Sokoto, which claimed three lives.
102	March 2, 2005	Ibaji, Kogi	Clash between farmers and normads over allegations of destruction of farmlands. Over 200 cows were killed by aggrieved farmers.
103	March 5, 2005	Ubeji, Delta	Communal clash between two factions over the installation of a new Town Head. Two persons were killed and three buildings razed.
104	March 5, 2005	Bauchi/Gombe	Communal clash between to border communities- Maruta (Jigawa) and Burmin (Bauchi) - over relocation of market. Eight people were confirmed dead in the renewed clash.
105	March 7, 2005	Joinkrama, Rivers	A bloody intra-communal clash between Joinkrama sub-communities—Ususu, Isua, Odawu and Edagberi. The crisis was fueled by the provision of electricity in one of the four sub-communities by oil company operating in the area. The three other sub-communities felt neglected. Six lives were lost in the clash.
106	March 7, 2005	Warri, Delta	A factional conflict resulting from the installation of a new Town Head (Olare-Aja) in Ubeji town. One person was reported killed.
107	April 11, 2005	Cross River/ Ebonyi	A bloody clash between Ukeli (Cross River) and Izzi (Ebonyi) communities over claims of ownership of land. The disputed is among speculated land owners (Ukelli) and tenants (Izzi). About 100 people died in nearly three weeks of violence.
108	May 3, 2005	Buruku/Katsina-Ala, Benue	A violent clash between Pursur and Ikyurav communities over ownership of piece of land. Several houses and farms were destroyed, and several women were abducted.
109	May 11,2005	Logo, Benue	Violent clash between two factions of Mbaikwe clan of Ugondo in Logo LGC. The violence was sparked off as a result of an alleged attack by one of the feuding parties.
110	May 11, 2005	Lere, Kaduna	A communal clash between the Guza and Mariri communities over naming of a secondary school. The Mariri people consider Guza (who are claiming indigeneship) as settlers. The naming of the school after Guza triggered the crisis but there is a lingering communal crisis resulting from installation of Village and Ward Heads. Three people were confirmed killed.
111	May 21,2005	Delta/Bayelsa	A cold war between Tuomo and Ayamasa communities, of Delta and Bayelsa States respectively, over ownership of land containing gas and oil deposits discovered by an oil company.
112	May21, 2005	Cross River	A renewed clash between the Izzi and Ukelle communities, which claimed nine lives.

113	May28, 2005	Sokoto, Sokoto	A sectarian violence between Shiites and Sunni which claimed 2 lives.
114	June 11,2005	Sokoto, Sokoto	A renewed clash between Sunni and Shiite sects over use of mosque. At least one person was killed.
115	July 24,2005	Lota, Ondo	Four people were feared dead over boundary dispute between Ijaw and Ikale. A bloody clash ensued in Taibor an Ijaw settlement in Odigbo following an alleged invasion of the Community by people suspected to be Inhabitants of neighbouring village.
116	August 9,2005	Akoko Edo, Edo	A woman and her 2 years old daughter were killed and 3 others declared missing following renewed hostilities between the Akuku and Ewan communities of Akoko Edo L.G.A.
117	August 9,2005	South Ukelle, Cross River.	Nine people were reported killed, when over 45 gunmen suspected to be Izzi militiamen from Ebonyi State invaded Ukelle–Agon Community of Ijigaton Clan firing sporadically killing and maiming peoples in the process.
118	August, 15,2005	Ilorin Kwara State	At least six people were reportedly killed and four houses burnt down in the aftermath of Sunday's turbaning of new chiefs by the Emir of Ilorin Alhaji Sule Gambari. Opposing sides of the chieftancy titles clashed. Assorted weapons such as guns, knifes, machetes and charms were deployed by them.
119	August 20, 2005	Isale–Eko, Lagos.	No fewer than 30 Muslim youths killed when cultists and members of the out-lawed Oodua Peoples Congress (OPC) attacked Muslims.
120	September 25,2005	Onitsha, Anambra.	No fewer than six persons were feared dead, when members of the Movement for the Actualization of the Sovereign State of Biafra (MASSOB) and men of the Nigeria police clashed in Onitsha.
121	September 25, 2005	Ringim-Taura/Maruta Jigawa.	Reports indicate that in 8 months more than 20 lives and properties worth millions of naira were lost in clashes between Fulani and farmers in the area.
122	September 28,2005	Khana, Rivers.	18 feared dead in a clash between two communities in Ogoniland River State. The clash which erupted around 6 a.m. was between the Bua–teyor Kaani and Gbor–Kaani communities over the imposition of a councilor on them.
123	September 28, 2005	Biase, Cross River.	Two communities in Biase council area of Cross–Rivers State engaged in a communal war which left scores dead. Both towns, Ufut and Ikot Ana communities had taken on each other in the past, but there was respite until recent encounter, which also claimed several houses.
124	October 14, 2005	Akure,Ondo.	At least seven people were killed as Irate youth and Islamic Militants engaged in bloody clash. When the youths followed the Ojomoluda of Ijebu Owo singing and dancing during the famous Igogo festival.
125	October 14,2005	Lagos	12 people were killed and 30 vehicles Burnt in (OPC) *Oodua People's Congress* rivals clashed.The problem started when some members of Gani – Adams led OPC were barred from operation motorcycles in Iyana Ipaja vicinity of the state for lack of proper registration.
126	October 21,2005	Southern Ijaw, Bayelsa	Two persons were found dead and several others injured in the riverine Igbo matoru community in southern Ijaw local government area of Bayelsa State in the aftermath of an Intra-Communal clash allegedly caused by disagreement over oil royalties.
127	October 21,2005	Minna, Niger	A policeman was reportedly Killed and three others missing as violent clash erupt between Fulani cattle rearers and Gwari farmers. Trouble started in the area when the farmers challenged a fulani boy who went into a Gwari farmland.

128	October 22, 2005	Okpe, Delta	One person was confirmed dead and several others injured in a communal clash between the people of Adeje and Okwued-jeda communities following a dispute over largesse from an oil company.
129	October 22, 2005	Onitsha, Anambra.	At least two people were feared dead as police and members of MASSOB clashed within the house of first indigenous president Dr Nnamdi Azikiwe severely property burnt.
130	November 11, 2005.	Ajah, Lagos.	10 persons were killed over the crises, which erupted in Ajah end of Lagos State. A source said the crises started over who was the actual owner of Ajah land and the decision of the state government to install an *Oba* in the area.
131	Nov 12, 2005	Shendam, Plateau.	Three people were feared dead following the protest that trailed the creation of development area in Plateau state at Namu in Shendam local government area. Trouble started when certain people were not happy with the choice of Namu, because it did not reflect linguistic and tribal composition.
132	December 6, 2005.	Onitsha, Anambra.	Some people were reportedly killed following the sit-at-home protest order by MASSOB. 20 people were feared dead in clashes between MASSOB members and the police. The group was demanding the release of its leader, Chief Ralph Uwazuruike.
133	December 12, 2005	Kankara, Katsina.	A violent clash between farmers and fulani herdsmen in unguwar Ibran Danmaraba community, leaving 5 persons dead and no less than 13 others injured. When the fulani herdsmen launched a reprisal attack on the affected village.
134	Jan 15, 2006.	Bayelsa	Not less than 14 soldiers lost their lives in the battle to regain Anglo-Dutch oil giants shell's Beneseide flow station from militant youth.
135	Jan 19, 2006.	Okene, Kogi	At least Two {2} people were confirmed dead when violence erupted in Okene the heartland of Ebira central senatorial district. The crises wasbetween Zango community in Ajaokuta local Government area and Ozuwaya, Okene local government of the district. The crisis was ignited by the arrest of a young boy from Zango community.
136	Jan 19, 2006.	Ado-Ekiti , Ekiti state	Five persons were feared killed and many others seriously injured following the violence that greeted the report that the court of appeal, Ilorin division in Kwara state had nullified the appointment and thus dethroned of the Arajaka of Igbara-Odo, Oba Edward Jayeola.
137	February 8, 2006.	Maiduguri, Borno.	No fewer than 58 persons were killed and 30 churches burnt in an outbreak of deadly protest. The Muslims were angered over controversial cartoons published by Danish and other European publications on prophet Mohammed.
138	February 18, 2006	Bauchi, Bauchi.	No fewer than sixteen persons were feared dead following a violent demonstration by Muslims, incensed by alleged seizure and desecration of the Quoran by a female teacher rebuking her listless people in a secondary school. Properties including about 40 churches where reportedly burnt by the rampaging rioters.
139	February 21, 2006	Onitsha, Anambra	At least 100 people were feared dead in a reprisal attack believed to be in retaliation of the alleged killing of Igbo Christians in Maiduguri, over the controversial prophet Mohamed cartoons published in a Danish newspaper.
140	March 21, 2006	Nnewi, Anambra	At least, no fewer than 10 people were reported dead in a fracas that broke out on the first day of the national head count. The exercise that began across the nation was marred in Nnewi and part of Onitsha as people said to be members of the Movement for the Actualization of the Sovereign State of Biafra (MASSOB) were said to have attacked enumeration officers and seized their materials.

141	March 25, 2006	Ikale/Ijaw, Ondo	No fewer than seven persons were killed and properties destroyed in a communal clash between the Ikale and Ijaw in Ondo State over boundary dispute, in the build up to the census exercise.
142	April 10, 2006	Shendam, Plateau	Communal clashes between two clans, Geomai and Kwalla, in Namu village fuelled by a combination of tribal, economic and political issues exploited by the educated people in the area. 100 people were reported killed, 70 injured and over 1000 displaced.
143	April 14,2006	Ihima, Kogi	No fewer than 30 people lost their lives in a bloody clash between Ihima, a district in Kogi central senatorial district. The crises were allegedly aggravated by the Ohi title introduced by the State Deputy Governor, Mr. Phillip Salawu to stem down restiveness to the over-bearing dominance of the Ohinoyi of Ebiraland.
144	June 18, 2006	Onitsha, Anambra.	At Least Seven persons were reportedly killed and police Armoured personel carrier (APC) destroyed, when some hoodlums operating under the guise of, MASSOB, National Association of Road Transport Owners (NARTO), BAKASSI, National Union of Road Transport Workers (NURTW) and Anambra Vigilance Services (AVS) continued to disrupt the peace attained with the inauguration of governor Peter Obi's administration in the state.
145	June 23, 2007.	Gungur , Konshisha, Benue	Indigenes and settlers clash over burial of a dead 'settler' in a community burial ground.
146	July 16, 2007.	Katsina-Ala, Benue	An unending hostility between the Tivs in Benue and the Kuteb in Taraba, resurfaced again when the Kuteb invaded Kwagbondo village in Mbayongo II ward in Katsina Ala LGA, killed five people and forced several others into refugee.
147	July 16, 2007.	Benue/Cross River	Communal clash between the Obaniku community in cross Rivers state and the Kwande community in Benue state, two persons were reported killed in the clash.
148	December 21, 2007	Maigatari, Jigawa	Farmers/herdsmen clash in Maigatari LGA. 8 people were killed.
149	January 2, 2008.	Akoko,	Communal clash between indigenes of Enwan and Akuku in Akoko Edo LGA.
150	January 21, 2008	Njaba, Imo	Three people have been reportedly dead and Property conservatively estimated at N1.5bn burnt, looted and/or destroyed when angry youths from Okwodor, stormed the neighboring Owere Ebiri, Nkume and Ihebino were Njaba LGA.
151	September 1, 2008	Yala, Cross River	Communal clash in Gabu community over ownership of land and granting of mining rights for mining Barite used by oil companies.
152	September 7, 2008	Ikot Udo/Eastern Obolo, Akwa Ibom	Indigene/settler clash between Andonis and Ikot Udo community over claims over land. The clash started from a disagreement between 2 motorcyclists from the 2 communities but the feud can be traced to the Andonis ('setters') attempt to acquire Ibibio (indigenes) lands in Ikot Abasi LGA. 11 people were feared dead.
153	September 8, 2008.	Obajana, Kog	Suspected O'odua People Congress (OPC) otherwise known as the *Oworo boys* attacked truck drivers over allegations of trucks being parked in a way that they blocked the Lokoja–Kabba express road.
154	September 8, 2008.	Apa, Benue	Communal clash between Antaganyi and Omelemu over ownership of and royalties from bush-mango trees.
155	November 28, 2008	Jos, Plateau	Ethno-religious clash between largely Hausa/Fulani-Muslims and Indigenous groups-Christians following a local government election. The Hausa/Fulanis are considered 'settlers' by other indigenous groups as both groups struggle for political space and control of the Jos-North LGA. Over 500 lives were lost in the conflict.
156	December 4, 2008	Ohaji/Egbema, Imo	Violent clash in Awara community was reported to have claimed over 9 lives. Details of the causes and feuding groups were not given.

157	December 4, 2008	Dan Musa, Katsina	Clash between farmers and herdsmen in Yashi village over allegation of damage to farm produce. Four people were feared dead.
158	December 8, 2008	Emohua, Rivers	Renewed inter-communal clash over kingship in Ibaa. The community has been in war with itself over who becomes its next traditional ruler following the demise of the former ruler. Ten people were reported dead in the latest orgy.
159	Nov 16-Dec 19, 2008.	Musawa, Malumfashi, Matazu and Bindawa, Faskari, Bakori and Kafur LGAs in Katsina State.	Clash between farmers and pastoralists that spread across a number of LGAs in the State. Not fewer than 15 persons lost their lives in attacks and reprisal attacks
160	January 17,2009	Birnin-Kudu, Jigawa	Clash between Fulani normads and farmers in Kwari village over allegation of cattle encroaching farmlands and destroying farm produce. Two people lost their lives in the clash.
161	January 17, 2009	Ukwuani, Delta	Renewed violence over age-long boundary dispute between Amai and 3 other communities (Ezionum, Umueba and Eziokpo). An elderly woman was killed in the fracas that ensued.
162	February 3, 2009	Osogbo, Osun	Communal violence between Erin-Ijesa and Omo-Ijesa communities over ownership of land. Two persons lost their lives.
163	February 20-22, 2009	Bauchi, Bauchi	Religious violence that claimed over 11 lives and destruction of property. Violence erupted ostensibly as a result of conflict between Christians and Muslims over the parking of vehicles in front of a church.
164	March/April,2009	Ohimini, Benue	Indigene/settler clash in Ankpechi rural community over succession to village headship, Ochaliya traditional ruler. The tussle started on December 9, 2008 between 'settler' community and indigenous inhabitants. There were renewed hostilities in late March 2009. The latest orgy of violence was a reprisal attack, which claimed over 30 lives. Over 150 were injured and 3000 displaced.
165	April 7,2009	Kaugama and Miga, Jigawa	Clash between pastoralists and farmers in Boyoni village and Marke town. Two farmers lost their lives in Marke town as a result of the pastoralists attack while two pastoralists were killed as a result of farmers' revenge in Boyoni village.
166	April 7, 2009	Guma, Benue	Violent communal clash between Mbagen and Mzoron communities in Guma LGA over ownership of disputed farmlands. Eight people were reported killed while several houses and farmlands were destroyed.
167	April 12, 2009	Shiroro, Niger	Attack by Muslim youth during an Easter procession in Gwada, Shiroro LGC. No life was lost but 2 churches were destroyed. The cause of the attack was not reported.
168	April 12, 2009	Gwer-West, Benue	Clash between Tiv peasants and Fulani herdsmen in Adaka community. The cause of the conflict, according to an unconfirmed source, was reportedly mild-misunderstanding of the mission of Tiv hunters sighted by Fulani cattle rearers. More than 3 people were reported to be killed while several others sustained various degrees of injuries.
169	July 21, 2009	Okene, Kogi	Violent conflict that resulted from a group celebrating Eche-Ane festival violated State Government's banning of masquerades due to incessant communal violence in the area. Three lives were lost.
170	July 25, 2009	Isihelu, Ebonyi	A renewed violent clash between Ezza and Ezillo communities over land disputes in Isihelu LGA. Violence first erupted 15 months earlier. Three lives were lost in the latest conflict.

171	July 25, 2009	Guma, Benue	Clash between Fulani herdsmen and Tiv farmers in Tse-Ande village of Guma LGA over alleged encroachment into farmland. Five people lost their lives.
172	July 26-30, 2009	Bauchi (Bauchi), Potiskum (Yobe), Wudi (Kano, Danja) and Maiduguri (Borno	A sectarian violence broke out in at least five states. Conflict started when a radical Islamic group, *Boko Haram,* attacked police station in Bauchi and later spread to Potiskum, Wudil, Danja and Maiduguri. The group threatened to retaliate the shooting of its members earlier by the police for not wearing crash helmet. Over 700 people (including security agents) were believed to have lost their lives where the violence occurred.
173	December 5, 2009	Ijebu-East, Ogun	A violent clash between police and youth in Ijebu-Ife town over alleged killing of a youth by vigilante group. The peaceful protest organized by the youth turned violent leading to the killing five persons including an Assistant Commissioner of Police.
174	December 19, 2009.	Nasarawa, Nasarawa	A violent farmers/herdsmen clash in Uden Gida village over allegation of destruction of rice farm by cattle. Conflict was reported to have started on December 6, 2009 when farmer protested against destruction of his rice and got killed in the process. Over 30 people lost their lives in the latest orgy of violence.
175	December 28, 2009	Bauchi, Bauchi	A religious violence following disagreement among followers of the *Kala Kato* sect, which led to the killing of people including security agents.
176	January 17-20, 2010	Jos and environs, Plateau	A communal clash with religious coloration which claimed over 362 lives and property worth billions destroyed. The immediate cause of the violence was reported to be an alleged attack of Muslim youths on Christian worshipers in a church. The conflict was also reported to have been caused by disagreement between two individuals over a property.
177	January 29, 2010	Ohaji/Egbema, Imo	A clash between members of Akanu, Umuapu community over mob action against a community member. Other members of the community protested and a bloody conflict ensued, which claimed over 30 lives.
178	January 30, 2010	Gombe, Gombe	A clash between students in secondary school following the outbreak of violence in Jos, Plateau State. A mosque and a church were destroyed.
179	February 19, 2010	Ishielu/Ebonyi	A communal clash between Ezza and Ezillo communities over disputed land. The battle actually started in May 2008 over the location of commercial pay phone booth. No fewer than six persons lost their lives including policemen caught in-between crossfire.
180	February 20, 2010	Ofu/Kogi	A clash between warring youth over killing of a youth leader in Ejule, who was accused of masterminding the killing of a youth activist. No fewer than six persons died.
181	February 21, 2010	Kazaure/Jigawa	A communal disturbance that took religious coloration. The conflict started after youth protested the alleged killing of a driver by the police. Aggrieved youth later took to the street and burned churches.
182	March 7,2010	Lavun/Niger	A communal clash between Emegi and Kuchita communities over the ownership of fish pond. The communities have been at dagger drawn for years over ownership of fish ponds located on the boundary between the two villages. Two people were reported dead in the last outbreak of violence.
183	March 7,2010	Jos South/Barkinladi, Plateau State	Attack on Dogo Nahauwa, Zot, Rasat and Kutgot villages in Barkin Ladi and Jos South LGAs by Fulanis. Police reported 109 killed; while State Govt reported over 500 killed

184	June 6, 2010	Lapai/ Niger State	Clash between local indigenes and Fulani herdsmen in Chekwu, Bina, Yelwa villages over farm lands. Houses burnt and no fewer than 14 lives lost.
185	June 11, 2010	Jos-Norht/Plateau State.	Clash between commercial motorcyclists and security operatives over Okada ban, 3 people died, several others injured.
186	June 25, 2010	Gwer/Benue State.	Clash between Fulani herdsmen and local Tivs in Anchiha. 4 persons confirmed dead.
187	June 29, 2010	Abia State.	Communal clashes between Okaiuga Nkwoegwu, Umuosu communities resulting in destruction of property with over 15 houses burnt.
188	July 3, 2010	Jos South/ Plateau State.	Displaced Fulani herdsmen were attacked by unknown persons in Doj village while returning to their hamlets. Severe injuries to both humans and cattle.
189	July 4, 2010	Jos North/ Plateau State.	Suspected Fulanis attacked the village burning houses and churches in Mazah village leaving 7 persons dead.
190	August 6, 2010	Tafawa Balewa/ Bauchi State.	Communal clash resulting in the death of 2 people, while 5 others were critically wounded.
191	August 7, 2010	Barkin ladi/ Plateau State.	Suspected Fulani Herdsmen attacked Mai Idon-Toro village village killing a middle-aged man, Chuwang Hwere, rustling his cattle and his niece, Victoria Dung was shot in the process.
192	September 4, 2010	Ovia/Edo State.	Clash between Binis and Ijaws in Gegele over the appointment of a traditional ruler, resulting in the destruction of property.
193	September 6, 2010	Bauchi/ Bauchi State.	Violent attack on Bauchi Federal prison by the Boko Haram sect. 721 inmates were released, 2 people killed and several others injured.
194	October 1,2010	Fct /Abuja	Abuja Bomb blast, 18 Killed, 26 Cars damaged by MEND over Resource control in the Niger Delta.
195	October 3, 2010	Ado-Odo/Ogun State.	Violent attack on the Olofin of Ado-Odo's palace by hoodlums over Obaship tussles. 6 persons killed and property destroyed.
196	October 18, 2010	Maiduguri/Borno State.	Boko Haram sect members attacked and killed Police Inspector Shettima Bukar in front of his residence.
197	October 21, 2010	Gokana/Rivers State.	Communal clash between two Ogoni communities leaving several houses burnt.
198	October 22, 2010	Boki and Nsadop L.G.As/ Cross River State.	Inter-communal clash over land dispute resulting in loss of many lives and destruction of property.
199	October 23,2010	Bauchi/Bauchi State.	Unknown gunmen killed a Community Leader and Ward head in Bauchi, Alhaji Tukur Ahmed.
200	October 24, 2010	Gulani/Yobe state.	Six armed men suspected to be Boko Haram sect members, attacked Gulani police station killing a policeman and leaving several others injured. They also set the station ablaze.
201	November 7, 2010	Maiduguri/Borno State.	Three suspected Boko Haram sect members attacked Alhaji Mohammed Mala, Ward Head of Bolori, attempting to kill him.
202	November 16, 2010	.	Chieftaincy tussles between two royal families resulting in the death of a policeman and injury to 15 others.
203	November 29, 2010	Mosogar, Delta State.	Violent clash between various youth factions resulting in loss of lives and property
204	December 1, 2010	Burutu, Delta State.	Joint Task Force (JTF) raid on Ayakoromor community leaving no fewer than 20 civilians dead
205	December 3, 2010	Bassa, Plateau State.	Reprisal attack on Kwal village by suspected Fulani herdsmen, killing 7 persons
206	December 5, 2010	Maiduguri, BornoState.	Clash between policemen and suspected Boko Haram gunmen leaving 5 persons dead

207	December 5, 2010	Bauchi State.	Violent clash between Karofi and Kofar Dumi youths leaving 2 persons dead and 7 others injured
208	December 7, 2010	Warri, Delta State.	Leadership tussle by various factions resulting in the death of 5 persons
209	December 9, 2010	Maiduguri, Borno State.	Suspected Boko Haram sect members attacked a joint military/police checkpoint causing panic and setting one of the patrol vehicles ablaze
210	December 21, 2010	Gokana, Rivers State	Communal clash between K-Dere and B-Dere communities leaving 5 persons dead and several others injured
211	December 21, 2010	Jos Plateau State	Suspected Fulani herdsmen attacked Kuru, Jos south L.G.A, killing 3 persons and rustling over 100 cows
212	December 24, 2010	Jos, Plateau State.	Multiple bomb explosions rocked Gada Biu, Kabong and Angwa Rukuba areas of Jos, killing over 10 people and leaving several others severely injured; and many property destroyed.
213	December 25, 2010	Maiduguri, BornoState.	Two churches were attacked by suspected Boko Haram members killing 6 persons and setting one of the churches ablaze
214	December 26, 2010	Jos, Plateau State	Escalation of violence in various parts of Jos as youths protested the Christmas eve bombings. No fewer than 8 persons killed, property destroyed
215	December 26, 2010	Oron, Akwa-Ibom State.	Communal clash between Eyo Abasi and Idua communities over a parcel of land. No fewer than 6 lives lost, property destroyed
216	December 27, 2010	Jos, Plateau State.	Reprisal attacks in Abattoir and Anglo-Jos areas, leaving scores of people dead with property destroyed.
217	December 28, 2010	Maiduguri, Borno State.	Suspected Boko Haram members attacked the University of Maiduguri Teaching Hospital leaving 3 people dead
218	December 29, 2010	Maiduguri, Borno State.	Suspected Boko Haram members attacked Bulunkuttu ward, killing 4 mobile policemen and 2 traders. 10 others sustained various degrees of injury
219	December 31, 2010	Abuja	Two explosions rocked Mogadishu cantonment leaving no fewer than 10 people dead and 30 others severely injured
220	January 1, 2011	Ikirun, Osun State.	3 people killed as police and youths clashed over the alleged killing of a motorcyclist by a police constable
221	January 9, 2011	Jos, Plateau State.	Incessant skirmishes resulting in loss of lives and property, with the igbo community suffering loss of no fewer than 40 lives and property
222	January 11, 2011	Barkin Ladi & Riyom, Plateau State.	Suspected Fulani herdsmen attacked Barkin Ladi killing 5 people and burning 14 houses. The attack in Riyom was carried out by people in military uniforms, leaving 13 people dead
223	January 15, 2011	Mushin, Lagos State.	Clash between rival groups of social miscreants leaving no fewer than 8 people dead and over 30 others injured
224	January 17, 2011	Jos, Plateau State.	Group of hoodlums attacked INEC ad hoc staff, leaving one of the staff dead while 2 soldiers were badly injured
225	January 18, 2011	Akoko, Ondo State.	Communal clashes between various factions in Arigidi-Akoko leaving no fewer than 4 persons injured and property destroyed
226	January 18, 2011	Maiduguri, BornoState.	4 unknown men attacked and killed a pastor and 3 of his neighbours causing panic and tension
227	January 26, 2011	Jos, Plateau State.	Hundreds of aggrieved women staged a public protest against the continued presence of soldiers at the central abattoir, alleging that the soldiers were aiding and abetting attacks on the people of the state
228	January 27, 2011	Barlin- Ladi, Plateau State.	12 people were allegedly killed in an attack by suspected Fulani herdsmen
229	January 28, 2011	Jos, Plateau State.	Violent clash between University of Jos students and Hausa youths resulting in the death of 2 students
230	January 29, 2011	Dutse, Jigawa State.	4 unknown persons attacked a police checkpoint killing a police officer
231	January 29, 2011	Jos, Plateau State.	16 lives were lost as armed youth took on soldiers in a free for all, as a fall out to the shooting of 15 students

232	January 30, 2011	Maiduguri Borno State.	Unknown gunmen attacked police officers at a police road block, leaving a policeman and 2 of the gunmen dead
233	January 30, 2011	Jos, Plateau State.	Militant youths attacked and killed a mobile policeman. This followed the violence between Hausa youths and students of the University of Jos
234	February 1, 2011	Maiduguri, Borno State.	Unidentified gunmen trailed DSP Gadzama and shot him dead
235	February 2, 2011	Borno State.	The dreaded Boko Haram sect threatened Jihad against the government, claiming responsibility for the killing of prominent citizens of the state
236	February 9, 2011	Makurdi, Benue State.	Hundreds of youths took over the Makurdi-Enugu highway protesting the killing of a 30-year-old man by a mobile policeman
237	February 10, 2011	Gwer, Benue State.	Armed Fulani herdsmen invaded Tyotegh ward killing 12 persons, in a reprisal attack over the purported killing of their cattle by indigenes of the area
238	February 10, 2011	Ikole -Ekiti, Ekiti State.	No fewer than 2 persons were killed as police and indigenes clashed over the relocation of a proposed Federal university from Ikole Ekiti to Oye Ekiti
239	February 10, 2011	Kuru, Plateau State.	Suspected Fulani herdsmen attacked the Federal College of Land Resources Technology quarters, killing 5 people and rustling about 30 cows. 9 others were left injured
240	February 12, 2011	Ilaje, Ondo State.	Hoodlums attacked the private residence of a deposed traditional ruler, razing the building with one of his wives and 3 daughters inside
241	February 15, 2011	Jos, State.	No fewer than 6 persons, including a mobile policeman were killed during the Eid'l Maulud celebration violent attacks
242	February 16, 2011	Ilorin, Kwara State.	Peaceful demonstration by youths, which turned violent over the slow pace of work on the Ipo/Kabba highway. Several people injured
243	February 18, 2011	Danbatta, Kano State.	Violent protest by angry youths over alleged police brutality, claiming no fewer than 5 lives, with several others injured
244	February 19, 2011	Agbor, Delta State.	Factional rivalry between NURTW members resulting in the death of 10 persons and several others injured
245	February 20, 201	Abeokuta, Ogun State.	Cultists invaded streets in an operation lasting about 3 hours. At least 10 persons shot
246	February 22, 2011	Bere, Plateau State.	At least 18 people were killed by suspected Fulani Herdsmen in a pre-dawn attack on the village. 19 cows were rustled and a house destroyed
247	February 28, 2011	Kuru, Plateau State.	At least 5 members of the same family killed by unknown assailants who invaded the village in the early hours of the morning.
248	February 28, 2011	Kaduna, Kaduna State	Suspected Boko Haram members attacked the residence of a senior police officer, killing 2 armed police men on duty.
249	March 3, 2011	Idumu-Igbo, Delta / Evbohighae, EdoStates	Communal clash as a result of land dispute leading to the death of 2 persons
250	March 10, 2011	Tafawa Balewa LGA, Bauchi State.	Renewed ethno-religious violence leading to the death of 3 persons and destruction of property.
251	March 15, 2011	Benin, EdoState.	Violent clash between supporters of the Oba of Benin and those of the chairman of the Road Transport Employers Association, resulting in the death of 4 persons
252	March 15, 2011	Jabi, Abuja	Clash between NURTW factions over installation of union leaders causing mayhem
253	March 15, 2011	Benin, Edo State.	40 suspected thugs burnt down the family house of suspended chairman of the Edo state task force on anti-pipeline vandalisation, Osakpamwan Eriyo over the killing of two of their own.

254	March 18, 2011	Abeokuta, Ogun State.	A member of NURTW, Ogun state was shot dead by a rival group during a traditional festival
255	March 20, 2011	Jos Plateau State.	At least 3 persons killed as explosive devices went off close to two churches. 2 of the deceased carried the explosives and died in the process of trying to detonate them.
256	March 20, 2011	Idemili, Anambra State.	Violent protests by youths over the killing of a youth by the police
257	March 21, 2011	Jos, Plateau State.	No fewer than 7 persons killed as Christians and Hausa-Fulanis clashed in Farin-gada. This was a sequel to the bomb explosions that rocked the town a day before
258	March 22, 2011	Kubau, KadunaState.	7 persons killed resulting from a crisis that erupted after a hoodlum attacked an Imam inside a Mosque
259	March 22, 2011	Maiduguri, Borno State.	2 gunmen attacked the ward head of Ummarari, killing him and leaving 2 other people injured
260	March 29, 2011	Ini, Akwa – Ibom State.	No fewer than 12 lives lost as a result of communal clashes
261	March 29, 2011	Maiduguri, Borno State.	Suspected Boko Haram gunmen shot and killed ANPP chieftain, Alhaji Modu Gana Makanike
262	March 29, 2011	Zugana, Sokoto State.	Property worth millions of naira destroyed as suspected political thugs ambushed the village
263	March 30, 2011	Kuru, Plateau State.	2 persons killed by unknown people in a fresh attack at the Federal School of Soil Conservation
264	March 30, 2011	Maiduguri, Borno/ Damaturu, Yobe States	Separate bomb explosions planted by suspected Boko Haram members rocked Maiduguri and Damaturu
265	March 30, 2011	Abavo/Evboghai, Delta State.	8 persons killed in a renewed land dispute between both communities
266	April 1, 2011	Bauchi State.	Bomb blast at a police station causing panic among residents
267	April 2, 2011	Bogoro, Bauchi State.	Gunmen attacked 3 villages killing 2 persons and burning houses
268	April 2, 2011	Dutsentanshi, Bauchi State.	Unknown gunmen attacked a police station, leaving 2 cops seriously injured
269	April 9, 2011	Shani, Borno State.	10 hoodlums stormed a police station killing 10 persons and leaving about 56 others injured
270	April 11, 2011	Ikorodu, Lagos State	2 lives lost as rival cult groups engaged in a free-for-all
271	April 12, 2011	Tafa, Niger State.	Irate youths protesting the avoidable death of 18 passengers in a commuter bus burnt down the FRSC office
272	April 28, 2011	Ojota, Lagos State.	3 persons killed as two NURTW factions clashed
273	May 5, 2011	Maiduguri, Borno State.	3 gunmen suspected to be Boko Haram members attacked the duty officer of the Borno State Government House, ASP Umaru Shehu at his residence, killing a teenager in the process
274	May 5, 2011	Bogoro, Bauchi State.	No fewer than 16 persons killed, 20 houses burnt as gunmen attacked the village at night
275	May 12, 2011	Maiduguri, Borno State.	2 gunmen attacked and killed Alhaji Abba Mukhtar Tijjani, District Head of Mairiri
276	May 13, 2011	Maiduguri, BornoState.	Suspected Boko Haram members shot and killed a police inspector, Maina Kadai, a District Head and another policeman in separate attacks
277	May 13, 2011	Maiduguri, Borno State.	2 persons killed as a bomb exploded in London Chiki, a populated community
278	May 14, 2011	Ododegho, Delta State.	3 youths killed in a violent intra-community clash, resulting from a leadership tussle

279	May 16, 2011	Onipanu, Lagos State.	3 persons killed and several others injured as two factions of street urchins, popularly known as "area boys" clashed in a battle for supremacy
280	May 16, 2011	Idemili north, Anambra State.	No fewer than 4 persons killed with property worth millions of naira destroyed in a communal clash over land sales
281	May 18, 2011	Maiduguri, Borno State.	3 bomb explosions rocked Maiduguri leaving a police officer dead, while 2 soldiers and 3 anti-riot policemen were seriously injured.
282	May 18, 2011	Maiduguri, Borno State.	No fewer than 10 lives lost as suspected Boko Haram members launched an offensive on a police station
283	May 22, 2011	Mubi, Adamawa State.	2 people killed as armed robbers and villagers clashed
284	May 22, 2011	Guma, Benue State.	No fewer than 30 persons killed in renewed skirmishes between Fulani herdsmen and native Tiv communities
285	May 24, 2011	Ibereko, Lagos State.	Soldiers of the 242 Recce battalion went on rampage killing 14 people including a police DPO and DCO, with 8 other police officers, protesting the alleged killing of one of their colleagues by policemen
286	May 27, 2011	Damboa, BornoState.	5 persons were killed in an attack by about 70 gunmen suspected to be Boko Haram members who attacked a police barrack and a bank, shooting sporadically and injuring many people in the process.
287	May 29, 2011	Bauchi, Bauchi State.	Bomb explosions rocked the 23 Artillery Brigade headquarters killing 5 people and leaving several others injured.
288	May 29, 2011	Bauchi, Bauchi State.	About 20 people died after two bomb blasts at the Mammy Market of Gadawanta barracks
289	May 29, 2011	Zuba, Abuja	3 people injured in a bomb blast at the Lagos park in Zuba, Abuja.
290	May 29, 2011	Zaria, Kaduna State.	Two bomb explosions left 2 children and many other people injured.
291	May 30, 2011	Maiduguri, BornoState.	Suspected Boko Haram members shot and killed Alhaji Abbah Ibn El-Kanemi, a younger brother of the Shehu of Borno.
292	May 31, 2011	Owerri, Imo State.	Violent clash between MASSOB and police officers lead to the death of 3 persons and destruction of property.
293	June 1, 2011	Katagum, Bauchi State.	Unknown gunmen attacked a police station with explosives and gunshots leaving a policeman dead and 13 others dead, 40 people sustained injuries.
294	June 7, 2011	Maiduguri, Borno State.	At least 10 people were killed; others severely injured as a result of several bomb blasts and a gunfight between the police and Boko Haram members.
295	June 9, 2011	Jos Plateau State.	2 persons, a woman and a motorcyclist were reportedly killed in Juwl village of Riyom Local Government area by unidentified gunmen.
296	June 11, 2011	Maiduguri, BornoState.	4 people died in an attack by Boko Haram sect at a drinking joint in Bulumkutu, Maiduguri
297	June 16, 2011	FCT, Abuja	10 people were killed, 76 cars burnt in the first suicide bomb in the Nigeria police headquarters.
298	June 20, 2011	Kankara, Katsina State	8 people died in an attack by Boko Haram sect in police station and a branch of bank PHB plc in Kankara LGA. Six policemen and two civilians died.
299	June 26, 2011	Maiduguri, BornoState.	Another strike by Boko Haram sect killed 25 people in three separate bomb explosions in Maiduguri.
300	July 3, 2011	Maiduguri, BornoState.	Boko Haram killed 10 persons in Maiduguri. Victims include a Local Government Chairman; many other persons were injured in attacks in different parts of the city.
301	July 5,2011	Maiduguri, Borno State.	2 policemen shot, seven others killed in an attack in Maiduguri. Boko Haram claimed responsibility.

302	July 6,2011	Bauchi, Bauchi State.	4 Soldiers injured in Boko Haram's attack. A police station in Toro was sacked and armoury looted in Bauchi, detainees freed.
303	July 10,2011	Maiduguri, BornoState.	17 persons dead as military team attacks Boko Haram sect in Maiduguri. 11 of the killed persons were members of Boko Haram.
304	July 10, 2011	Kaduna, Kaduna State	7 persons injured at a relaxation Joint in Facodos Road, near popular Obalande Relaxation Centre in Kaduna. The attack was suspected reprisal attack by members of Boko Haram group.
305	July 11, 2011	Suleja, Niger State.	Bomb killed 4 in a church in Suleja. The bomb was thrown into a church in Suleja Niger State.
306	July 11, 2011	Lau, Taraba, Taraba State	7 persons killed and property destroyed In communal clash between the Jukun kona and Mumuye people in Lau Local Govt Area of Taraba. The immediate cause was a dispute over a parcel of land. The Councilor representing Jalingo Ward, Mr. Damjuma Kyamo lost his life; over 200 others fled their residences.
307	July 11, 2011	Maiduguri, Borno State	2 JTF members seriously injured, 3 Boko Haram members killed by crossfire gunshots as Boko Haram sect continued their reign of terror in Maiduguri with two bomb blasts.
308	July 30,2011, 2011	Jos, Plateau State	Two Bomb explosions in Jos, one near an Islamic leader's home (Sheikh Seidu Hassan Jengri, the Deputy National Chairman of Izala group) in Sarikin Mangu Street, and the other at Angwan Rimi.
309	August 7, 2011	Bauchi, Bauchi State	5 policemen injured by bomb blast that rocked Bauchi metropolis while on duty at Central Market Roundabout on Sunday night, The parcel bomb was thrown on them by motor-cyclists, who ran away.
310	August 9, 2011	Gwange, Maiduguri, Borno State	2 persons killed , a 40 year old school teacher, Mallam Nurudeen Umar and his friend, Sulaiman Bangini were shot dead in Maiduguri by gunmen suspected to be members of Boko Haram sect at Gwange.
311	August 9, 2011	Jos, Plateau State	2 persons killed and Four others injured over cow theft in a night raid of Fulani Settlement in Bisichi, South LGA. It was reported that over 400 cows were rustled by unknown raiders.
312	August 11, 2011	Biu, Biu LGA, Borno State	One Person – a Nursing Mother, Hadiza Mohammed was Killed during a Soldier/Youth clash as Soldiers raid an Islamic school at Mandara Abdu Ward in Biu town. 2 other people were injured while 5 scholars suspected to members of Boko Haram were arrested. The Local Govt Secretariat vandalized by protesting youths. The Army later denied killing a nursing mother.
313	August 11, 2011	Foron District, Barkin Ladi LGA, Plateau State	3 persons were killed by unknown gunmen at Raffa Village in Foron District of Barkin Ladi LGA. The victims were a man, son and a relation.
314	August 14, 2011	Jos, Plateau State	Tension in Jos over the murder of Okada rider (Motorcyclist) at Eto Baba area in Jos North LGA. The corpse of the Okada rider, Mr. Kamilu Yahaya was discovered in a stream in Eto Baba. His motorcycle was made away with.
315	August 16, 2011	Tambuwal, Sokoto State	4 Policemen and 2 other Persons were killed by Boko Haram at Tambuwal LGA Of Sokoto State.
316	August 16, 2011	Jos, Plateau State	4 persons were killed in Jos at different flash points in Jos. Among those killed was a student, Mr Tony Ojukwu who came to Jos to write his post UME examination at University of Jos.
317	August 19, 2011	Maiduguri, Borno State.	Boko Haram militants killed a policeman and injured 3 others in attack at Bolori in Maiduguri.
318	August 21, 2011	Jos, Plateau State	6 persons were reportedly killed in an attack of Joi and Kwi villages of Riyom Local Government Area of Plateau State.

319	August 26,2011	UN building Abuja	UN house attack in Nigeria claimed 23 lives. Eleven of the people confirmed to have died in the attack were UN staff, including one international staff member. 32 received treatment in different hospitals.
320	August 29, 2011	Jos, Plateau State.	15 people were killed in another religious violence between Christian and Muslim youths during the salah celebration at Rukuba road. Over 200 vehicles were burnt.
321	August 30, 2011	Jos, Plateau State.	1 person was killed in Dogon Karfe area of Jos South Local Government Area.
322	August 30, 2011	Kafanchan, Kaduna State	4 persons were killed in Kafanchan area of Kaduna State during a reception for the State's Deputy Governor.
323	September 1, 2011	Yola, Adamawa State.	Soldiers killed 2 suspected members of the Boko Haram sect in Adamawa state.
324	September 1, 2011	Jos, Plateau State.	Several people were killed in a fresh violence that erupted at Dutse Uku area in Jos North Local Government Area.
325	September 1, 2011	Jos, Plateau State.	42 persons were feared death in a renewed Jos crisis in the city. Residents blamed soldiers for causing an increased number of the casualties through indiscriminate shooting.
326	September 2, 2011	Maiduguri, Borno State.	6 persons were killed and 8 sustained injuries as soldiers and youths clashed in Borno.
327	September 3, 2011	Ibadan ,Oyo State.	2 Policemen died in a clash with members of O'odua People's Congress in Oyo.
328	September 4, 2011	Jos, Plateau State.	The family of 8 was wiped out by assailants at a village in Heipang District of Barkin -Ladi Local Government Area.
329	September 13, 2011	Maiduguri, BornoState.	4 persons were killed at a bar in Maiduguri, the Borno state capital.
330	September 21,2011	Maiduguri Borno State.	Boko Haram killed 3 in an attack in Bulumkutu ward in Maiduguri.
331	October 1, 2011,	Maiduguri/ BornoState.	2 people were killed in a bomb blast explosion in Mauduguri the Borno state capital.
332	October 1, 2011	Baga road Market, Maiduguri, BornoState.	1 person was killed by some unidentified gunmen in Maiduguri the Borno state capital.
333	October 1, 2011	Maiduguri, Borno State.	Two separate bomb blasts occurred in Dalashuwari and Nganaram wards of Borno state. Number of casualties was not ascertained at the time of the report.
334	October 2, 2011	Linyado Village, Zamfara State.	19 people killed by a group of 150 assailants that invaded Lingyado village in Zamfara. The group attacked in the early morning hours. The attack was believed to be a planned retaliatory action by another village last August.
335	October 2, 2011	Maiduguri, Borno State.	3 persons were killed as Joint Task Force shuts Maiduguri markets. Some gunmen killed three people in Maiduguri, Borno state Capital within 12 hours.
336	October 5, 2011	Enugu, Enugu State.	4 Persons murdered In Enugu: - 3 police men and 1 welder murdered In cold blood at Amawobia Street, Uwani Area While Igwe Pius Delibe Uzochukwu of Mgbidi Autonomous Community in Awgu was abducted.
337	October 8 , 2011	Kaura Namoda, Zamfara state	3 persons died within a month in a ritual killing in Kaura Namoda in Zamfara state.
338	October 11, 2011	Maiduguri, Borno state	4 people were reportedly killed in another struck by the Boko Haram sect. Three of the casualties were traders at Baga international fish market, a soldier died when a bomb exploded in the area.
339	October 15, 2011	Jos, Plateau State.	3 people died in Jos when a soldier was killed. The ward head of Ali Kazaure and a young man died in the process.

340	October 15, 2011	Maiduguri, Borno State.	1 person was murdered in malanch Kambai area in Borno state by some gunmen.
341	October 16, 2011	Kwamu, GombeState	1 Police man and three attackers were killed when gunmen lunched a pre-down bomb attack on a Mobile Police base in Kwami, Gombe state.
342	October 16, 2011	Maiduguri, Borno State.	1 person was shot dead in front of his private residence at Gomari area of Maiduguri metropolis.
344	October 19, 2011	Maiduguri, BornoState.	5 people were killed in a three separate attacks by gunmen in London Chika area of Maiduguri.
345	October 20, 2011	Kagadama, Bauchi State.	2 people died and several others injured in a crisis at Kagadama Yelwa a suburb of Bauchi Metropolis.
346	October 22,2011	Maiduguri, Borno State.	Gunmen Suspected to be Boko Haram members killed a reporter with the Nigeria Television Authority (NTA) in Maiduguri.
347	October 23,2011	Maiduguri, Borno State.	A Roadside bomb hit a military patrol vehicle in Maiduguri, the Borno State Capital, the blast occurred in Zinnari area of the city, killing dozens.
348	October23,2011	Saminaka, KadunaState.	Gun men bomb two Banks in Saminaka, number of people killed not identified.
349	October 24,2011	Damaturu, Yobe State.	Some unidentified gunmen shot dead a policeman at his home in Damaturu, the Yobe state capital.
350	October 29, 2011	Maiduguri Borno State.	Unidentified gunmen killed a cleric in the Borno state Capital in another explosion in Bulabul in Ngarnam area of the Capital city.
351	October 31, 2011	Ekpoma, Edo State.	14 year old allegedly killed his pal after a disagreement over a girlfriend.
352	October 31, 2011	Maiduguri BornoState.	1 soldier was killed by unknown gunmen suspected to be Boko Haram along the popular Monday Market in Maiduguri
353	November 4, 2011	Maiduguri Borno State.	Three suicide bombers suspected to be Boko Haram sect died and six injured as they were denied access to military base at Bombari Bye pass. The Vehicle exploded as they moved away.
354	November 4, 2011	Zonkwa, Kaduna State	2 women were killed by unknown assailants while in a church attending a night vigil in Tabok village
355	November 4 & 5 , 2011	Maiduguri Borno, Potiskum and Damaturu in Yobe states.	150 people were killed, worship places torched and several public building including a bank vandalized in a multiple attacks in Borno state capital Maiduguri, Potiskum and Damaturu in Yobe state by Boko Haram sect.
356	November 5 , 2011	Zango-Kataf, Kaduna State	1 person died and others injured in an attack by unknown gunmen in Karmin Bi village, Zango-Kataf LGA in Kaduna state.
357	November 6, 2011	Maiduguri, Borno State.	A Police Inspector was killed while on his way back from Eid prayer ground in Maiduguri. The incident took place in the London ciki area of the metropolis.
358	Novermber 6 , 2011	Omaba Village in Ibaji LGA, Kogi State.	Chief James Onyekwe was reportedly killed by unidentified gunmen in his domain during a communal crisis over the traditional stool of the village.
359	November 7, 2011	Damaturu, Yobe State.	1 suspected suicide bomber shot dead in Yobe by security men on guard at the post while the suspect was attempting to explode some of the containers of explosive devices in his vehicle.
360	Novermber 9, 2011	Kafancha, Kaduna State	Three people were killed and many others injured following out-break of religious violence in Kafanchan town of Jema'a Local government area of Kaduna State.
361	November 11,2011	Wuntin-Dada Bauchi State.	A device went off in an un-occupied building, at Wuntin-Dada, a densely populated suburb of Bauchi, injuring five people.
362	November 17,2011	Yola, Adamawa State.	One Man was shot death while three others got wounded after two gunmen opened fire on them in Luka memorial Store.

363	November 18,2011	Sabon-line Gwange ward MaiduguriBor noState.	Boko Haram engaged JTF in shoot-out, 3 killed.
364	November 19,2011	Gangare Village, Bogoro LGA, Bauchi State.	4 killed, 5 injured in over night attack in Gangare Village, Gobbiya District in Bogoro LGA
365	November 20,2011	Rokot Village, Barkin-Ladi Local Government Area, Plateau State.	Seven Killed in two separate attacks in Plateau State .In the first attack on Sunday night,four persons were reportedly ambushed by about 20 assailants at Rokot village in Barkin-Ladi Local Government Area and three of three of them were killed.During a protest by youths in the area, four people were reportedly died.
366	November 21, 2011	Bulumkutu Market and Gomari area, Maiduguri, Borno State.	3 Solidiers and a number of civilians including members of the sect, died in clash between JTF and Boko Haram.
367	November 22,2011	Ughelli North Local Government Area, Delta.	A member of a vigilante' group on Aroh road in Ughelli North Local Government of Delta State was killed by unidentified assassins.
368	November 23,2011	Barkin Ladi, Plateau State.	10 killed, 20 houses burnt in renewed Plateau Violence.
369	November 24,2011	Nasarawa and Benue States.	Four persons were killed in a renewed hostility between Tiv Communities and Fulani herdsmen in a boundary area between Nasarawa and Benue State.
370	November 26,2011	Gaidam State	4 Policemen were killed, 20 injured, 8 Churches, 20 Markets Stalls and Geidam Council Secretariat were destroyed as Boko Haram attack Gaidam area in Yobe State.
371	November 27,2011	Gwange Ward, Maiduguri, Borno State.	Unknown gunmen believed to be members of the Boko Haram Sect shot and killed a Borno State Government House Protocol officer Kala Boro and Malam Garba Abdullahi a herbalist in the same attacks
372	November 28,2011	Orile- Coker, Lagos State.	Two People were killed in a clash between rival groups at Orile-Coker Lagos.
373	November 28,2011	Mile Two area of Diobu Port Harcourt Rivers State.	Unknown Gunmen killed one Policeman and injured two others at the Mile Two area of Diobu, Port Harcourt.
374	December 1,2011	Gwasari Ward and Barga road, Maiduguri Borno State.	Members of the Boko Haram and JTF (Operation Restore Peace) clashed in Maiduguri, the Borno State Capital, a Bomb blast along Barga road, near the Timber market. The casualty figure was not immediately known in both incidents.
375	December 1, 2011	Uzere, Isoko South Local government, Delta State.	Three youths were allegedly killed by Soldiers attached to Shell Petroleum Development Company (SPDC).There was a protest after the killings, which led to distortion of properties.
376	December 2, 2011	Gwange area& London Chiki area of Maiduguri Metropolis	Boko Haram engages JTF; unconfirmed report revealed that there were some casualties on both sides.
377	December 3,2011	Maiduguri, Borno State.	Unknown gunmen shot and killed a former councilor from Shehuri North at a wedding ceremony and injured two others.

378	December 3,2011	Azare, Bauchi State.	More than 100 gunmen suspected to be from the Boko Haram sect raided Azare, Bauchi State ,bombed two police stations and two banks in an attack that killed 3 people,3 gunmen and injured several others.
379	December 4,2011	Hasusari ward, Maiduguri, Borno state.	Two killed as gunmen attacked a Mosque (Duriya Tandari Mosque) in Maiduguri.
380	December 4,2011	Naka, Guma, Gwe, Benue State.	Number of deaths, unknown; 350 were missing following invasion of Fulani herdsmen who staged persistent attacks on Benue communities and villages leaving in their trail deaths and destruction.
381	December 7,2011	Kaduna, Kaduna State.	10 killed many others injured, 11 shops and rooms were destroyed in a blast in Kaduna.
382	December 10,2011	Bauchi -Ring road, Jos, Plateau State.	One killed, 11 injured in multiple bomb blasts.
383	December 11,2011	Kukum Daji village, Kaura Local Government Area, Kaduna State.	One killed, two injured in Southern Kaduna Village attack.
384	December 13, 2011.	Ali Goshe, Maiduguri, Borno State.	Four people were reportedly killed in a suicide Bomb attack targeted at members of the Joint Task Force (JTF).
385	December 14,2011	Santimari polo Road, Gwange, Maiduguri, Borno State.	Gunmen suspected to be members of Boko Haramsect, killed two people and injured three.
386	December 14, 2011	London Ciki, Borno State.	Scores feared dead in Borno explosion.
387	December 15, 2011	Gamboru 2area,Maiduguri, Borno State	5 killed by unknown gunmen, one injured.
388	December 15, 2011	Igbogbo/Bayeku Local council Development Area, Lagos State.	Clash in Lagos community claims 21 kidnapped, several injured
389	December 16, 2011	Air Force school, Kano state	Gunmen suspected to be members of the militant Boko Haram Sect killed three Air force officers and injured one other in Kano
390	December 17, 2011	Jwol & Foron Riyom Local government area, Plateau State.	Three killed, one missing in fresh Jos attack.
391	December 18, 2011	Shehuri 2, Bolori Ward, Borno State.	An explosion that took place in a Bomb Factory in Maiduguri claimed the live of three persons.
392	December 19, 2011	Damaturu, Kaduna State.	One dead, six injured, building destroyed in an explosions.

393	December 19, 2011	Darmunawa quarters in Kano State.	7 killed,14 arrested in a police shoot-out with members of the Boko Haram Islamic Sect.
394	December 21, 2011	Angwan Rami-Kagoro Kaura LGA, Kaduna State.	5 killed in fresh Southern Kaduna village attack and others hospitalized.
395	December 21, 2011	Ramin Daji, Southern Kaduna State.	Five dead as gunmen invaded Southern Kaduna village.
396	December 23 2011	Damaturu, Yobe State.	The assault on Boko Haram members left death toll near 70.
397	December 24, 2011	Mubi, Adamawa State.	Two persons were injured in an Explosion in Mubi, Adamawa.
398	December 24, 2011	Ohaji, Imo State	Assassins kill 1 cop, 2 civilians.
399	December 25,2011	Madalla, Niger State.	Christmas day Bomb blast in Madalla, Niger State, claimed about 40 lives, Maimed numerous others and destroyed over 10 vehicles and buildings at St. Theresa Catholic Church.
400	December 25, 2011	Ibeno,Akwa Ibom State	50 Houses were razed on Christmas day by suspected members of a rival community.
401	December 27, 2011	Lagos Carnival, Lagos State.	Two dead, scores injured in Lagos Carnival.
402	December 27, 2011	Wereng Village, Riyom Local Government Area, Plateau State.	Three killed in an attack by suspect Fulani herdsmen.
403	December 29, 2011	Sapele, Delta State.	Eight Children were injured following a bomb blast at an Arabic school.
404	December 30, 2011	Maiduguri, Borno State.	Four people were killed in Maiduguri, Borno State, following a bomb blast near a Mosque.
405	December 30,2011	Maiduguri Borno State.	Four people were killed after Joint Task Force clash with gunmen.
406	December 30, 2011	Maiduguri, Borno State.	Five killed as Boko Haram attack a private house and Market raid in Maiduguri.
407	December 31, 2011	Ezillo, Ishielu LGA, Ebonyi State.	Gunmen killed 53 persons in Ebonyi State.
408	January 1,2012	Kaura LGA, Kaduna state.	Unknown gunmen on New Year day invaded a community in Kaduna State and shot three people.
409	January 4,2012	Sabon Layi quarters, Gombe State.	Gunmen killed 2 in Jubilee Hotel, Gombe
410	January 4,2012	Dala ward, Maiduguri Borno State.	A Father and Son were killed and one injured by Boko Haram Sect.
411	January 5,2012	Gombe State.	Three people were killed and others wounded after gunmen attacked a church in Gombe.
412	January 5,2012	Adamawa State.	Gunmen killed 13 people in Adamawa.
413	January 5,2012	Mubi, Adamawa State.	Boko Haram kills 30 Southerners in Mubi.

414	January 6,2012	Owerri North LGA, Imo State.	15 persons, including a lady were injured in a communal clash in Owerri North LGA
415	January 6,2012	Mubi, Adamawa State.	Boko Haram members killed over 10 in Mubi.
416	January 7,2012	Christ Apostolic Church, Jimeta, Yola, Adamawa State.	Boko Haram killed 16 in Yola.
417	January 7,2012	Borno State.	Boko Haram kills three in Borno
418	January8,2012	Maiduguri, BornoState.	One killed, Two injured in Maiduguri
419	January 8,2012	Damaturu, Yobe State.	Boko Haram kills 8 in Damaturu.
420	January 10,2012	Benin, EdoState	5 killed in Benin Mosque attack.
421	January 10, 2012	Potiskum, Yobe State.	Gunmen kill 5 Police, 3 Civilians in Potiskum.
422	January 10, 2012	Pyakman Village, Tafawa Balewa local government area, Bauchi State.	Unknown gunmen killed Three people in Pyakman Village in Tafawa Balewa Local Government Area.
423	January 11 ,2012	Jimeta-Yola, Adamawa State	A Police corporal was shot and killed by unknown gunmen in Jimeta-Yola.
424	January 11, 2012	Potiskum, Adamawa State	Gunmen kill 4 travellers in Potiskum.
425	January 11 ,2012	Ebonyi State.	One killed, Three injured in Ebonyi communal clash.
426	January 13, 2012	Adamawa State	Reprisal attacks claimed two lives in Adamawa State
427	January 14, 2012	Yola, Gombe State.	Gunmen kill 4 persons in Yola, Gombe
428	January14,2012	Vwak Village Riyom, Plateau State	1 person was killed in Vwak Village.
429	January 16, 2012	BornoYobe	Gunmen kill Five in Borno,Yobe.
430	January 17, 2012	Maiduguri, Borno State.	Boko Haram kills 2 Soldiers, wounds 5 Soldiers in Maiduguri.
431	January 17,2012	Yobe State.	Gunmen kill 3 Chadians in Yobe
432	January 17, 2012	Maiduguri. BornoState.	4 killed many injured as JTF clash with suspected Boko Haram
433	January 20, 2012	Kano State.	200 people were killed in Kano multiple explosion.
434	January 22, 2012	Bayelsa State	Gunmen attack Ex-militant leader's Home in Bayelsa State; kill Policeman and an ex-militant Youth.
435	January 22, 2012	Tafawa Balewa, Bauchi State.	Unknown gunmen killed a DSP of Police, Soldier and 8 others.
436	January 23, 2012	Bauchi State	Explosions at two Churches in Bauchi.

437	January 25 ,2012	Shaka Police station,Kano	Explosions at the Shaka Police station, casualty figure at that time unknown by reporters.
438	January 27, 2012	Kano State.	Two Killed in Kano attack.
439	January 28, 2012	Maiduguri, BornoState.	Soldiers kill 11 Boko Haram suspects in Borno
440	January 29 ,2012	Air force Barracks, Maiduguri, Borno State.	Boko Haram attacks Air force Barracks killing five in Maiduguri.
441	January 29 ,2012	Eggon, Nasarawa State.	13 killed in Tiv, Eggon Communal clash
442	January 29, 2012	Zaria Road, Kano State.	One civilian killed as Gunmen attacked a Police Station
443	February 1, 2012	Amagba and Evbukhu, Edo State.	Benin crisis between two communities in Oredo local government Area of Edo State, Amagba and Evbukhu over the ownership of a large parcel of land. No live was lost in the dispute, property worth millions of Naira was destroyed.
444	February 1, 2012	Maiduguri, BornoState.	Boko Haram kills six in Borno
446	February 1, 2012	Adamawa State	Gunmen killed Alhaji Lawan Kabu, former Local Government Chairman in Borno
447	February 2, 2012	Ebonyi State.	Nine killed in renewed Ebonyi Communal clash.
448	February 2, 2012	Maiduguri, BornoState.	7 found butchered after all-night bombing in Maiduguri
449	February 2, 2012	Delta State.	Unidentified assailants beheaded a Traditional Chief in Delta State.
450	February 5, 2012	Damaturu, Yobe State.	Gunmen killed SSS officer in Damaturu.
451	February 6, 2012	Law fab Hotel, Delta State.	Suspected militants bombed Law Fab Hotel in Delta leaving several persons injured and properties of the Hotel destroyed.
452	February 6, 2012	Lagos State.	Two Suspected assassins gunned down in Lagos
453	February 6, 2012	Mariri, KanoState.	5 killed in Kano shoot out between Joint Security Team and Boko Haram
454	February 7, 2012	Kawo, Kaduna State	Suicide bomber hits Army Barracks in Kaduna,3 killed,Scores injured
455	February 7, 2012	Enugu State	Tension in Enugu community as Rival Vigilantes kill resident
456	February 8, 2012	Niger Delta.	MEND Attacks.
457	February 11, 2012	Potiskum, Yobe State.	Gunmen killed 3 in Potiskum.
458	February 11, 2012	Jere Local Government Area, BornoState.	Gunmen killed 3 in Borno
459	February 11 ,2012	Kataf Local Government Area, Kaduna State.	2 killed in Kaduna Village attack.
460	February 12, 2012	Maiduguri, Borno State.	12 killed in Boko Haram and Soldier's attack.
461	February 14 ,2012	Kaduna State	Anti-bomb Cop dies in Kaduna twin bomb Explosions.
462	February 20, 2012	Baga Fish market, Maiduguri	20 killed as JTF pursues Boko Haram
463	February 20, 2012	Lagos State	Four killed, Twenty Vehicles vandalized as transport workers clash in Lagos-NURTW
465	February 21, 2012	Yobe State.	Gunmen kill Cleric, Teacher in Yobe

466	February 24, 2012	Gombe State.	14 killed as Boko Haram attack Police Station in Gombe.
467	February 24, 2012	Kano State.	Boko Haram kills 4 in Kano.
468	February 26, 2012	Jos, State.	10 died in Jos Church suicide Bombing, reprisals.
469	February 26, 2012	Kahagu Village, Kaduna.	4 Villagers shot dead in Kaduna.
500	February 26, 2012	Kaura Local government, Kaduna	Unknown Gunmen kill two, injure one in Kaduna.
501	February 27, 2012	Bauchi State.	Boko Haram attacked a Police Station and Bank killing a Policeman.
502	February 27, 2012	Madagali local government, Adamawa state.	Unknown gunmen killed three Police Corporals in an attack on the Shuwa Divisional Police Station.
503	February 27, 2012	Yobe State	Gunmen kill 2 ward heads in Yobe.
504	February 28, 2012	BornoState.	Gunmen kill immigration officer in Borno state.
505	February 28, 2012	Danbatta road, Kano state.	Gunman shot dead a man along Danbatta road, Kano.
506	March 1, 2012	Yenagoa, Bayelsa State.	4 soldiers, 4 Cops killed in Bayelsa state.
507	March 1, 2012	Borno State	Boko Haram 3 schools burnt in Borno.
508	March 2, 2012	Kaleri Maiduguri	Boko Haram's bomb factory explodes, kills 3 members.
509	March 3, 2012	Kano State.	Boko Haram kills Corporal in Kano
510	March 4, 2012	Gamboru Market, Maiduguri, BornoState.	Boko Haram kills 4 in fresh Maiduguri attacks.
511	March 4, 2012	Kano State.	Unknown Gunmen kills Bridegroom in Kano
512	March 4, 2012	Gwer-West, Benue state.	10 killed as Fulani herdsmen invade Benue Communities.
513	March 4, 2012	Maiduguri, Borno State.	4 Boko Haram suspects killed in Maiduguri
514	March 6, 2012	Yobe State.	Gunmen kill Yobe, Borno Customs' Comptroller.
515	March 6, 2012	Gwer west, Benue State.	Gunmen kill 21 women, Children in Benue.
516	March 6, 2012	Lagos State.	One killed others injured as Area Boys clash in Lagos.
517	March 7, 2012	Port Harcourt, River State.	Militants kill Ghanaian professor in Port Harcourt.
518	March 7, 2012	NURTW, Lagos State.	Four killed, 20 injured, 50 Vehicles damaged in Lagos NURTW clash.
519	March 9,2012	Gombe State.	Gunmen murder Gombe Village head
520	March 11, 2012	Jos, plateau State.	11 killed in Jos as suicide bomber attack church.
521	March 11, 2012	Tse Yaji village, Nasarawa state.	Police confirmed 8 killed in Tse Yaji village in Nasarawa state.
522	March 11, 2012	Bayelsa state.	3 killed in Bayelsa cult clash.
523	March 12, 2012	Yelwa, Mubi, Adamawa State.	6 bullet-ridden bodies dumped in Mubi.
524	March 12, 2012	Kano state.	Gunmen kill Policeman in Kano.

525	March 17, 2012	Rigasa, Kaduna State.	Unknown gunmen suspected to be members of Boko Haram Sect shot a Policeman and his wife in Kaduna.
526	March 20, 2012	Kano State.	Unknown gunmen killed three persons while another teenager was also killed by a stray bullet in Kano.
527	March 20, 2012	Jos, Plateau State.	Gunmen attack Jos Police College and shot two Policemen on duty.
528	March 20, 2012	Adamawa State	Gunmen kill 2 in Adamawa.
529	March 21, 2012	Okene, Kogi State.	Unknown gunmen killed a prominent clan Leader in Okene Local Government Area of Kogi State.
530	March 21, 2012	Ekiti State.	20 injured in Okada riders' clash in Ekiti.
531	March 21, 2012	KanoState	Soldiers ambushed Boko Haram killed 9 sect members, arrested 2 in Kano
532	March 22, 2012	Borno State.	Cleric, 2 others shot dead by gunmen in Borno
533	March 23, 2012	Abraka, Delta State	Youths burn Mosque in Abraka, attack Northerners.
534	March 24, 2012	Kano State.	Boko Haram car bomb killed two in Kano
535	March 24, 2012	Abagannaram / Railway quarters, Maiduguri	The Sect opened fire on a Joint Task force (JTF) team killing 10.
536	March 25, 2012	Maiduguri, Borno State.	Boko Haram killed three in Maiduguri
537	March 25, 2012	Borno State.	Gunmen kill ex-Police Inspector, friends in Borno
538	March 25, 2012	Maiduguri, Borno State.	Boko Haram killed Spokesman's (Abu Qaqa) Father in Maiduguri
539	March 28, 2012	Borno State.	Gunmen kill Police Inspector in Borno
540	March 29, 2012	Damagum police Station Yobe State.	4 killed as Gunmen attack a Police station in Yobe to free inmates.
541	March 29, 2012	Kaduna State.	Suicide bomber killed self, injures others in Kaduna
542	April 1, 2012	Maiduguri, Borno State.	Gunmen suspected to be Boko Haram members killed Caretaker Chairman of Chibok Local Government in Maiduguri
543	April 1, 2012	Potiskum and Nangere, Yobe State.	Two people were killed when Gunmen suspected to be Boko Haram attacked Police stations in Yobe State.
544	April 1, 2012	Plateau State	One person was killed, while Rioters burn Police station in plateau village.
545	April 1, 2012	Kaduna State.	Kaduna Polytechnic Lecturer, Policeman killed in Kaduna.
546	April 1,2012	Takum LGA Taraba State	8 killed in Taraba communal clash between Tiv and Fulani
547	April 2, 2012	Borno state.	Gunmen killed an SSS operative in Borno
548	April 8, 2012	Riyom, Plateau State	Pregnant Fulani Woman killed in Plateau.
549	April 10, 2012	Banki Town, Borno State	10 killed as gunmen attacked Borno
550	April 11, 2012	Makarfi road/Makera in Rigasa, Kaduna State.	Gunmen suspected to be members of the Boko Haram sect killed 22 years-old in Kaduna
551	April 12, 2012	Maiduguri Market, BornoState.	One killed as gunmen storm Maiduguri Market.
552	April 12, 2012	Katsina State.	One killed, 2 injured in Katsina Market attack.
553	April 15, 2012	Cross River State.	Man killed in Cross River communal clash among Nko in Yakurr LGA and Obubra LGA.
554	April 17, 2012	Borno State.	Seven killed, 13 arrested as JTF engaged gunmen in Borno

555	April 18, 2012	Kaduna state.	Unknown Gunmen shot a Sergeant in Rigasa, Kaduna
556	April 19, 2012	Borno State.	Boko Haram killed 5 bakery workers.
557	April 19, 2012	Idemili South LGA, Anambra state.	Gunmen killed three Movements for the Actualization of the Sovereign state of Biafra members in Anambra.
558	April 19,2012	Kano state	Gunmen shoot 2 cops in Kano
559	April 20,2012	Maiduguri, Bornostate.	Two suspected Boko Haram members killed in Maiduguri
560	April 20, 2012	Riyas Village in Bokkos, Plateau State.	Two Vigilante' members were killed in Plateau village.
561	April 21,2012	Umuahia, Abia State.	Gunmen killed Petroleum marketer in Umuahia.
562	April 21, 2012	Bornostate.	JTF killed two Boko Haram suspects, recovered arms and ammunition in Borno state.
563	April 22, 2012	Biu, Borno state.	Five sect members killed in Biu.
564	April 22, 2012	Kano State.	Soldier killed in Kano
565	April 23, 2012	Mubi, Adamawa state.	SSS officer, Businessman killed in Mubi.
566	April 24, 2012	Gashish, Barkin-ladi, Plateau state	Unknown Gunmen killed three people and their bodies set ablaze in Barkin- Ladi.
567	April 24, 2012	Maiduguri, Borno State.	3 Boko Haram members killed in Maiduguri, Borno State.
568	April 25, 2012	Plateau, Yobe, Kogi States.	Gunmen killed 17 in Plateau, Yobe, Kogi.
569	April 25, 2012	Damaturu, Yobe State.	Gunmen killed Policeman, 4 others in Yobe
570	April 25, 2012	Riyom LGA, Plateau State	Five killed in Gwarim village of Riyom LGA in Plateau State by suspected Fulani herdsman.
571	April 25, 2012	Tudun Wada, Plateau State	STF confirms 1 dead, 3 injured at Tudun Wada Blast.
572	April 26, 2012	Boki Local Government Area, Cross River State.	Communal clash claims 3 in Cross River between Nasadop and Boje communities.
573	April 26, 2012	Jabi, Abuja and Kaduna State	Boko Haram bombed *ThisDay* Newspaper Headquarters in Abuja. Bombed the offices of *The Sun* and *The Moment* Newspaper in Kaduna
574	April 26, 2012	Gaida, Kano	Unknown Gunmen suspected to be Boko Haram members killed four in Kano
575	April 25,2012	Bajoga area command, Gombe State.	Two policemen were killed in Gombe attack by Boko Haram
576	April 25, 2012	Kano State.	Unknown Gunmen killed two in Kano
577	April 27, 2012	Yola, Adamawa	Attacks claim 3 more lives in Yola by unknown Gunmen suspected to be Boko Haram member.
578	April 28, 2012	Jimeta, Adamawa State	Five persons were killed in Adamawa state by unknown gunmen suspected to be members of Boko Haram
579	April 29, 2012	Bayero University, Kano State.	A Prof, 15 others died in University Church attack in Bayero University, Kano by Boko Haram members.

580	April 29, 2012	Maiduguri, Borno State.	Boko Haram killed prison warden in Maiduguri
581	April 29, 2012	Maiduguri, Borno State.	Gunmen kill pastor, 2 other worshippers in Maiduguri
582	April 29, 2012	Enugu state.	Unknown Gunmen killed a D.P.O in Enugu.
583	April 30, 2012	Taraba State	11 killed, 20 others injured in Taraba State commissioner of Police convoy bomb attack by suspected to be from Boko Haram
584	April 30, 2012	Riyom, Plateau State	1 killed, 4 houses burnt in Plateau by suspected Fulani herdsmen.
585	April 30, 2012	Adamawa State	Boko Haram killed 45 Policemen in Adamawa.
586	April 30, 2012	Nasarawa State.	Policemen were killed in gunmen's attack in Nasarawa.
587	May 2, 2012	Potiskum, Yobe State.	56 killed in Yobe Market attack by Gunmen suspected to be Boko Haram members.
588	May 4, 2012	Borno Prison, Borno State.	Gunmen invaded Borno Prisons, freed inmates, and killed Two Wardens, 23 were arrested.
589	May 5, 2012	Dananaca village, Taraba State	Gunmen in Army uniforms executed Five in Taraba.
590	May 5, 2012	Ogbomoso, Oyo State	One Farmer was killed and several others injured as Fulani herdsmen attacked Ogbomoso Farmers in Oyo.
591	May 6, 2012	Kano State.	JTF raid militants' hideout in Kano killed four.
592	May 7, 2012	Zaria LGA, Kaduna State.	Gunmen killed 2, kidnapped another in Kaduna
593	May 8, 2012	Udege, Nasarawa State.	Gunmen stormed police station killed two Fulani detainees in Udege, Nasarawa State.
594	May 8, 2012	Mbaitoli LGA, Imo State	Gunmen killed a Monarch, Eze Stanley Akuneto, traditional Ruler of Umueze-Abazu, and Ogwa in Imo State
595	May 9, 2012	Umuahia, Abia State	Unknown Gunmen killed a Salesman in Umuahia.
596	May 9, 2012	Rinyam-Tahoss, Riyom, Plateau State	Seven dead in Plateau attack by Gunmen suspected to be Fulani herdsmen.
597	May 10, 2012	Banki, Borno State.	Gunmen killed Police, Immigration officers, three others in Borno
598	May 11, 2012	Rigasa community, Kaduna state.	Gunmen killed a Village Head, 4 others in Rigasa community, Kaduna
599	May 12, 2012	Misau LGA, Bauchi State.	Unknown Gunmen attacked a Divisional Police headquarters in Misau local Government Area in Bauchi killing 2 Policemen - Mobile police officer and a Sergeant.
600	May 12, 2012	Mafa L.G.A, BornoState.	2 Policemen killed, 13 suspects arrested in Borno
601	May13, 2012	Budun area, Maiduguri, BornoState.	Gunmen killed Prisons officer in Borno
602	May13, 2012	Zamfara/Borno States.	Gunmen killed six Policemen three others in separate incidents in Zamfara and Borno States.
603	May 13, 2012	Tukuntawa area, Kano State.	Unknown Gunmen killed 5 Civilians in Kano
604	May 14, 2012	Yan Lemu area, Kano State.	Gunmen killed Man in Kano

605	May 14, 2012	Benin, Edo State.	Gunmen killed Journalist in Benin.
606	May 16, 2012	Kaduna State.	Gunmen killed Zaria Businessman.
607	May 17, 2012	Rumoukoro area, Port Harcourt, River State.	Explosion killed 2 in Port Harcourt.
608	May 19, 2012	Mbo LGA, Akwa Ibom State.	1 killed in communal clash between Ebughu and Efiat communities in Mbo Local Government Area of Akwa Ibom State.
609	May 19, 2012	Mbaagbwu District, Gwer West LGA, Benue State	10 killed, 46 Houses burnt by suspected Fulani herdsmen in Gwer West LGA, Benue State
610	May 20, 2012	River State.	Gunmen killed two Policemen, injured one in River State.
611	May 21, 2012	Onitsha, Anambra State	Unknown gunmen killed Deputy Superintendent of Police in Onitsha.
612	May 21, 2012	Benesheikh, Kaga Local Government Area, Borno State.	Gunmen raid Borno Police Station, killing one.
613	May 21, 2012	Damaturu, Yobe State.	Gunmen killed Police officer in Yobe
614	May 23, 2012	Sokoto State.	Two died as security agents, gunmen clashed in Sokoto.
615	May 26, 2012	Potiskum, Yobe State.	Gunmen killed Cleric, ex-prison guard in Yobe
616	May 27, 2012	Yobe State.	Unknown Gunmen attack Muslim worshippers in Yobe killing Two and injuring others.
617	May 27, 2012	Ezza North LGA, Ebonyi state.	Unknown gunmen on Motorcycles shoot Ebonyi Council boss, Legislative leader.
618	May 27, 2012	Luusue and Gior, Khana LGA, Rivers State.	2 killed, 10 houses burnt in fresh Ogoni Crisis among Luusue and Gior communities in Khana LGA, Rivers State.
619	May 28, 2012	Odukpani LGA, Cross River State and Ibiono Ibom LGA, Akwa Ibom State.	40 reported killed in communal clash in Cross River.
620	May 30, 2012	Danbare suburb, opposite the campus Bayero University, Kano	Kidnapped German killed in Kano after gun fight between Joint Task Force (JTF and suspected Terrorists.
621	June 1, 2012	Kpong-Asnsun, Madakiya district, Zangon Kataf LGA, KadunaState.	Unknown gunmen attacked some communities in Zangon Kataf Local Government Area of Kaduna State killing 2, injuring one and houses burnt.

622	June 2, 2012	Assakyo, headquarters of Lafia East, Nasarawa State.	30 killed in Assakyo, Headquarters of Lafia East caused by violence between Alago and Eggon communities in Nasarawa state.
623	June 2, 2012	Lawan Bukar ward, Maiduguri, Borno State.	A Groom, 2 others slaughtered by suspected Boko Haram members in Maiduguri
624	June 3, 2012	Harvest Field Church of Christ, Yelwa area, Bauchi State.	15 people were killed while 4 others were injured as a Suicide bomber detonated a bomb at Harvest Field Church of Christ in Yelwa area of Bauchi State.
625	June 5, 2012	Sauna/Kawaji, Kano State.	Unknown Gunmen suspected to be Boko Haram members killed retired DIG, Abubakar Saleh Ningi; 2 others in Kano
626	June 5, 2012	Ikwuano LGA, Abia State	Unidentified Gunmen attacked and shot dead a Businessman in Ikwuano local government area of Abia state.
627	June 6, 2012	Tanjol Village, Riyom, Plateau State	Unknown Gunmen killed 3, and a Cop missing in fresh Riyom attack.
628	June 6, 2012	Rabah road, Kaduna State.	Unknown Gunmen killed a staff of the Federal Airport Authority of Nigeria (FAAN) in Kaduna
629	June 7, 2012	Sauna, Kano state.	Police Inspector killed while repelling an attack by Unknown Gunmen in Sauna, Kano State.
630	June 8, 2012	State Police headquarters, Maiduguri Borno State.	5 killed as suicide bomber targets Borno Police Headquarters.
631	June 9,2012	Hotoro store, Nassarawa LGA, KanoState.	Unknown Gunmen killed an SSS officer, and a Customs officer in Kano
632	June 10, 2012	Karim Lamido, Taraba State	13 Fulani herdsmen were killed in a reprisal attack by Bachama farmers from Numan, Adamawa State in Karim Lamido Local Government area of Taraba State
633	June 10, 2012	Christ Chosen Church, Rukuba road, Plateau State	3 killed, 41 injured in Jos Suicide bombing at Christ Chosen Church, Rukuba road in Plateau State
634	June 10, 2012	EYN church, Nassarawa, Biu town, Bornostate.	Unknown gunmen attacked EYN church in Nassarawa area in the outskirt of Biu town killing a Woman and injured many people.
635	June 13, 2012.	Bukuru area, Jos South LGA, Plateau State	Unidentified Gunmen killed 3 in Jos
636	June 13, 2012	Nassarawa, Jalingo, Taraba State	Unknown Gunmen killed a Policeman in Jalingo.

637	June 15, 2012	New Garage area, Wadata, Makurdi, Benue State	Two children were allegedly killed in the Wadata area of Makurdi by Men of the Police force, during a gun fire battle between the Police and angry Muslim Youths. The protest by the Muslim Youths, Brick layers was over demolition of a Mosque, houses and Shops by the Benue State Urban Development Board.
638	June 15, 2012	Unguwa Uku area, Kano State.	Joint Task Force (JTF uncovers Militants media center, killed 4 in Unguwa Uku area of Kano town. The media centre is for the Terrorist elements operating in Kano.
639	June 16, 2012	Imbur and Ngbalang Village, Numan, Adamawa	2 killed in Adamawa communal attacks on Numan Muslim by Imbur Christians.
640	June 17, 2012	Sabon Gari, Zaria, KadunaState.	72 killed in Kaduna, Zaria bombings, Reprisal attacks. Evangelical Church Winning All (ECWA) Wusasa, Zaria 3 people were killed; in Christ the King Catholic Church (along Yoruba street) 3 people were killed; in Sabon Gari, Zaria 16 persons were killed; in Shalom Church 3 people were killed and in Reprisal attack 50 were killed.
641	June 17, 2012	Jeka-Dafari Quarters, Gombe State.	Unidentified Gunmen shot and killed 25 years-old Bello Faruk and 18 years-old Mashood Hassan at Jeka-dafari quarters of Gombe metropolis.
642	June 18, 2012	Damaturu, Yobe State.	Many people, including civilians, attackers and operatives of various security agencies were killed; when over a dozen bombs exploded and gunmen fired gun shots for several hours in many parts of Damaturu the Yobe State capital.
643	June 19, 2012	Kumbiya Quarters, GombeState.	Unknown gunmen killed Malam Adamu Mamman, the Acting Director of Security matters, Government House.
644	June 19, 2012	Damaturu, Yobe State.	40 killed in clash between members of the Joint Task Force(JTF) and gunmen suspected to be members of the Boko Haram sect.
645	June 20, 2012	Eziokpor Road, Obiaruku, Ukwuani LGA, Delta State	Unknown gunmen killed farmer in Delta community.
646	June 22, 2012	Tibiu Village, Kombum ward, Mangu LGA, Plateau State.	Unknown Gunmen invaded Tibiu village in Mangu Local Government of Plateau State killing Six members of Dakibang Family, injured four other persons.
647	June 23, 2012	Jan-block quarters, Kano State.	The Joint Task Force (JTF) in Kano killed four gunmen suspected to be Boko Haram members in a shoot-out.
648	June 24, 2012	Prison, Damaturu, Yobe State.	Unknown Gunmen suspected to be members of the Islamist sect Boko Haram, attacked a Satellite Prison in Damaturu killing 8 and freeing 40 inmates.
649	June 24, 2012	Bariga, Lagos State.	Five persons were killed in Bariga, Lagos when factions of street gangs clashed over the control of a canoe park.
650	June 25, 2012	Ugwuleru community, Umunneochi LGA, Abia State.	The Traditional ruler Eze Iroha Nwankwo was allegedly beaten to death in his palace allegedly by Youths in the community who invaded his palace in Abia.
651	June 25, 2012	Damaturu, Yobe State.	Three suspected Islamic Militants were, killed in a gun dual between the sect members and the sect members and the Joint Task Force (JTF) in Damaturu, Yobe State.

652	June 25, 2012	Ugwuleru, Umunneochi LGA,Abia	Eze Iroha Nwankwo a traditional ruler of Ugwuleru community was allegedly beaten to death by youths in Abia State.
653	June 25, 2012	Damaturu,Yobe	Three suspected Islamic militants were killed in a gun dual between the sect members and Joint Task Force (JTF) in Damaturu, Yobe State.
654	June 29, 2012	Gulak, Madagali LGA, Adamawa	Unknown gunmen attacked a Divisional Police headquarters in Gulak community in Madagali LGA of Adamawa State, killing three Policemen and two other Policemen on duty in a nearby Bank.
655	June 30, 2012	Damaturu,Yobe	Two soldiers, two Policemen and three suspected members of the Boko Haram sect were killed during a military raid on Boko Haram hideout in Damaturu.
656	July 1, 2012	Kurna Asabe, Kano	Unknown Gunmen killed a former local government councilor, a lady and a teenager in Kurna Asabe area in Kano.
657	July 1, 2012	Gwandu Quarters, Shamaki ward, Gombe	Unknown Gunmen kill Two, injure one in Gombe.
658	July 2, 2012	Bolori Quarters, Borno	Suspected Boko Haram members slaughtered Nine Mosque Builders in Borno.
659	July 7, 2012	Gashish district in Barkin Ladi LGA, Kakuruk, Kuzen Ngyo, Kogoduk, Ruk and Dogo villages of Plateau State.	23 killed, 50 injured in fresh Plateau violence by suspected mercenaries who stormed seven Berom villages of Barkin Ladi LGA of Plateau State.
660	July 13, 2012	Maiduguri central Mosque, Borno.	Five people were killed when a suicide bomber targeted the Shehu of Borno Alhaji Abubakar Umar Ibn Garbai Al-Amin El-Kanemi and the Borno State Deputy Governor Alhaji Umar Zanna Mustapha in front of the Maiduguri Central Mosque.
661	July 15, 2012	Limanti area, Maiduguri, Borno.	Unknown gunmen killed Hajja Bayayi Local Government Councilor in Bolari Ward 1 in Maiduguri
662	July 16, 2012	Police area command,CID and a Division, Damaturu, Yobe.	Unknown gunmen Suspected to be members of Boko Haram attacked a Police station in Damaturu, two people were killed.
663	July 17, 2012	Azikoro,Yenagoa, Bayelsa State.	Unknown gunmen killed two persons along Azikoro, in Yenagoa, Bayelsa State.
664	July 17, 2012	Bukuru ,Jos, Plateau.	Three rocket-propelled grenades were fired in Jos, one at an Islamic school packed with students taking exams and two near an office of the Special Task Force. a Boy and 5 others were killed.
665	July 18, 2012	Ishi Ozalla, Nkanu West LGA, Enugu.	One person and two cows were killed when habitants of Ishi Ozalla community in Nkanu West LGA of Enugu State clashed with some Fulani herdsmen.

666	July 21, 2012	Egun community, Makolo, Lagos	A Policeman allegedly killed Timothy Huntoyanwha, Egun community leader in Makolo during a protest at the site of demolition in the area.
667	July 22, 2012	Bayan-Gari, Bauchi.	Two people were killed while several other were injured when an explosion rocked the Bayan-Gari area of the Bauchi metropolis.
668	July 23, 2012	Ganaram, Maiduguri, Borno.	Unknown gunmen shot dead five persons including three brothers in Maiduguri.
669	July 25, 2012	Gum Arabic factory, Bayan Quarter, Maiduguri, Borno	Unknown Assailants Slaughtered Two Indians at Gum Arabic factory in Maiduguri.
670	July 25, 2012	Gubio, Borno State.	Unknown gunmen killed two Policemen in a local government secretariat and a Divisional Police headquarters in Gubio town in Borno State.
671	July 26, 2012	Gombe road, Bauchi.	Unknown Gunmen kill 3 Policemen in Bauchi Gombe road, Bauchi State.
672	July 29, 2012	Na'ibawa Yanlemo-Zaria Road, Kano.	Unknown gunmen killed two Air force personnel at Na'ibawa 'Yanlemo along Zaria road in Kano. Two civilans were also killed in an earlier attack at Hotoro Walaiwa by Unknow gunmen.
673	July 29, 2012	Janbulo Mosque-Bayero University Kano Road, Kano State.	Suicide bomber, 3 gunmen killed during failed attack on Janbulo Mosque along Bayero University Kano Road, Kano.
674	July 30, 2012	Tudun Wada, Zaria, Kaduna State.	Unknown gunmen attacked Vice President Namadi Sambo's family home in Tudun Wada, Zaria, injured two Policemen and killed a cobbler.
675	July 30, 2012	Ungwar Rogo Police Station Arkilla Divisional Police Station Sokoto State.	Suicide bombings in Sokoto, four persons were killed, among them a Police Corporal and two suicide bombers, 30 people were injured.
676	August 4, 2012	Old Maiduguri & Gwange ward, Borno	Unknown Gunmen killed five people in Maiduguri.
677	August 5, 2012	JTF post in Shagari Quarters, Damaturu, Yobe State	Suicide bomber kills six soldiers, two civilians in Damaturu, Yobe.
678	August 5, 2012	Maiduguri, Borno State.	A former commissioner in Borno State, Alhaji Abdulkadir Kaasa was shot dead in an attack.
679	August 5, 2012	Damaturu, Yobe.	Nine soldiers and one mobile police officer were killed in an attack on security patrol team in Damaturu, Yobe state.
680	August 6, 2012	Otite, Okene, Kogi State.	Unknown gunmen killed 16 Worshippers at Deeper Life Bible Church Okene during service.
681	August 7, 2012	Central Mosque Okene, Kogi State.	Unknown gunmen attack the central Mosque adjacent to the local government secretariat in Okene, killing two soldiers on patrol.

682	August 8, 2012	Gubi village- Ningi/Kano road. Bauchi State	Unknown gunmen killed two Policemen at a patrol centre in Gubi village along Ningi/ kano road in Bauchi State.
683	August 8, 2012	Gomari area, Maiduguri, Borno.	Unknown gunmen shot and killed a tea vendor at his shop in Gomari area of Maiduguri, two other people were injured.
684	August 8, 2012	Otukpo, Obi Local Government Area, Benue State.	Five persons were killed in a renewed land dispute between two border communities of Otukpo and Obi local government areas in Benue State.
685	August 9, 2012	Okene, Kogi State	Unknown gunmen shot dead three worshippers while praying inside a Mosque in Okene, Kogi State.
686	August 12, 2012	Gaidamari, Bulabulin Ngarnam, Maiduguri, Borno State.	One soldier, 20 suspected Boko Haram insurgents were killed in Maiduguri during hours-long shootout between Joint Task Force (JTF) and Boko Haram members in Borno.
687	August 12, 2012	All Saints Catholic Church, Kanoyel, Gombe State.	Unknown gunmen attacked the All Saints Catholic Church, Kanoyel in Gombe State, killing a Policeman who was on duty at the Church.
688	August 12, 2012	Karofi, Bauchi State.	Suspected thugs belonging to the *Sara Suka* group killed three persons and injured three others in Karofi area in Bauchi Local Government Area of Bauchi State.
689	August 15, 2012	Nayi-Nawa, Yobe State.	Nine people were killed as Boko Haram fights fake members in Nayi- Nawa, Yobe state.
690	August 19, 2012	Customs Area, Maiduguri, Borno.	Two suspected Boko Haram members were killed in a botched suicide attack on a military patrol van at the Customs area in Maiduguri.
691	August 18, 2012	Polo area, Maiduguri, Borno.	Unknown gunmen killed former secretary Borno emirate council, Alhaji Mustaph El-Kanemi, in the Polo area of Maiduguri.
692	August 18, 2012	Sho, Rott district of Barkin- Ladi, Plateau State.	Two Fulani men were killed and two others injured in Sho, Rott district of Barkin- Ladi LGA of Plateau State.
693	August 19, 2012	Sabon- Layi, Mubi, Adamawa State.	Unknown gunmen killed two persons in Mubi, in an attack which left one person injured.
694	August 20, 2012	Goniri town, Yobe State.	Unknown gunmen kill two, raze sharia court, school, police station in Goniri town in Yobe state
695	August 23, 2012	Sho Village, Barakin Ladi LGA, Plateau	Two people were killed by suspected Fulani herdsmen who attacked residents of Sho Village in Barakin Ladi LGA of Plateau State.
696	August 23, 2012	Michika, Adamawa State.	Unknown Gunmen killed two brothers, injured another in Michika, Adamawa state.
697	August 26, 2012	New market Layout, Owerri, Imo.	Suspected assassins killed a former direction at the Central Bank of Nigeria (CBN), Mr. Charles Nwosu, along New market layout in Owerri, Imo State.
698	August 26, 2012	Nsukwa, Asaba, Delta.	One (Chizoba Opute) person was killed over leadership Tussle in Nsukwa community, near Asaba, Delta State.

699	September 1, 2012	Ruwan Zafi, Dikwa-Gamboru Road, Maiduguri, Borno.	The Joint Task Force (JTF) in Borno State killed five members of the Islamist sect, Boko Haram in an encounter at Ruwan Zafi, Dikwa-Gamboru road in Maiduguri, 3 persons were injured.
700	September 1, 2012	Ruku, Gashish District, Barkin Ladi, Plateau.	Unknown gunmen suspected to be Fulani herdsmen ambushed and killed five in Ruku in Gashish District of Barkin Ladi LGA of Plateau State.
701	September 1, 2012	New Marte, Marte LGA, Borno.	Unknown gunmen suspected to be members of Boko Haram sect killed a Police Sergeant and two civilians at New Marte in Marte LGA of Borno State.
702	September 3, 2012	Marte LGA, Borno State	Men suspected to be Boko Haram sect killed police sergeant and two civilians.
703	September 4, 2012	Barkin Ladi, Plateau State	Five killed, in Berom Fulani clash in Barkin Ladi, Plateau State.
704	September 17, 2012	Zango area, Bauchi State	Gunmen suspected to be members of the Boko Haram sect. killed five people and injured seven.
705	September 17, 2012	Kano, Kano State.	Gunmen suspected to be Boko Haram members shot a Nigerian Civil Defence officer, his wife, two children and a physically challenged dead.
706	September 17, 2012	Umuode, Nkanu East LGA, Enugu State	One person killed another seriously injured and seven houses were destroyed in Communal clash between Umuode and Oruku communities.
707	September 18, 2012	Bauchi, Bauchi State	Gunmen believed to be members of the Boko Haram sect stormed Bauchi, killing nine people on Sunday night.
708	September 18, 2012	Maiduguri, Borno State	A gun duel between men of the Joint Task Force (JTF) and the Boko Haram men led to the death of 10 gunmen. Some JTF members were injured and some houses were burnt.
709	September 18, 2012	Mariri, Kano State	A JTF official said Boko Haram spokesman and commander of its members in Kano State Abu Qaqa was shot dead and two members of the sect arrested.
710	September 19, 2012	Bama, Borno State	Gunmen suspected to be members of Boko Haram sect shot dead Borno State Commissioner for Justice and Attorney-General Zanna Malam Gana.
711	September 19, 2012	Azare, Bauchi State	Former Comptroller-General of Prisons Alhaji Ibrahim Jarma, shot on Monday, Sep tember 17, 2012 by gunmen in front of a mosque; he died at the hospital September 18, 2012.
712	September 21, 2012	Maiduguri-Kano Road	JTF's Spokesman confirmed the killing of two *Boko Haram* top commanders coordinating the sect's activities in Mubi and Yola in Adamawa and Yobe State, respectively, by a combined team of JTF and DSS.
713	September 24, 2012	St. John Catholic Church Bauchi, Bauchi State	A suicide bomber attacked Saint John Catholic Church killing three people and injuring 46 others.
714	September 25, 2012	Damaturu, Yobe State	The Joint Task Force (JTF) claimed killing 35 and arrested 156 suspected Boko Haram members in a crack down on the insurgent group in Damaturu, the Yobe State capital.

715	September 27, 2012	Ikot Uko in Ika LGA Akwa Ibom and Okirika community in Abia State	Not fewer than six persons have been reportedly killed while several others sustained various degrees of injuries following weekend deadly border clash involving Ikot Uko in Ika Local Government Area of Akwa Ibom and Okirika Local community in Abia State.
716	September 30, 2012	Abor Akuzor in Umusiome village in Nkpor, Idemili Council Area of Anambra State	A middle-aged woman was killed in a land dispute between the Abor Akuzor kindred and their neighbouring Oramadike village in Ogidi, also in the same council, in recent times, was clashes between the two communities which led to loss of lives and destruction of property.
717	October 1, 2012	Kpakungu, Minna Niger State	Two policemen were Saturday night shot to death at Kpakungu, along Bida road in Minna by gunmen suspected to be members of Boko Haram sect.
718	October 1, 2012	Gaskiya Lay-out, Zaria, Kaduna State	Residents of the university town woke up to sounds of gunshots as security men and members of the Boko Haram sect slugged it out in Gaskiya. Two members of the sect were killed.
719	October 2, 2012	Mubi, Adamawa State	Massacre of over 40 students of Federal Polytechnic, Mubi, Adamawa State University and the School of Health Technology, Mubi last Monday in their hostel in Mubi, after a prolonged shooting by gunmen.
720	October 2, 2012	Maiduguri, Borno State and Zaria, Kaduna State	Six suspected members of Boko Haram sect were killed by the Joint Task Force in Maiduguri, the Borno State capital and Zaria, the university town in Kaduna State. One was killed in a gun duel in Zaria; five were gunned down in Maiduguri.
721	October 2, 2012	Lagos Street Maiduguri, Borno State	A member of the Joint Task Force (JTF) in Borno State was killed while about four others were injured when an Improvised Explosive Device (IED) which was targeted at their patrol vehicle exploded along Lagos Street in Maiduguri.
722	October 2, 2012	Danmagaji area of Zaria, Kaduna State	The Joint Task Force (STF) killed one suspected member of Boko Haram, and arrested another in a hideout after a fierce exchange of gun shots.
733	October 4, 2012	Zaria, Kaduna State	Gunmen suspected to be members of Boko Haram shot dead a Police Corporal attached to the Zaria Area Command of Kaduna State.
734	October 4, 2012	UNIMAID, Borno State	Two students of the University of Maiduguri were reportedly killed following an attack on their off campus hostel on Bama Road in Maiduguri metropolis by yet to be identified gunmen.
735	October 4, 2012	Abaganaram ward, Maiduguri, Borno State	Twenty people have been killed by gunmen suspected to be members of Boko Haram sect who went from house to house in their selective and silent killings of 20 residents at State Low Cost Housing Estate (SLHE) in Abaganaram ward, Maiduguri, Borno State, by slitting their throats.
736	October 5, 2012	Jalingo, Taraba State	A man was reportedly killed in Jalingo, the Taraba state capital, after an explosion rocked Doruwa area of the city. Eleven others were injured.
737	October 5, 2012	Zaria, Kaduna State	Ten persons, including commercial sex workers and hotel workers, were injured in an explosion at Cosmopolitan Hotel, in Sabo-Garin area of Zaria, Kaduna State.
738	October 7, 2012	Dogon Kuka, Yobe State	Unknown gunmen opened fire on Dogon Kuka, a village along Potiskum-Damaturu road, in Yobe State, leading to the killing of unconfirmed number of persons.

739	October 8, 2012	Kandahar, a notorious suburb of Damaturu and Gwange area of Yobe State	The Joint Task Force (JTF) in Yobe State, in an early morning operation killed the Yobe State Commander of the Boko Haram sect, named Bakaka and 30 others suspected Boko Haram insurgents in a gun battle.
740	October 8, 2012	Zaria, Kaduna State	Some unknown gunmen shot dead a doctor and two other persons, while a woman sustained gunshot wound at King's Road, Sabon Gari, Zaria, Kaduna State.
741	October 8, 2012	Madauchi, Zangon Kataf LGA, Kaduna State	Unknown gunmen killed a woman trader and injured a young man.
742	October 9, 2012	Maiduguri, Borno State	Thirty civilians and insurgents were killed in Maiduguri when security operatives allegedly went berserk after the killing of an Army Lieutenant and six other military personnel in an explosion. This was denied by Army Headquarters.
743	October 13, 2012	Riyom and Barkin Ladi LGA's Plateau State	Fourteen persons including a 75-years old grandma were allegedly killed in separate attacks between 7th to 10th October, 2012 by suspected Fulani herdsmen. This led to a declaration of 24-hour curfew on affected communities.
744	October 15, 2012	Dogon Dawa, Kaduna State	Unknown gunmen allegedly killed 24 persons in Dogon Dawa village in Kaduna State.

NOTES:

1. *The News*, June 21, 1999 p. 20-23.
2. *This Day*, July 25, 1999, p.1
3. *This Day*, July 24, 1999, p.1
4. *This Day*, August 9, 1999, p.1
5. *New Nigeria*, December 25, 1999, p.8.
6. *The week*, November 15, 1999, p.10.
7. *Daily Champion*, October. 22, 1999, p.1.
8. *New Impression*, January. 2000, p.8.
9. *Daily Champion*, November. 19, 1999, p.1.
10. *New Nigeria*, December. 25, 1999.p.8
11. *Newswatch*, March 6, 2000. P.8
12. *Newswatch*, March 13, 2000, p.20.
13. *Tell*, March 2000, p.27.
14. *The Punch*, March 20, 2000.
15. *The Punch*, April 13, 2000.
16. *Daily Champion*, April 17, 2000, p.1.
17. *The Punch*, May 8, 2000.
18. *Sunday Champion*, May 21, 2000 .p.1.
19. *This Day*, June 6, 2000, p.1.
20. *The Punch*, July 18, 2000.
21. *The Punch*, September 11, 2000.

22. *Tell*, Feb. 18, 2002. p.30.
23. *Newswatch*, October 30, 2000, p.22.
24. *This Day*, October 20, 2000, p.1.
25. *This Day*, October 24, 2000.
26. *The Punch*, December. 7, 2000.
27. *This Day*, June 29, 2001, p.1.
28. *This Day*, September 9, 2001, p.1.
29. *This Day*, September 17, 2001, p.1
30. *This Day*, October 14, 2001, p.1.
31. *This Day*, October 14, 2001, p.1.
32. *This Day*, November 6, 2001.
33. *Tell*, November 5, 2001, p.30.
34. *This Day*, January 2, 2002.
35. *The Punch*, January 21, 2002.
36. *The Insider* Weekly, February 18, 2002.
37. *The Punch*, March 28, 2002.
38. *The Punch*, February 28, 2002.
39. *This Day*, May 5, 2002. p.3.
40. *This Day*, May 15, 2002. p.11.
41. *This Day*, May 19, 2002. p.7.
42. *The Punch*, June 18, 2002.
43. *The Punch*, June 30, 2002. p.1.
44. *The Punch*, July 15, 2002. p.1
45. *Vanguard*, January 21, 2003, p.7.
46. *Vanguard*, February 5, 2003, p.1.
47. *Vanguard*, February 13, 2003, p.6.
48. *Vanguard*, February 28, 2003, p. 6.
49. *Vanguard*, March 2, 2003, p.3.
50. *Vanguard*, March 20, 2003, p. 10.
51. *Vanguard*, March 26, 2003, p. 6.
52. *Vanguard*, May 7, 2003, p. 3.
53. *Vanguard*, May 2, 2003, p. 7.
54. *Vanguard*, May 15, 2003, pp. 1 and 2.
55. *Vanguard*, July 10, 2003, p.6.
56. *Vanguard*, July 17, 2003, p. 7.
57. *Vanguard*, July 17, 2003, p.7.
58. *Vanguard*, August 6, 2003, p. 2.
59. *Vanguard*, August 16, 2003, p. 2.
60. *Vanguard*, October 17, 2003, p. 3.
61. *Vanguard*, November 12, 2003, p. 7.
62. *Vanguard*, November 24, 2003, pp. 1 and 2.
63. *Vanguard*, November 26, 2003, pp. 1 and 2.
64. *Vanguard*, November 26, 2003, p.5.
65. *Vanguard*, December 17, 2003, p.6.
66. *Vanguard*, January 16, 2004, p. 5.
67. *Vanguard*, January 15, 2004, p. 11.
68. *Vanguard*, January 14, 2004, p. 7.
69. *Vanguard*, January 13, 2004, p. 6.

70. *Vanguard*, January 8, 2004, pp. 1 and 2.
71. *Vanguard*, January 30, 2004, p. 6.
72. *Vanguard*, January 21, 2004, p. 6.
73. *Vanguard*, January 21, 2004, p.7.
74. *Vanguard*, January 20, 2004, p.7.
75. *Vanguard*, February 18, 2004, p. 10.
76. *Vanguard*, January 19, 2004, pp. 1 and 2.
77. *Vanguard*, March 24, 2004, p. 10.
78. *Vanguard*, March 16, 2004, p. 4.
79. *Vanguard*, March 30, 2004, pp. 1 and 2.
80. *Vanguard*, April 29, 2004, p. 11.
81. *Vanguard*, April 7, 2004, p. 1.
82. *Vanguard*, April 11, 2004, p. 1.
83. *Vanguard*, April 28, 2004, pp. 1 and 11.
84. *Daily Trust,* May 4, 2004, pp. 1 and 2.
85. *Vanguard*, May 13, 2004, p. 3.
86. *Vanguard*, May 26, 2004, pp. 1 and 2.
87. *Vanguard*, June 7, 2004, p. 9.
88. *Vanguard*, June 13, 2004, p.3.
89. *Vanguard*, June 18, 2004, p. 6.
90. *Vanguard*, July 15, 2004, p. 3.
91. *Vanguard*, August 6, 2004, pp. 1 and 6.
92. *Vanguard*, August 20, 2004, p. 6.
93. *Vanguard*, August 26, 2004, p. 2.
94. *Vanguard*, August 31, 2004, pp. 1 and 2. Also see, *Daily Sun*, September 22, 2004, p. 2.
95. *New swatch*, September 20, 2004, pp. 10-23.
96. *Vanguard*, September 28, 2004, pp. 1 and 2.
97. *This Day*, November 12, 2004, pp. 1 and 6.
98. *Vanguard*, November 24, 2004, p. 6.
99. *Daily Independent*, December 13, 2004, pp. A1 and 2.
100. *This Day*, December 16, 2004, p. 19.
101. *Daily trust*, January 17, 2005, p. 1.
102. *This Day*, February 10, 2005, p. 6 and *Newswatch*, March 14, 2005, pp. 10-11.
103. *Vanguard*, February 9, 2005, p. 11.
104. *Daily Sun*, March 9, 2005, p. 6.
105. *Vanguard*, February 14, 2005, p. 12.
106. *Daily Sun*, February 24, 2005, p. 4.
107. *Daily Sun*, March 9, 2005, p. 6.
108. *Daily Trust*, February 24, 2005, p. 5.
109. *Thisday*, February 25, 2005, pp. 1 and 4.
110. *Daily Trust*, March 2, 2005, p. 12.
111. *Vanguard*, March 4, 2005, p. 7.
112. *Daily Trust*, March 7, p. 1 and March 8, 2005, p. 3.
113. *Vanguard*, March 9, 2005, p. 7.
114. *Vanguard*, March 4, 2005, p. 7..
115. *Vanguard,* May 1, 2005, p. 19 and *This Day,* April 30, 2005.

116. *Daily Trust,* May 6, 2005, p. 3.
117. *Daily Trust,* May 11, 2005, p. 3.
118. *Daily Trust,* May 12, 2005, p. 3 *and Vanguard,* May 19, 2005, p. 32.
119. *Vanguard,* May 12, 2005, p. 8.
120. *Vanguard,* May 18, 2005, p. 7.
121. *Daily Sun,* May 25, 2005, p. 1.
122. *Daily Independent,* June 2, 2005, pp. 1 and 2.
123. *Vanguards*, December 5, 2007, pp. 1,5,&7.
124. *Daily Trust*, December 21, 2007, p.24
125. *The Punch*, January 2, 2008, p.6.
126. *Vanguard*, February 21, 2008, p.5
127. *This Day*, January 23, 2008, p. 15
128. *Vanguard*, January 21, 2008 p.13.
129. *This Day,* April 7, 2008, p.2.
130. *Vanguard*, September 7, 2008, p.17.
131. *Daily Trust,* September 8, 2008, pp. 1 & 5.
132. Daily Trust, November 18, 2010 p5
133. Vanguard, June 25,2010,p.6
134. Saturday Sun,October2,2010,p.3-7
135. Sunday Trust, October 24,2010,p.3
136. The Nation, December 2, 2010 p7
137. Leadership, December 4, 2010 p1
138. Daily Trust, December 6, 2010 p2
139. Vanguard, December 6, 2010 p1
140. Daily Trust, December 7, 2010 p2
141. Vanguard, December 6, 2010 p10
142. Leadership, December 10, 2010 p7
143. The Nation, December 22, 2010 p7
144. The Nation, December 22, 2010 p8
145. Saturday Sun, December 25, 2010 p11
146. The Nation, December 27, 2010 p57
147. Leadership, December 27, 2010 p1
148. Leadership, December 27, 2010 p2
149. The Nation, December 28, 2010 p1
150. The Nation, December 30, 2010 p2
151. Leadership, December 31, 2010 p2
152. The Nation, January 1, 2011 p3
153. Sunday Tribune, January 2, 2011 p11
154. Sunday Vanguard, January 9, 2011
155. Daily Trust, January 10, 2011 p7
156. The Nation, January 12, 2011 p2
157. The Nation, January 17, 2011 p6
158. Daily Trust, January 18, 2011 p1
159. The Nation, January 20, 2011 p7
160. Vanguard, January 21, 2011 p1
161. Daily Trust, January 27, 2011 p4
162. The Nation, January 28, 2011 p9
163. Weekly Trust, January 29, 2011 p6

164. Weekly Trust, January 29, 2011 p6
165. Leadership, January 30, 2011 p1
166. Daily Trust, January 31, 2011 p2
167. The Nation, January 31, 2011 p9
168. Daily Trust, February 2, 2011 p2
169. Leadership, February 3, 2011 p1
170. Leadership, February 5, 2011 p1
171. The Nation, February 10, 2011 p4
172. Leadership, February 11, 2011 p2
173. Leadership, February 11, 2011 p8
174. The Nation, February 12, 2011 p3
175. Vanguard, February 13, 2011 p8
176. Leadership, February 16, 2011 p1
177. Vanguard, February 21, 2011 p15
178. The Nation, February 21, 2011 p3
179. Leadership, February 21, 2011 p2
180. Leadership, February 21, 2011 p8
181. Leadership, February 23, 2011 p1
182. Leadership, March 1, 2011 p1
183. Leadership, March 2, 2011 p12
184. The Nation, March 4, 2011 p7
185. Daily Trust, March 11, 2011 p2
186. Daily Trust, March 16, 2011 p2
187. Daily Trust, March 16, 2011 p47
188. The Nation, March 17, 2011 p8
189. Leadership, March 19, 2011 p9
190. Leadership, March 21, 2011 p1
191. The Nation, March 21, 2011 p10
192. The Nation, March 22, 2011 p9
193. Daily Trust, March 23, 2011 p2
194. Daily Trust, March 23, 2011 p8
195. Vanguard, March 23, 2011 p9
196. Daily Trust, March 28, 2011 p1
197. Leadership, March 30, 2011 p6
198. Daily Trust, March 31, 2011 p2
199. The Nation, March 31, 2011 p4
200. Leadership, March 31, 2011 p7
201. The Nation, April 2, 2011 p2
202. Daily Trust, April 4, 2011 p8
203. Daily Trust, April 4, 2011 p8
204. Daily Sun, April 7, 2011 p12
205. Leadership, April 10, 2011 p1
206. Vanguard, April 13, 2011 p17
207. Vanguard, April 14, 2011 p14
208. Leadership, April 29, 2011 p2
209. Daily Trust, May 6, 2011 p6
210. Leadership, May 7, 2011 p2
211. Daily Trust, May 13, 2011 p5

212. Saturday sun, May 14, 2011 p12
213. Sunday sun, May 15, 2011 p14
214. Vanguard, May 17, 2011 p9
215. Daily sun, May 17, 2011 p6
216. Daily sun, May 17, 2011 p10
217. Nigerian Compass, May 20, 2011 p1
218. Nigerian Compass, May 20, 2011 p1
219. Daily Trust, May 25, 2011 p11
220. Vanguard, May 25, 2011 p2
221. Daily Trust, May 25, 2011 p1
222. Weekly Trust, May 28, 2011 p5
223. Leadership, may 28, 2011 p5
224. Daily Sun, May 30, 2011 p7
225. Leadership, May 30, 2011 p1
226. Daily Sun, May 31, 2011 p11
227. Vanguard, June 1, 2011 p12
228. Daily Trust, June 2, 2011 p2
229. Daily Trust, June 8, 2011 p1
230. Daily Trust, June 10,2011 p 7
231. Leadership June 14,2011 p2
232. Leadership June 17,2011 p 1&5
233. Leadership June 21, 2011 p1
234. Leadership June 27,2011 p1&5
235. The Nation, July 4, 2011 p2
236. The Nation, July 6, 2011 p2
237. Daily sun, July 6, 2011 p5
238. The Nation, July 7, 2011 p1&2
239. The Nation, July 11,2011
240. Daily trust, July 12, 2011
241. This day, July 12,2011 p8
242. The Nation, August 1,2011 p6
243. Daily Trust, August 9, 2011 p9
244. The Nation, August 9, 2011 p5
245. National mirror, August 12, 2011 p6
246. Daily Trust, August 15, 2011 p2
247. Leadership, August 17, 2011 p5
248. National Mirror, August 17,2011 p4
249. Leadership, august 21, 2011 p5
250. Leadership, August22, 2011 p5
251. The Nation, August 30,2011 p53
252. The Nation, August 31,2011 p4
253. Leadership, September 1, 2011 p8
254. Leadership, September 2, 2011 p6
255. Daily Trust, September 2,2011 p 2
256. The Nations, September 3, 2011 p6
257. The Nation, September 4, 2011 p4
258. Leadership, September 4, 2011 p6
259. Vanguard, September 5, 2011, p8

260. The Nation, September 14, 2011 p1
261. The Nation, September23,2011
262. Sunday Mirror, October 2,2011 p2&50
263. The Nation, October 2, 2011 p5
264. Daily Trust, October 4,2011 p2
265. Weekly trust, October 8, 2011 p3&5
266. The Nation, October 12, 2011 p1
267. Daily Trust, October 17, 2011 p1,2,&5
268. Leadership, October 20,2011,p.6
269. Daily Trust, October 21,2011,p.16
270. The Nation, Friday, October 21,2011,p10
271. Leadership Sunday,October23,2011,p.7
272. The Nation Monday,October24,p7
273. Leadership, October 24,2011,p.5
274. The Nation, October 26, 2011, p 9
275. Daily Trust, October 31, 2011, p2
276. Vanguard, November 3, 2011 p12
277. Daily Trust, November 4, 2011 p4
278. The Nation, November 5, 2011 p5
279. Leadership, November5, 2011 p2
280. Leadership, November 6, 2011 p4&6
281. The Nation, November 6, 2011 p1&4
282. Daily Trust, November 7, 2011 p1&5
283. The Nation, November7, 2011 p 1&2
284. Leadership, November 8 2011 p2
285. Leadership, November 10,2011,p1-8
286. The Nation, Thursday, November 10,2011,p58
287. The Nation on Sunday November 13, 2011, p.5
288. Daily Trust, November 17, 2011, p2
289. Leadership Sunday, November 20, 2011, p.4
290. The Nation Sunday, November 20, 2011, p.4
291. Sunday Trust, November 20, 2011, p.4
292. The Nation ,Tuesday, November 22,2011,p.9-10
293. The Nation, Wednesday, 23 November 2011,P.10
294. The Nation, November 25,2011,p.2&57
295. Leadership ,November 25,2011,p.5
296. The Nation ,November 28,2011,p.2
297. Daily Trust ,Monday, November 28, 2011,p6
298. Leadership ,November 28,2011,p1&5
299. The Nation, November 29,2011,p.6
300. Leadership ,November 29,2011,p.48
301. The Nation, December, 2, 2011,p.56
302. The Nation, December 3,2011,p.4
303. Leadership, December 3,2011,p.12
304. Leadership ,December 4, 2011,p.10
305. Vanguard, December 4,2011,p.34
306. Leadership ,December 5,2011,p.5
307. Daily Trust, December 5,2011,p1&6

308. Daily Trust, December 8,2011,p.2
309. National Mirror ,December 8,2011,p.2
310. The Nation, December 8,2011,p.2,3&4
311. Daily Trust, December 12,2011,p.2
312. Daily Trust, December 12,2011,p.6
313. Leadership,December14,2011,p.2
314. The Nation, December 15,2011,p.7
315. Vanguard, December 15,2011,p.24
316. Vanguard ,December 16,2011,p.7
317. The Nation, December 17,2011,p.5
318. Weekly Trust, December 17,2011,p.9
319. Leadership weekend, December 17,2011
320. Saturday Vanguard, December 17,2011,p.5
321. Weekly Trust, December 17,2011,p.5
322. Sunday Vanguard ,December 18,2011,p.6
323. The Nation, December 18,2011,p.4
324. The Nation ,December 18, 2011,p.5
325. Sunday Daily Trust, December 18,2011,p.6,
326. The Nation, December 19,2011,p.2
327. Vanguard December 19,2011,p.5
328. The Nation, December 20,2011,p.6
329. Daily Trust, December 20,20,2011,p.2
330. Vanguard, December 20,2011,p.5
331. The Nation, December 21,2011,p.60
332. Leadership, December,21,2011,p.5
333. Leadership,December,25,2011,p.7&10
334. The Nation, December 25,2011,p.1&2
335. Sunday Trust ,December 25,2011,p.1&9
336. Vanguard, December, 27,2011,p.5
337. Vanguard, December 28,2011,p.8
338. The Nation, December 29,2011,p2,.56&,54
339. The Nation, December 31,2011,p.2
340. Saturday Vanguard, December 31,2011,p.5
341. Weekly Trust, December 31,2011,p.6
342. Leadership Sunday, January 1,2012,p.7
343. Daily Trust, January 2,2012,p.6
344. The Nation, January 2, 2012,p.8
345. Sunday Sun, January 1,2012,p.11&13
346. Leadership ,January 2,2012,p.12
347. Daily Trust, January6, 2012, p.5&7.
348. Leadership, January 6,2012,p.5
349. Vanguard, January 6,2012,p.14
350. Saturday Vanguard, January 7,2012,p.5
351. Weekly Trust, January 7,2012
352. Leadership,January,7,2012,p.5
353. The Nation, January 8,2012,p.2
354. Sunday Trust, January 8,2012,p.2&3
355. This Day, January 11,2012,p.11

356. The Nation, January 9,2012,p.6
357. Daily Trust, January 9,2012,p.2
358. Daily Trust, January 11,2012,p.2
359. Daily Trust, January 11,2012,p.8
360. Daily Trust, January 12,2012,p.5
361. Weekly Trust, January 14,2012
362. Sunday Sun, January 15,2012,p.13
363. Leadership, January 16,2012,p.11
364. The Nation, January 16,2012,p.57
365. Leadership, January 18,2012,p.5&43
366. Daily Trust, January 18,2012,p.6
367. Sunday Trust, January 22,2012,p.2
368. Vanguard ,January 23,2012,p.6
369. Daily Trust, January 23,2012,p.2
370. The Nation, January 23,2012,p.4
371. Leadership, January 23,2012,p.13
372. Vanguard, January 23,2012,p.8
373. The Nation, January 25,2012,p.4
374. Vanguard, February 1,2012,p.4&5
375. The Nation ,February 1,2012,p.3,6&10
376. National Mirror ,February 1,2012
377. Leadership, February 1,2012,p.11
378. The Nation, February 3,2012,p.56
379. Daily Sun, February 3,2012,p.9&10
380. Daily Trust, February 6,2012,p.2&5
381. Leadership, February 7,2012,p.15
382. Vanguard, February 7,2012,p.49
383. Leadership, February 8,2012,p.5&7
384. The Nation, February 8,2012,p.5
385. Daily Sun, February 8,2012,p.6
386. The Nation, January 29,2012,p.4
387. Daily Sun, January 30,2012,p.6&12
388. The Nation, January 30,2012,p.4
389. Daily Trust,February13,2012,p.7&9
390. Leadership ,February 13,2012,p.14
391. The Nation, February 14,2012,p.2
392. Daily Sun, February 14,2012,p.5&13
393. Vanguard, February 15,2012,p.5
394. Daily Trust ,February 15,2012,p.5
395. Daily Trust ,February 21,2012,p.5
396. The Nation, February 21,2012,p.4,7&8
397. Leadership, February 21,2012,p.11
398. Daily Trust, February 23,2012,p.2
399. Saturday Sun, February 25,2012,p.10
400. The Nation ,February 26,2012,p.1& 4
401. Vanguard, February 27,2012,p.5
402. Daily Trust, February 28,2012,p.2&6
403. Vanguard, February 28,2012,p.51

404. The Nation, February 29,2012,p.58
405. Leadership, February 29,2012,p.5
406. Daily Sun, March 2,2012,p.5&15
407. Vanguard, Mach3, 2012, p.7
408. Leadership weekend, March 3,2012,p.5&9
409. Sunday Sun, March 4,2012,p.12
410. Vanguard, March 5,2012,p.8
411. Leadership, March 5,2012,p.6
412. Leadership, March 5, 2012, p.14.
413. The Nation ,March 5,2012 ,p.1
414. Daily Trust, March 5,2012,p.7
415. The Nation ,March 8,2012,p.7&8
416. Vanguard, March 7,2012,p.11,15&16
417. The Nation, March 12,2012,p.60
418. Leadership, March 12,2012,p.1&5
419. Daily Trust, March 13,2012,p.5,6&7
420. Sunday Trust, March 18,2012,p.56
421. Daily Trust, March 21,2012,p.2 &6
422. Vanguard March 22,2012,p.10&16
423. Daily Sun, March 22,2012,p.6&17
424. Saturday Vanguard, March 23,2012,p.6
425. Weekly Trust, March 24,2012,p.3
426. The Nation, March 25,2012,p.4
427. The Nation, March 26, 2012, p.4.
428. Daily Trust, March 26,2012,p.2
429. The Nation, March 28,2012,p.4
430. Daily Trust, March 29,2012,p.2
431. Leadership, March 30,2012,p.4
432. Leadership ,April 2,2012,p.5
433. The Nation, April 2,2012,p.4
434. Daily Trust, April 2,2012,p.5
435. Daily Trust, April 3,2012,p.2,6&7
436. Leadership, April 3,2012,p.5
437. Daily Trust, April 11,2012,p.3&6
438. Daily Trust, April 12,2012, p.5&6.
439. Leadership ,April 12,2012,p.6
440. Daily Trust, April 13,2012,p.2
441. Sunday Trust, April 15,2012p.56
442. Vanguard, April 18,2012,p.11
443. Daily Trust, April 18,2012,p.6
444. Daily Sun, April 20,2012,p.7
445. The Nation, April 20,2012,p.58
446. Daily Trust, April 20, 2012, p.6.
447. Weekly Trust ,April 21,2012,p.4
448. The Guardian ,April 22,2012,p.3
449. Vanguard, April 23,2012,p.7
450. Daily Trust, April 23,2012,p.2
451. Daily Trust ,April 24,2012,p.6&7

452. Leadership, April 25,2012,p. 5&7
453. Vanguard, April 26,2012,p.16
454. Daily Trust, April 26,2012,p.7
455. The Nation, April 26,2012,p.2
456. Leadership, April 26, 2012, p.41.
457. Leadership, April 27,2012,p.5
458. Daily Sun, April 27,2012,p.5
459. The Nation, April 27, 2012, p.59&60.
460. The Nation, April 29,2012,p.4
461. Sunday Trust, April 29,2012,p.3
462. The Nation, April 30, 2012, p.4.
463. Leadership ,April 30,2012,p.1,5&7
464. Vanguard, April 30,2012,
465. The Nation, May 1,2012,p.1&2&59
466. Leadership,May1,2012,p.5
467. National Mirror, May 4,2012,p.1,2&5
468. The Nation, May 4,2012,p.4
469. The Nation, May 5,2012,p.58
470. The Nation,May6,2012,p.5&8
471. Vanguard, May 7,2012,p.6
472. Leadership, May 8,2012,p.45
473. Daily Trust,May9,2012,p.8
474. Vanguard, May 9,2012,p.14
475. Daily Trust, May 10,2012,p.8
476. The Nation, May 11,2012,p.58
477. Leadership Sunday, May13,2012,p.1&5
478. Vanguard, May 14,2012,p.5& 15
479. Leadership, May 14,2012,p.5
480. Daily Trust, May 15,2012,p.2& 6
481. Vanguard, May 17, 2012, p.11.
482. Daily Trust, May 17,2012,p.7
483. Daily Trust, May 18,2012,p.2
484. Daily Trust, May 21,2012,p.4
485. Vanguard ,May 22,2012,p.5,11,&16
486. Leadership, May 22,2012,p.6
487. Daily Trust, May 22,2012,p.5
488. Vanguard, May 24,2012,p.16
489. Sunday Vanguard ,May 27,2012,p.7
490. Sunday Trust, May 27,2012,p.3
491. The Guardian, May 28,2012,p.5
492. Leadership, May 28, 2012, p.6.
493. The Nation, May 29,2012,p.59
494. Leadership, May 29,2012,p.12
495. The Guardian, May 29,2012,p.4
496. Daily Trust, May 30,2012,p.2
497. The Guardian, May30,2012,p12
498. Daily Trust,June1,2012,1&6
499. Sunday Vanguard, June 3,2012,p.5

500. Sunday Trust, June 3,2012,p.3
501. Leadership, June 4, 2012, p.1&5,
502. Daily Trust, June 4, 2012, p.6&7.
503. Daily Trust, June 6,2012,p.6&12
504. Daily Trust, June 7, 2012, p.6.
505. The Nation, June 8,2012,p.59
506. Weekly Trust, June 9,2012,p.6
507. Sunday Trust, June 10,2012,p.57
508. Daily Trust, June 11, 2012, p.2&5.
509. Daily Trust, June 12,2012,p.8
510. Daily Trust, June 14, 2012, p.7&9
511. Leadership weekend, June 16, 2012, p.8.
512. Weekly Trust, June 16,2012,p.7
513. Sunday Trust, June 17,2012,p.56
514. Leadership, June 18,2012,p.6
515. Daily Trust, June 19, 2012, p.1, 4 & 5.
516. Leadership, June 20,2012
517. Daily Trust, June 20,2012,p.1&5
518. Leadership, June 21, 2012, p.13.
519. Leadership Weekend, June 23,2012,p.8
520. Sunday Tribune ,24 June,2012,p.4
521. The Nation, June 24,2012,p.4
522. The Nation, June 25,2012,p.4&8
523. Sunday Vanguard ,July 1,2012,p.7
524. Leadership weekend, June 30,2012,p.5
525. Sunday Vanguard, July 1,2012,p.7
526. Daily Trust, July 2,2012, p.2
527. The Nation, July 2,2012,p.5
528. Daily Trust, July 3,2012,p.2&5
529. Leadership Sunday, July 8,2012,p.1&5
530. Weekly Trust, July 14,20012,p.5
531. Daily Trust, July 17.2012,p.2
532. Daily Trust, July 17,2012,p.6
533. Daily Trust, July 18,2012,p. 5&12
534. Leadership, July 18,2012,p.5
535. Leadership, July 19,2012,p.12
536. The Nation on Sunday, July 22,2012,p.5
537. The Nation, July 24,2012,p.59
538. Daily Trust, July 23,2012,p.2
539. Daily Trust,July26,2012,p.5
540. Daily Trust, July 30,2012,p.2
541. Leadership, July 30,2012,p.5
542. The Nation, July 31,2012,p.2
543. The Nation, July 31,2012,p.2
544. Sunday Trust, August 5,2012,p.16
545. Leadership, August 6,2012,p.12
546. The Nation, August 7,2012,p.4
547. Leadership, August 8,2012,p.5

548. Leadership, August 9,2012,p.8
549. Daily Trust, August 9,2012,p.6
550. Daily Trust, August 10,2012,p.4&6
551. Daily Trust, August 13,2012,p.2,6&8
552. Weekly Trust, August 18,2012,p.6
553. Leadership, August 16, 2012,p.4
554. The Nation, August 16,2012,p1&2
555. Leadership, August 21,2012,p.4
556. The Guardian, August 23,2012,p.3
557. Leadership, August 24,2012,p.6&7
558. Leadership, August 27,2012,p.12
559. Leadership, August 28,2012,p.11
560. The Nation on Sunday, September 2,2012,p.4
561. The Nation, September 3,2012,p.53
562. Daily Trust, September 6,2012,p.8
563. *The Nation*, September 3, 2012 p. 53
564. *The Nation,* September 4, 2012 p. 1
565. *The Nation*, September 17, 2012 p.1, 59
566. *Vanguard,* September 18, 2012 p.1, 3
567. *The Nation,* September 19, 2012 p. 1, 6
568. *Daily Trust,* September 24, 2012 p. 1
569. *The Nation,* September 25, 2012 p. 1
570. *Leadership*, September 27, 2012 p. 6
571. *Sunday Sun*, September 30, 2012 p. 14
572. *The Nation,* October 2, 2012 p. 1
573. Daily Trust, October 2, 2012 p.1, 2
574. The Guardian, October 4, 2012 p. 5
575. *The Nation,* October 1, 2012 p. 1
576. *The Nation,* October 5, 2012 p. 6
577. *The Nation,* October 4, 2012 p. 4
578. Leadership, October 4, 2012 p. 1

INDEX

N

O

P

R

S

T

U

V

W

Y